BLACK SEA

•NICE

CONSTAN-
TINOPLE
•CHALCEDON

PAPHLAGON

LAMPSACUS
CYZICUS

NICAEA

HELLESPONTUS

BITHYNIA

ANCYRA

PERGAMUM

LYDIA

PHRYGIA

GALAT

2

PÉPUZA

ASIA

PISIDIA

CARIA

ICONIUM

SOZOPOLIS

LYCAONIA

MEDITERRANEAN SEA

PAMPHYLIA

LYCIA

TELMESSUS

•SIDE

ISAURIA

PATARA

CORYDALA

SEL

PHELUS

LIMYRA

MEDITERRANEAN SEA

LEGEND
1 PONTUS
2 ASIA
3 ORIENS

Del
B.P.W.

CYPRUS

ASIA MINOR
in the time of
ST BASIL

0   KM   100

THE CHURCH
AND THE CHARISMA
OF LEADERSHIP
IN BASIL OF CAESAREA

BY

PAUL JONATHAN FEDWICK

Wipf and Stock Publishers
150 West Broadway • Eugene OR 97401

The Church and the Charisma of Leadership in Basil of Caesarea

By Fedwick, Paul Jonathan
Copyright©1979 by Fedwick, Paul Jonathan
ISBN: 1-57910-823-7

Reprinted by *Wipf and Stock Publishers*
150 West Broadway • Eugene OR 97401

Previously published by Pontifical Institute of Mediaeval Studies, 1979.

To June, Jason and Katie

379-1979
on the sixteenth-hundredth anniversary
of the death of Saint Basil

Contents

List of Abbreviations

(See Bibliography for details.)

1. Abbreviations of the Works of Basil of Caesarea

We refer to the works of Basil of Caesarea by the abbreviated Latin title and sub-division of the work. Books, chapters and paragraphs are indicated by arabic numerals. All references are to the Greek text either of Migne's Patrologia Graeca (= PG) volumes 29-32 quoted by volume, column and letter, or, if available, to the modern partial editions quoted by the name of the editor, volume and page number. Unless otherwise noted, English translations are my own. When used, the translations of others have always been checked against the Greek text and, if necessary, slightly revised. All such revisions are signalled by the abbreviation "rev." in parenthesis. The translations of W. K. L. Clarke and B. Jackson have been preferred to those of R. Deferrari, A. Way and M. Wagner as being more accurate.

C. Eun. 1-3	*Contra Eunomium libri tres*, PG 29, 497-669.
De fide	*De fide*, PG 31, 676-692; Eng. trans. Clarke, *Ascetic Works*, pp. 90-99.
De jud.	*De judicio Dei*, PG 31, 653-676; Eng. trans. Clarke, *Ascetic Works*, pp. 77-89.
De leg.	*De legendis libris gentilium*, PG 31, 564-589; ed. and Fr. trans. Boulenger, *S. Basile, Aux jeunes gens*; ed. and Eng. trans. Deferrari, "Address to Young Men," in *Saint Basil, The Letters*, 4: 363-435.
De sp. s.	*De Spiritu Sancto*, PG 32, 68-217; ed. Johnston, *The Book of Saint Basil the Great on the Holy Spirit*; ed. and Fr. trans. Pruche, *Basile de Césarée, Traité du Saint-Esprit*; Eng. trans. Jackson, SLNPF, 8: 2-50.
Ep. 1-366	*Epistolae 1-366*, PG 32, 220-1112; ed. and Fr. trans. Courtonne, *Saint Basile, Lettres* 1-3; Eng. trans. Jackson, SLNPF, 8: 109-327; ed. and Eng. trans. Deferrari, *Saint Basil, The Letters. Epp.* 2, 150 and 173 are edited in Rudberg, *Etudes sur la tradition*, pp. 151-211.
Hex. 1-9 (11)	*Hexaemeron homiliae* 9, PG 29, 4-208; ed. and Fr. trans. Giet, *Basile de Césarée, Homélies sur l'Hexaéméron*; Eng. trans. Jackson, SLNPF, 8: 52-107; *Homilies 10* and *11* are edited and translated into Fr. in Smets and van Esbroeck, *Basile de Césarée, Sur l'origine de*

	l'homme; see also the excellent edition of Hörner, *Auctorum incertorum ... sermones.*
Hom. 1-29	*Homiliae variae*, PG 31, 163-481; 489-617; 1437-1476; 1488-1496. *Homily 3* is edited in Rudberg, *L'homélie de Basile.*
In ps.	*Homiliae in psalmos* 1, 7, 14.1-2, 28, 29, 32, 33, 44, 45, 48, 59, 61, 114, 115 (PG 29, 307-494; 30, 104-116; Eng. trans. A. C. Way, *St. Basil, Exegetic Homilies*, pp. 151-359).
Interrog. 1-203	*Interrogationes fratrum*, PL 103, 483-554. Known also as *Small Asceticon*; see Gribomont, *Histoire*, pp. 237 ff.
Proem. ad hyp.	*Proemium ad Hypotyposin*, PG 31, 1509-1513. Cf. Gribomont, *Histoire*, pp. 278 ff.
Proem. in reg. br.	*Proemium in regulas brevius tractatas*, PG 31, 1080; Eng. trans. Clarke, *Ascetic Works*, p. 229.
Proem. in reg. fus.	*Proemium in regulas fusius tractatas*, PG 31, 889-901; Eng. trans. Clarke, *Ascetic Works*, pp. 141, 151.
Reg. br. 1-313	*Regulae brevius tractatae*, PG 31, 1080-1305; Eng. trans. Clarke, *Ascetic Works*, pp. 230-351; for the additional 7 *Interrogations*, see Gribomont, *Histoire*, pp. 179-186.
Reg. fus. 1-55	*Regulae fusius tractatae*, PG 31, 905-1052; Eng. trans. Clarke, *Ascetic Works*, pp. 152-228.
Reg. mor. 1-80	*Regulae morales*, PG 31, 700-869; Eng. trans. Clarke, *Ascetic Works*, pp. 101-131.

2. *Other Abbreviations*

AB	*Analecta Bollandiana* (Brussels)
Aug	*Augustinianum* (Rome)
BAC	Biblioteca de Autores Cristianos (Madrid)
BBGG	*Bollettino della Badia greca di Grottaferrata*
BZ	*Byzantinische Zeitschrift* (Munich)
CC	*Collectanea Cistercensia* (Rome)
CH	*Church History* (Chicago)
COVG	*Der christliche Osten in Vergangenheit und Gegenwart*
CSCO	Corpus Scriptorum Christianorum Orientalium (Louvain)
CSEL	Corpus Scriptorum Ecclesiasticorum Latinorum (Vienna)
DACL	*Dictionnaire d'archéologie chrétienne et de liturgie*, 15 vols., edd. J. B. Chabot et al. (Paris: Letouzey, 1907-1953).
DCB	*Dictionary of Christian Biography*, 4 vols., edd. W. Smith and H. Wace (London: Murray, 1877-1887).

DHGE	*Dictionnaire d'histoire et de géographie ecclésiastiques*, edd. A. Baudrillart et al. (Paris: Letouzey, 1912—).
DIP	*Dizionario degli Istituti di Perfezione*, edd. G. Pelliccia and G. Rocca (Rome: Edizioni Paoline, 1973—).
DOP	*Dumbarton Oaks Papers* (Washington, D.C.)
DR	*Downside Review* (Bath, England)
DSp	*Dictionnaire de la spiritualité*, edd. M. Viller et al. (Paris: Beauchesne, 1937—).
DTC	*Dictionnaire de théologie catholique*, 15 vols., edd. A. Vacant et al. (Paris: Letouzey, 1902-1972).
EC	*Enciclopedia cattolica*, 12 vols., edd. P. Paschini et al. (Vatican City, 1949-1954).
EChQ	*Eastern Churches Quarterly* (Oxford)
ED	*Euntes docete* (Rome)
EO	*Echos d'Orient* (Paris)
EThL	*Ephemerides theologicae lovanienses* (Louvain)
FZPhTh	*Freiburg Zeitschrift für Philosophie und Theologie* (Freiburg, Switzerland)
GCS	Die griechischen christlichen Schriftsteller (Berlin)
GOTR	*Greek Orthodox Theological Review* (Brookline, Mass.)
HSCP	*Harvard Studies in Classical Philology*
JEH	*The Journal of Ecclesiastical History* (London)
JThS	*Journal of Theological Studies* (Oxford)
LR	*Lutherische Rundschau* (Stuttgart)
MEPREO	*Messager de l'exarcat du patriarche russe en Europe occidentale* (Paris)
MS	*Mediaeval Studies* (Toronto)
NAR	*North American Review*
NCE	*New Catholic Encyclopedia*, 16 vols., ed. Catholic University of America (New York: McGraw-Hill, 1966-1974)
NRTh	*Nouvelle revue théologique* (Turnhout)
NTT	*Nederlands theologisch tijdschrift* (Wageningen)
OCP	*Orientalia christiana periodica* (Rome)
OCh	*Oriens christianus* (Wiesbaden)
OS	*L'orient syrien* (Paris)
PC	*Palestra del clero* (Rovigo)
PG	Patrologia graeca, 161 vols., ed. J. P. Migne (Paris, 1857-1866).
PGL	*A Patristic Greek Lexicon*, ed. G. W. H. Lampe (Oxford: Clarendon, 1961-1965).
PhS	*Philippiniana sacra* (Manila)
PL	Patrologia latina, 221 vols., ed. J. P. Migne (Paris, 1844-1855).

POCh	*Le Proche-Orient chrétien* (Jerusalem)
Progr.	Programme
RAM	*Revue d'ascétique et de mystique* (Toulouse)
RB	*Revue bénédictine* (Maredsous)
RCCM	*Rivista di cultura classica e medievale* (Rome)
REB	*Revue des études byzantines* (Paris)
REG	*Revue des études grecques* (Paris)
RHE	*Revue d'histoire ecclésiastique* (Louvain)
RHLR	*Revue d'histoire et de littérature religieuses* (Paris)
RHPR	*Revue d'histoire et de philosophie religieuses* (Strasbourg)
RHR	*Revue de l'histoire des religions* (Paris)
RR	*Ricerche religiose* (Rome)
RSCST	*Rivista storico-critica delle scienze teologiche*
RSPT	*Revue des sciences philosophiques et théologiques* (Paris)
RSR	*Recherches de science religieuse* (Paris)
RT	*Revista de teología* (La Plata)
SC	*La scuola cattolica* (Milan)
SCh	Sources chrétiennes (Paris)
SCM	Student Christian Movement (London)
SE	*Sacris erudiri* (Bruges)
SLNPF	A Select Library of Nicene and Post-Nicene Fathers of the Christian Church (New York: Grand Rapids)
SMSR	*Studi e materiali di storia delle religioni* (Rome)
SP	*Studia patristica* (Berlin)
SPCK	Society for Promoting Christian Knowledge (London)
STh	*Scripta theologica* (Pamplona)
SVThQ	*St. Vladimir Theological Quarterly* (New York)
TB	*Therapeutische Berichte*
TDNT	*Theological Dictionary of the New Testament*, 10 vols., edd. G. Kittel et al. (Grand Rapids: Eerdmans, 1964-1976).
TE	*Teología espiritual* (Valencia)
ThG	*Theologie und Glaube* (Paderborn)
ThL	*Theologische Literaturzeitung* (Leipzig)
ThQ	*Theologische Quartalschrift* (Stuttgart)
VC	*Verbum caro* (Taizé)
VCh	*Vigiliae christianae* (Amsterdam)
VChr	*Vetera christianorum* (Bari)
VM	*Vita monastica* (Arezzo)
VS	*La vie spirituelle* (Paris)
VSSt	*La vie spirituelle, Supplément* (Paris)
ZK	*Zeitschrift für Kirchengeschichte* (Stuttgart)
ZKTh	*Zeitschrift für katholische Theologie* (Innsbruck)
ZNW	*Zeitschrift für neutestamentliche Wissenschaft* (Giessen)

Introduction

In recent times several attempts have been made to explore the ecclesial consciousness of Basil of Caesarea (330-379).[1] Whereas P. Batiffol had tried to explain the "ecclesiology" of Basil mainly in terms of orthodoxy and charity, V. Grumel has in his turn argued in favour of Basil's adopting a more loyal stance in relation to the church of Rome and its bishop Damasus.[2] S. Giet, in a study devoted to Basil's social ideas and activities, largely subscribed to the conclusions of Grumel.[3] For L. Vischer, the question of Roman primacy in the "ecclesiology" of Basil of Caesarea does not seem to play a major role; rather it is the bishops, united by the confession of the same faith, who, according to this author, constitute the core of ecclesiastical unity in the thought of Basil of Caesarea.[4] In a revised article on the subject of Basil's relations with the major centers of communion in the fourth century, E. Amand de Mendieta compared and contrasted the ecclesial consciousness of Basil with that of Damasus and tried to explain thereby the failure of the negotiations with the Westerners which Basil undertook in order to settle some of the problems that troubled Eastern Christianity.[5] According to this author, the consciousness that Basil formed of

---

[1] Although most of the authors whose works are surveyed in this Introduction speak of the "ecclesiology" or "doctrine of the church" of Basil of Caesarea, throughout my work I have instead preferred to use the less "systematic" term "consciousness." Faith, and all that it entails, is not a subject for strictly systematic reflection or rigid definitions; its contents can perhaps be best expressed through images and metaphors (see the constitution *Lumen Gentium* of the Second Vatican Council). Also for Basil of Caesarea faith and church were dynamic realities of whose presence he was aware both in himself and others, and to whose call to service he tried to respond throughout his whole life. To express this awareness and unreflective understanding of his I employ the term "consciousness."

[2] P. Batiffol, "L'ecclésiologie de s. Basile," *EO* 21 (1922) 9-30 ; V. Grumel, "S. Basile et le siège apostolique," *EO* 21 (1922) 280-292.

[3] S. Giet, *Les idées et l'action sociales de s. Basile* (Paris, 1941), pp. 352-355; see also p. 353, n. 6.

[4] L. Vischer, *Basilius der Grosse* (Basel, 1953), pp. 52 ff. Very similar views are found in B. Krivocheine, "L'ecclésiologie de s. Basile le Grand," *MEPREO* 17 (1969) 75-102.

[5] E. Amand de Mendieta, "Basile de Césarée et Damase de Rome. Les causes de l'échec de leurs négociations" in *Biblical and Patristic Studies in Memory of R. P. Casey* (Freiburg im Breisgau, 1963), pp. 122-166; the previous article of Amand de Mendieta from 1954 is cited in the Bibliography. His views of a complete split of ecclesiologies in the case of Basil and Damasus have been rebutted by J. Taylor, "St. Basil the Great and Pope St. Damasus

the universal church was more of a mystical than a juridical nature, more pneumatic than institutional, based more on faith, charity and the brotherly union of all orthodox bishops than on the authority of one superior bishop. According to N. Corneanu, Basil, by repeatedly calling on the Western episcopate, envisioned in the ecumenical synod the only supreme authority in the church competent to solve the dogmatic or institutional conflicts.[6] Among the elements constituting unity, Basil would accord priority to tradition, to charity and peace, and to friendship among the ecclesiastical coryphaei exhibited in the exchange of letters and visits. There would also be an intrinsic relationship between the unity in creation and the order sought for the church. B. Bobrinskoy has analyzed in a paper the theology of the Holy Spirit in the writings and liturgy of Basil.[7] A brief reference is also made in his presentation to the trinitarian (or rather pneumatological) "ecclesiology" of the bishop of Caesarea. "The church," affirms Bobrinskoy, "is conceived by Basil as a brotherhood and community of love ruled and inspired by the Holy Spirit" (p. 24). Ecclesial unity would manifest itself chiefly in the Eucharist. Also P. Scazzoso in his posthumous work emphasizes the pneumatological (trinitarian) and eucharistic aspects of Basil's "ecclesiology."[8] Despite its title this study rightly stresses the precedence of experience over conceptualization in Basil's approach to the church.[9]

If there is an area of agreement in the most recent Basilian scholarship with regard to Basil's ecclesial consciousness it is perhaps in the realization of the importance Basil attributed to the role of the Holy Spirit in the building and growth of the church. It is almost a cliché to say today that Basil is one of the most important theologians of the Holy Spirit to have flourished before the First Council of Constantinople.[10] However, even his work *On the Holy Spirit* is less a dogmatic treatise than an essay on the spirituality of the church; that is, a demonstration of the energizing

---

I," *DR* 91 (1973) 186-203; 262-274. See also the reservations of J. Gribomont, "St. Basil," *NCE* 2 (1966) 143-146, and "Rome et l'Orient. Invitations et reproches de s. Basile," *Seminarium* 27 (1975) 336-354.

[6] N. Corneanu, "Les efforts de s. Basile pour l'unité de l'Eglise," *VC* 90 (1969) 43-67.

[7] B. Bobrinskoy, "Liturgie et ecclésiologie trinitaire de s. Basile," *VC* 89 (1969) 1-32. See also the article of M. Hornus, "La divinité du Saint-Esprit comme condition du salut personnel selon Basile," *VC* 89 (1969) 33-62.

[8] *Introduzione alla ecclesiologia di san Basilio* (Milan, 1975). I became acquainted with this work only after my own research was completed. Cf. also below, n. 15.

[9] The work of O. Papadopoulou-Tsanana (see Bibl.) is known to me only through the review of E. Amand de Mendieta, *BZ* 65 (1972) 81-84.

[10] Cf. H. Dörries, *De Spiritu Sancto. Der Beitrag des Basilius zum Abschluss des Trinitarischen Dogmas* (Göttingen, 1956).

presence and power of the third divine hypostasis in the life, experience and practices of the Christian community. Already in the third book *Against Eunomius* appears the argument *ad absurdum* which Basil continually brandishes against the Pneumatomachi in his *De Spiritu Sancto*: "Were the Holy Spirit not divine, how could he then sanctify, as it is believed in traditional Christianity, angels and humans?"

It must be said, however, that in recent scholarship rather insufficient attention has been paid to the charismatic aspect of Basil's ecclesiology. As somewhat onesidedly exemplified in Hans von Campenhausen's study on ecclesiastical authority and charisma in the early church, the tendency among some scholars has been to see a conflict rather than complementarity between charisma and institution in early Christianity.[11] Some authors who approached Basil in this way, tried to unravel the alleged dilemma of an opposition in his conception of the church as an established body and the charismatic operation of the Spirit, while others reduced the experience of the Spirit to the merely miraculous or sensational.[12] Another seeming difficulty with which some authors endeavoured to cope in their study of Basil's ecclesial consciousness was a too rigid separation between Christian and ascetic (or rather "monastic") life.[13] The tendency to classify Basil as a "monastic" legislator has prevented many scholars from utilizing a great deal of his writings since they considered them as dealing exclusively with a narrow range of Christian issues.[14]

The present essay constitutes a modest attempt at studying Basil's consciousness of the Christian church within the totality of his life as an ascetic *and* a churchman. I pay careful attention to the historical period in which

---

[11] H. von Campenhausen, *Kirchliches Amt und geistliche Vollmacht in der ersten drei Jahrhunderten* (Tübingen, 1953; Eng. trans. London, 1969). This type of approach is less prominent in the most recent study of A. M. Ritter, *Charisma im Verständnis des Joannes Chrysostomos und seiner Zeit: Ein Beitrag zur Erforschung der griechisch-orientalischen Ekklesiologie in der Frühzeit der Reichskirche* (Göttingen, 1972), because Ritter, a disciple of Campenhausen, tries to integrate also the views of other scholars who dealt with the subject. For an alternate valuation of the charismatic experience in the early period see the works of E. Schweizer, E. Käsemann, J. D. G. Dunn cited below, p. 24, n. 127. In addition see L. Goppelt, *Apostolic and Post-Apostolic Times* (London, 1970).

[12] See e.g. W. K. L. Clarke, *The Ascetic Works of St. Basil* (London, 1925), p. 46, whose contention that charisma in Basil means something miraculous like healings (cf. *Reg. fus.* 55) is rightly criticized by P. Humbertclaude, *La doctrine ascétique de s. Basile* (Paris, 1932), pp. 315 f. See also below, p. 30 for a different interpretation of the *Shorter Interrogation 114* from e.g. J. Gribomont's in "Obéissance et évangile selon s. Basile le Grand," *VSSt* 21 (1952) 203.

[13] This is apparent in L. Vischer's dissertation cited above, n. 4.

[14] See below, pp. 161 ff.

Basil lived—in particular the emperorships of Julian and Valens—and the problems of religious and ecclesiastico-political order confronting fourth-century Christians in Asia Minor. As much as I can, throughout this essay, I deliberately try to preserve Basil's own terminology and ways of perceiving things as he often through a different choice of words implied a different understanding of the topics which are dealt with also by other contemporary writers, for instance, Gregory of Nazianzus or Gregory, his brother.[15] My conclusions are based largely on my own textual and historical interpretation of the original documents, although I have also tried, whenever possible, to take into account the perceptions of other scholars whose works are listed in the Bibliography. By demonstrating sensitivity to the problems of identity, chronology, and authenticity of Basil's writings, I hope to contribute not only to theological knowledge as such but to the internal and external criticism of Basil's works as well.[16]

As I deal with Basil's life throughout my book,[17] here I shall recall only the most salient moments of his career. Basil (*ca.* 330-379) was born, lived most of his life, and died in Caesarea of Cappadocia, the modern Kayseri,

[15] An instance of this is the fact that Gregory of Nazianzus saw Basil as involved in reviving and organizing monastic institutes whereas Basil himself totally avoided, and not without reason, this type of terminology. Also for the most part I preserve Basil's manner of referring to some church members as leaders (προεστῶτες) rather than bishops, presbyters, etc. The lumping together of the three Cappadocians under one common name often generates the difficulty of duly appreciating the nuances of their thought. K. Holl in his remarkable work, *Amphilochius von Ikonium in seinem Verhältnis zu den grossen Kappadoziern* (Tübingen, 1904) has avoided this pitfall by carefully differentiating between the individual particularities of the trinitarian teaching of the three Cappadocians. In my opinion, somewhat less successful in his attempt is P. Scazzoso; his constant references in the *Introduzione* to the other Cappadocians and some later Greek (Orthodox) authors seem to obfuscate rather than illumine Basil's originality in and contribution to the theology of the church. In my work such cross-references are reduced to a minimum because I feel that it is too early to draw comparisons among authors whose particular positions have not yet been thoroughly studied. (A limited number of references is made to the works of E. Bellini, *La chiesa in Gregorio Nazianzeno* [Venegono Inferiore, 1970], and A. M. Ritter cited above n. 11.)

[16] In Appendix A the reader will find a Chronological Table of the life and works of Basil of Caesarea, and also a list of the works that have been excluded from the present investigation either because of serious doubt about their authenticity or because modern scholarship has proved them to be spurious. For the social aspect of Basil's teaching which for reasons of space could not be dealt with more thoroughly in this book the reader is referred to the work of S. Giet (above n. 3; see also the important critical remarks and most recent bibliography in J. Gribomont, "Un aristocrate révolutionnaire, évêque et moine: saint Basile," *Aug* 17 [1977] 179-191) but particularly to the very valuable historical study of R. Teja, *Organización económica y social de Capadocia en el siglo ιv, según los Padres Capadocios* (Salamanca, 1974).

[17] Besides Appendix A, see the Analytical Index s.v. Basil of Caesarea.

Turkey. Descended from a family of affluent landowners with holdings scattered over the provinces of Cappadocia, Armenia Minor, perhaps Galatia, and the two provinces of Pontus, Basil could also count Christian heroes of the great persecutions among his forebears.

His education, which started at home with his father, Basil completed at Caesarea, Constantinople and Athens; it was the education of a rounded humanist in Greek literature, philosophy, and oratory. Basil's total commitment to Christian asceticism led him to a monasticism conceived as a way of life based on the biblical witness but also marked by the best humanism of the time. The ascetic movement Basil deployed for works of social utility in order to make of its practitioners what he termed "Complete Christians."[18] In a time of drought and its attendant famine, the winter of 368, Basil spent himself on the relief of Christians, pagans, and Jews alike. On a property of his outside Caesarea, he devoted a complex of buildings to the housing of travellers, the sick, and the poor, an early form of public charity called "The Brand New City" or "Basiliada."

In 370 Basil was elected bishop of Caesarea and in that office pursued with vigour his ideal of deepening the sense of unity among the various Christian churches in the name of their common bond in Christ. His forceful defense of the faith, his immense learning, and his effective charity combined to make him an exemplary aristocrat, statesman, pastor, theologian, in short, a saint and an authentic father and doctor of the Christian church.

* * *

I would like to express my gratitude to the Canada Council for a fellowship toward the preparation of this work. My sincere thanks go also to Professor Walter H. Principe for his assistance and guidance in the preparation of the first draft of this work. For critical reading of the whole manuscript and for many valuable suggestions I thank Professors Leonard Boyle, and in particular Walter M. Hayes who has helped to eliminate many inaccuracies from the text. Dr. Wolf D. Hauschild I thank for reading and commenting critically on the first draft of Appendix A. The reader will also thank, as I do most warmly, Miss Beryl Wells for the valuable map of fourth-century Asia Minor on which are shown all the locations mentioned in Basil's writings. I wish also to record my gratitude to the members of the

---

[18] I owe this rendering of οἱ τέλειοι Χριστιανοί to Edward A. Synan, President and Professor of the Pontifical Institute of Mediaeval Studies, Toronto; also the translation of ἡ καινὴ πόλις by "The Brand New City."

editorial staff of the Institute for their help and kindness. Last but not least
I thank my wife June for her support and assistance. For the many imper-
fections that remain, I am solely responsible.

Pontifical Institute of Mediaeval Studies   P.J.F.
Toronto
January 1978

1

The Church in the Life and Works
of Basil of Caesarea

The term by which Basil of Caesarea most commonly addresses the communities of Christians is "church," "churches of God."[1] Obviously referred to are not simply liturgical gatherings but established bodies of Christians living in a locality.[2] It would be inappropriate to ask whether Basil employs the term ἐκκλησία with reference to the universal or local church. Throughout his writings the bishop of Caesarea shows no awareness of such a distinction as every local body is for him but the manifestation of a universal reality—the reality of being reached and grasped at a certain point of time by the saving action of God the Father acting for man's sake through the Son in the Holy Spirit.[3] The church is the body of Christ and the fellowship of the Spirit.[4] As the work of God, the Almighty,

---

[1] Other expressions include: "house of God," "church of Christ," "body of Christ," "dove of Christ," "bride of Christ," "city of God," "daughter of God," and also very frequently, "brotherhood." The names applied to Christians include: "brethren," "people of God," "members of the body of Christ," "believers in Christ," "God's flock," "disciples of the Lord," and "disciples of the gospel." Some of these expressions are studied below pp. 6 ff. In his work, *Early Christian Doctrines* (London, 1968), p. 401, J. N. D. Kelly quotes with approval the "customary" (*sic!*) view according to which "as contrasted with that of the West, Eastern teaching about the Church remained immature, not to say archaic, in the post-Nicene period." One could reply that all such time-honoured designations, although obviously derived from the Bible, by being repeated in new historical contexts, reflect new realities, in the case of Basil the situation of the "imperial" church under Julian and Valens.

[2] See e.g. *In ps.* 45 and 59 quoted below p. 10. On the fourth-century church as an organization (society) competing with the state see A. Momigliano, *The Conflict between Paganism and Christianity in the Fourth Century* (Oxford, 1963), pp. 9 ff.

[3] See *In ps.* 48.1 discussed in n. 7, below; *Ep.* 161.1: Courtonne, 2:93; *De jud.*, 1:653A-B; *Ep.* 243.1: Courtonne, 3:68, and chapters 8 and 9 of the book *On the Holy Spirit.* For the theological impossibility of a distinction between universal and local church in general see H. M. Legrand, "The Revaluation of Local Churches: Some Theological Implications," *Concilium* 71 (1972) 57, and K. L. Schmidt, "Ἐκκλησία," in *TDNT* (1965) 3: 501-536; see also J. D. G. Dunn, *Jesus and the Spirit* (London, 1975), pp. 262 ff.

[4] See below, pp. 41 ff., and 23 ff.

the church cannot be confined to one people, culture, or social order. Neither can it be circumscribed spatially.[5] By its very essence, the church provides the place and opportunity for humans to rediscover their common nature,[6] so that those who were before their calling (κλῆσις) opposed to each other because of social, cultural or national differences might become "through the instrumentality of the church habituated to each other in love."[7] Consequently, the end of the Christian church and the general end of human existence converge: both consist in being totally possessed and ruled by God.[8]

Basil first experienced the church in the bosom of his religious family. Although in his panegyric Gregory of Nazianzus speaks foremost of the cultural and intellectual upbringing of the future leader of the church of Caesarea, Basil himself, in recalling his childhood, maintains an eloquent silence on the matter. He acquaints us instead with his early contacts with religion in its various applied forms. The fullness of assurance (πληροφορία) that Scripture and tradition are of equal weight and authority in the establishment of orthodoxy, which echoes throughout Basil's writings, seems to have originated from his domestic experience.[9] Whereas from his

---

[5] See *Ep.* 161.1: Courtonne, 2:93; *In ps.* 59.2: 464B-C.

[6] See *Reg. fus.* 2.1: 908B ff.; *In ps.* 44.2: 392A f.

[7] *In ps.* 48.1: 433C-D. This important homily provides the essential elements of Basil's view on the universality (intrinsic and intentional catholicity) of the church. Before speaking of the Holy Spirit as the architect of the church (ὁ ἐκκλησιάζων) and of the church as the community of universal love (433A-D), Basil surveys the theories of the various philosophical schools concerning the end of human existence (432A-B). After the statement of the Christian position according to which the end of human life is "to be totally ruled by God," there follows a comprehensive list of all those called by the kerygma of the Holy Spirit to form the universal fellowship (433A). In order that no one may be left without the church's aid in the path to salvation, "there are three pairs of those called, in which every race of men is included" (ἐν αἷς ἅπαν τὸ τῶν ἀνθρώπων περιέχεται γένος, 433B). Among those called by the Spirit are: non-Romans and Roman citizens (ἔθνη καὶ οἱ κατοικοῦντες τὴν οἰκουμένην); people of primitive culture and civilized men (γηγενεῖς καὶ οἱ υἱοὶ τῶν ἀνθρώπων); the rich and the poor (πλούσιοι καὶ πένητες) whereby all social classes are comprised. See also *Hex.* 11.5: Smets-Esbroeck, 238: "Πληθύνεσθε". ἐκκλησίας ἡ εὐλογία. Μὴ ἐν ἑνὶ περιγραφήτω ἡ θεολογία · ἀλλ' εἰς πᾶσαν τὴν γῆν κηρυχθήτω τὸ Εὐαγγέλιον τῆς σωτηρίας. For the historical background of Basil's statements see Momigliano, *The Conflict*, pp. 12-16. On Gregory of Nazianzus' concept of universality and unity see Ph. Muraille, "L'église, peuple de l'oikouménè d'après s. Grégoire de Nazianze. Notes sur l'unité et l'universalité," *EThL* 44 (1968) 154-178, and E. Bellini, *La chiesa nel mistero della salvezza in san Gregorio Nazianzeno* (Venegono Inferiore, 1970), pp. 71-74. On Origen see briefly G. Bardy, *La théologie de l'église de saint Irénée au concile de Nicée* (Paris, 1947), pp. 160-161.

[8] Besides *In ps.* 48.1, see *De jud.*, 2:656A f.

[9] See *De jud.*, 1:653A. For the interpretation of *De sp. s.* 66: Pruche, 478 ff., see G. Florovsky, "The Function of Tradition in the Ancient Church," *GOTR* 9 (1963) 181 ff.;

parents Basil and Emmelia, Basil learned "from infancy the Holy Scriptures," Macrina, his grandmother, was the link for his acquaintance with an evolved (spiritual rather than speculative) form of Origenism, embodied since the time of Gregory Thaumaturgus in the liturgical tradition of the church of Neocaesarea.[10] There can be little doubt that Basil became first acquainted with the "words and sayings" of Gregory before he knew anything about the symbol of Nicaea.[11] One of the fundamental principles of Neocaesarean theology, the radical distinction between creator and creature, lord and servant, will later find wide application in Basil's controversy with the Arians (Son as the intermediate hypostasis), Anomoeans (unlikeness of Father and Son), and the Pneumatomachi (creaturehood of the Son and of the Holy Spirit).[12]

Another distinctive characteristic acquired by Basil early in his life was a strong awareness of the Christian faith as a holocaust not only of human freedom but also, whenever necessary, of human life.[13] Macrina and her husband, it is known, barely managed to escape the persecution of the second Maximinus.[14] The narrative of the severe hardships, the long wan-

---

also T. Špidlík, *La sophiologie de saint Basile* (Rome, 1961), pp. 172-186. For the quite different domestic experience of the church of Gregory of Nazianzus see Bellini, *La chiesa*, pp. 13-14.

[10] See *De jud.*, 1:653A; *Epp.* 204.6: Courtonne, 2:178; 210.1: ibid., 190; 223.3: ibid., 3:1 ff. Whenever his orthodoxy was attacked or questioned Basil would appeal to the ties of his family with Gregory Thaumaturgus, apostle and founder of the church of Neocaesarea. K. Holl in *Amphilochius von Ikonium in seinem Verhältnis zu den grossen Kappadoziern* (Tübingen, 1904), pp. 117-119, has tried to show Basil's indebtedness to the theology, mainly as contained in the *Expositio fidei*, of Gregory Thaumaturgus. See also J. Gribomont, "L'origénisme de saint Basile," *L'homme devant Dieu. Mélanges H. de Lubac* (Paris, 1963), p. 281, and H. Dehnhard, *Das Problem der Abhängigkeit des Basilius von Plotin* (Berlin, 1964), pp. 19-32. But the authenticity of Gregory's *Expositio fidei* attributed to him by Gregory of Nyssa (PG 46, 912D-913A) has lately been challenged by L. Abramowski, "Das Bekenntnis des Gregor Thaumaturgus bei Gregor von Nyssa und das Problem seiner Echtheit," *ZKG* 87 (1976) 145-166. However, it is not at all impossible that Gregory of Nyssa is quoting in the symbol most or some of the *ipsissima verba* of the founder of the church of Neocaesarea as they were transmitted orally through his disciples, notably Macrina. There could be posterior additions by some of his successors in the see of Neocaesarea. The term χορηγός does not have to be necessarily derived from Plotinus; it is found already in Clement of Alexandria and Origen (see *PGL, s.v.*). For a comparison of Gregory's *Expositio fidei* with Arius' *Thalia* see A. Grillmeier, *Christ in Christian Tradition*, 2nd ed. (Atlanta, 1975), 1: 232-238.

[11] See the *Epistles* cited above, n. 10.

[12] For the evidences see Holl, *Amphilochius*, pp. 127 ff., and n. 10, above.

[13] See *De sp. s.* 75: Pruche, 516; *Reg. mor.* 8.1: 712C-D; 70.19: 832B.

[14] See Gregory of Nazianzus, *Oration* 43.5-6: PG 36, 500B-D; Gregory of Nyssa, *Vita Macrinae*, 2 and 20: Maraval, 142 ff. (with the notes), and 206.

derings of his ancestors through the wilderness of Pontus, put Basil from the beginning in contact with a church of martyrs, a church founded on the blood of Christ and that of many of his followers.[15]

If one may assume that the church of Neocaesarea was at the time under the influence of Eustathian asceticism, Basil must also have perceived a continuity between the family type of religion as practiced in his household and the religion of the ascetics living in communities nearby the urban churches.[16] This experience further establishes in his consciousness the close link and even total inseparability of Christian life and ascetic practice which we find prominently represented in his early writings.

Outside the family environment there was another aspect of the church which Basil was soon destined to discover and which was to fill his heart not only with sorrow and grief but also with the desire to correct it later in life. The fellowship that claimed apostolic origin and martyrdom within its ranks was to reveal itself also as a community of sinners whose members hindered its expansion rather than contributed to its growth.[17] His own words in the first preface to the *Moralia* seem to indicate the uneasiness he experienced from having become acquainted during his travels abroad with the state of many churches strongly divided against each other:

> Seeing a great and exceeding discord on the part of many men both in their relations with one another and their views about the divine Scripture, ... and what was most horrible of all, its very leaders differing so much from one another in sentiment and opinion and wondering, moreover, what and whence was the cause of so great an evil, first of all I lived as it were in profound darkness and was inclining, as it were on scales, first in this direction and then in that. Now one man would attract me, now another.[18]

---

[15] On the inclusion of the cult of martyrs in the homilies of the Cappadocians see J. Bernardi, *La prédication des Pères cappadociens. Le prédicateur et son auditoire* (Paris, 1968), pp. 398-400.

[16] Probably Musonius, the bishop of Neocaesarea, was an ascetic (see *Ep.* 28.1: Courtonne, 1: 66-67). That many of the urban churches and schools were under the supervision of the Eustathians see below, pp. 162 ff., and 160 ff. Probably the whole family of Basil practiced the family type of asceticism which until 350 was in full vigour in Syria and Asia Minor; see E. Amand de Mendieta, "La virginité chez Eusèbe d'Emèse et l'ascéticisme familial dans la première moitié du IVᵉ siècle," *RHE* 50 (1955) 777-820, esp. pp. 800 f.; Id. and M. C. Moons,. "Une curieuse homélie grecque inédite sur la virginité adressée aux pères de famille," *RB* 53 (1953) 18-69; 211-238; also R. Metz, *La consécration des vierges dans l'Eglise romaine* (Paris, 1954).

[17] On the defection of Dianius, the bishop of Caesarea who baptized Basil, see *Ep.* 51.2; Courtonne, 1: 132-133. There was also the downfall of Hosius and Liberius.

[18] *De jud.*, 2 and 1 (conflated): 653c and B; Clarke, pp. 77 f. See also below, pp. 69, n. 149, and 75, n. 175.

That Basil did not let this negative dimension prevail over his consciousness we find evidenced in his early decision to give up a promising career as a sophist-rhetorician, and in his rejection of the eremitic type of asceticism on grounds that it does not serve the common interests of Christians but tends to separate one individual from the other, thus aggravating even more the dissension in the churches. As we shall see Basil's full support and further elaboration of the communal type of asceticism was aimed at healing the church's wounds caused by internal divisions.

After these preliminary remarks based mostly on Basil's own recollections and those of others regarding his first experiences of the church, we will now briefly review some of his writings. We shall consider only those in which some reference is made to the church and its ministerial structure. Because of the uncertainty surrounding the exact chronology of Basil's writings, we can review them here in only an approximate order.

A. *CONTRA EUNOMIUM* 1-3

One of the earliest writings to be considered in which the term "church" occurs is the *Against Eunomius*, Books 1-3, written *ca.* 364.[19] The overall plan of the work is to refute Eunomius' attempt to couch Christian truths in Aristotelian categories and to expose the danger which might follow for Christians from the encroachment of philosophical ideas upon the "simplicity" of expression of their ecclesiastical faith.[20] Prior to writing his apologies, Basil had taken part in a public debate with the Semi-Arians at the Council of Constantinople in January of 360, but apparently without attracting much attention. Thus the treatises against Eunomius constitute his first major contribution to the defence of orthodox Christianity. The rationale for writing the refutation was to protect the faith of those members of the orthodox community who were unskilled ("weak") in Arian sophistries.

What emerges from the opening paragraphs of the first apology against Eunomius is Basil's awareness of a church founded on the "simplicity"

---

[19] This, if we are to place the *Moralia* after 370; see below, pp. 149 ff., our Chronological Table. On Eunomius see M. Spanneut, "Eunome," in *DHGE* 15 (1963) 1399-1405 (with Bibliography). Among the most recent studies should be noted, L. R. Wickham, "The Date of Eunomius' *Apology*: A Reconsideration," *JThS* 20 (1969) 231-240 (Eunomius has *indeed* delivered his *Apology* at the Council of Constantinople), and E. Cavalcanti cited below, n. 22.

[20] *C. Eun.* 1.1: 497A ff.; 5: 516B ff.; 9: 532A. Cf. Kelly, *Early Christian Doctrines*, p. 249.

(ἁπλότης) of the evangelical witness and the apostolic traditions.[21] By emphasizing simplicity Basil shows opposition to any "private" reelaboration or restatement of the ecclesiastical formulae handed down by past generations. He is not so much opposed to knowledge as to the arrogance and self-sufficiency that a man like Eunomius exhibits by calling into question the viability of past formulae and by trying to replace them with some of his own.[22] Also salient throughout Basil's treatises is a strong consciousness of the centrality of the person of Christ in the economy of salvation. Only through Christ is there access to true knowledge (γνῶσις).[23] People who do not believe in the divinity of Christ are, as it were, dead and nonexistent (μὴ ὄντα).[24]

Very characteristic of Basil's understanding of the church's role in establishing the truth is the inclusion of past authorities in the apologies.[25] The use of authorities is most conspicuous in the third book, in which the main thesis that the Spirit is not a creature is entirely drawn from liturgical evidence.[26]

B. The Theme of the Church and Its Charismatic Structure in the Homilies

The hearers of Basil's homilies belonged to varied classes and occupations, with the poor class predominating. Among the people attending his sermons were architects, builders, merchants, husbandmen, soldiers, probably members of the clergy, and also ascetics of the family and communal type.[27] The catechumens seem to have constituted the majority of

---

[21] See *C. Eun.* 1.1: 497A f.

[22] See *C. Eun.* 1.3: 505-508; 2.30: 641A; 7: 584B. Cf. *Ep.* 52.1: Courtonne, 1: 134; Špidlik, *Sophiologie*, pp. 211 ff. See also E. Cavalcanti, *Studi eunomiani* (Rome, 1976), pp. 34-46, and M. Girardi, "Le 'nozioni communi sullo Spirito Santo' in Basilio Magno," *VChr* 13 (1976) 278-283.

[23] See *C. Eun.* 1.26: 569c. Cf. *De sp. s.*, 17-19: Pruche, 302 ff.; *In ps.* 28.3: 288A-B.

[24] See *C. Eun.* 2.19: 612B-C.

[25] See *C. Eun.* 2.5: 585B-C; 19: 612C; 1.3: 508A ("multitude of Christians ... endowed with all sorts of spiritual charismata").

[26] See in particular *C. Eun.* 3.2-3: 657c ff.

[27] The presence of clergy seems to be implied in *Hom.* 3.5: Rudberg, 30. See also the remark on *Hom.* 11.5 below, p. 7. On the two types of ascetics see Appendix B and C below, pp. 156-165. In his otherwise valuable work on the preaching of the Cappadocians Bernardi has failed to take notice of the preface to the *Small Asceticon* (PG 31: 1080A-B) which, in my opinion, implies the regular attendance of Basilian ascetics at the services and instructions held in the local churches. Moreover, many of the so-called *Shorter Rules* seem to have been occasioned by questions put to Basil following his homilies in the church. In

church members at the time belonging to all of the aforementioned walks of life with the exception of the clergy and the ascetics. Thus, most of Basil's homilies can be interpreted as exhortations to baptism and thereby the acceptance of the ascetic life.

Indeed, *Homily 11*, chronologically the first of those to be reviewed here, deals with the subject of envy. It was probably in replying to an outbreak of jealousy that Basil made an excursus on the charismatic structure of the church. Some of his colleagues—the custom then being that several preachers addressed the public on a single occasion—or perhaps some members of the congregation, coveted his charisma of brilliant eloquence. At any rate, the point was made by Basil that neither natural endowments, nor riches, nor strength, nor power are ends in themselves but instruments (ὄργανα) of virtue.[28] They only provide blessedness if used for the purpose of serving the neighbours. Particularly practical wisdom (φρόνησις) and the competence to interpret the words of God are devices and charismata of the Holy Spirit given for the good of others.

> It is your good, and it is for your sake that your brother was endowed with the gift of teaching, if only you are willing to accept it. ... Why then do you refuse to lend your ears gladly to the spiritual word so profuse in the church, and gushing forth like a river from the pious heart filled with the charismata of the Spirit? Why do you not with gratitude take advantage of the benefits? [29]

Per se charismata are instruments intended more for the good of others than the one possessing them.[30] The lesson for the church conveyed in this incidental remark is that, like material possessions, spiritual gifts are also to be regarded not as a private good but as the common property of all.

Homily 3 hinges upon the instrumentality of the *logos* as a means of communication and discipleship among people.[31] Basil speaks with approval of the exercise of the various crafts (τέχναι) in the church. These crafts, whose introduction is elsewhere attributed to the period after the Fall, are highly regarded as outstanding achievements of the human *logos*.[32] Despite their characteristic of being not "us" or "ours" but things "around us,"

---

some cases they appear as further explanations of some points raised during the sermons. As instances cf. *Reg. br.* 301: 1296A f. with *Hom.* 3.4: Rudberg, 28 f.; *Reg. br.* 164: 1189B ff. with *Hom.* 3.5: Rudberg, 30, etc.

[28] *Hom.* 11.5: 381C-D.
[29] Ibid., 384B.
[30] A similar thought is expressed in *Interrog.* 3: 495A.
[31] *Hom.* 3.1: Rudberg, 21 ff.
[32] Cf. *Hom.* 9.9: 394A-B; 3.6: Rudberg, 32-33.

they are used by Basil as incentives to cheer up the poor and destitute.[33] They should, however, be put in the perspective of the gospel requirements. Basil feels that each disciple of the *logos* is a minister (ὑπηρέτης) in charge of one of the activities (πράξεις) demanded by the gospel.

> In the great house, which is the church, there are not only vessels of every kind—golden and silver, of wood and earthenware—but also manifold crafts. Indeed the house of God, that is, the church of the living God, houses hunters, travellers, architects, builders, husbandmen, shepherds, athletes, soldiers.[34]

Basil then proceeds to attribute a higher meaning to each of these occupations, interpreting them symbolically, as significant of higher mysteries.[35]

The theme of the church as a house is developed also in the *Homily on Psalm 29*. The church is the new house of David, built by Christ. "The renovation of the church must be understood as the renewal of the mind, which takes place through the Holy Spirit in each, individually, of those who complete (συμπληρούντων) the body of the church of Christ."[36] Again, the *Homily on Psalm 48* represents the church as housing people of all walks and pursuits of life "in order that no one may be left without its aid."[37] Through the kerygma of the Holy Spirit people of all races and cultures are called to fill its ranks. The church's function in history is described as that of leveling all differences of racial and cultural background or origin. There is one common goal assigned to all: strive to be ruled by God.

In the *Homily on Psalm 44* the church is treated within a christological perspective. The homily relates the words of the psalm to the various aspects of Christ's divinity and humanity: Christ the Word of the Father (393A), Christ the Man anointed by the Spirit (405A), Christ Man and the church, his body (397C), the preaching and the preachers of the gospel (396C; 401A). According to this homily, every believer is a member of the body of Christ.[38] The church is the only perfect dove of Christ "which admits to the right hand [χώραν] of Christ those who are conspicuous by their

---

[33] *Hom.* 3.3: Rudberg, 26. Cf. *Reg. fus.* 55: 1044B ff.

[34] *Hom.* 3.4: Rudberg, 28 f.; see *Hom.* 8.8: 328B.

[35] *Hom.* 3.4: Rudberg, 29-30. For a similar procedure see *In ps.* 28.1: 281A-B; 29.1: 308A; 48.1: 433B.

[36] *In ps.* 29.1: 308A.

[37] *In ps.* 48.1: 433B. See also above, p. 2, n. 7.

[38] *In ps.* 44.5: 397D.

good works, discerning [διαϰρίνουσα] them from the evil ones, as a shepherd discerns the sheep from the goats."[39] Then the preacher proceeds to talk about the soul not subject to sin whom he calls queen and bride standing at the right hand of the "bridal Word."[40] "As the doctrines [δόγματα] are not of one kind but variegated and manifold, comprising moral, natural and mystical sayings [ἠθιϰούς τε ϰαὶ φυσιϰοὺς ϰαὶ τοὺς ἐποπτιϰοὺς λόγους], Scripture [ὁ λόγος] declares that the garment of the bride is variegated."[41]

Returning again to the church, Basil refers to it by the names bride of Christ and daughter of the King, adopted through love.[42] Through the words of the psalmist, God summons the church to abjure its former parent who begot it for destruction, to reject the teachings of the demons and instead to apply itself to the study and observance of the commandments. Through love for God the church becomes his daughter.[43] Only after the church's mind (νοῦς) has been purified of evil teachings and its natural pride overcome through obedience to the humble account of the gospel does it acquire a mind capable of ascending (ἀναβαίνειν) from contemplation (θεωρία) of the visible order to recognition of its Creator.[44] Although he ascribes to the church many of the attributes of Christ the Man, Basil maintains that not the church, but Christ its head is the object of Christian worship (προσϰύνησις).[45]

The church is not only endowed with words but also with many deeds, and therefore it is capable of bringing virgins to the King, but only virgins that keep close to the bride of the King and "do not deflect from the ecclesiastical discipline [εὐταξία]."[46] In the context of the church generated through the proclamation of the gospel, Basil regards the Old Testament patriarchs as the fathers of the church "because for them through Christ were born children doing the works of Abraham."[47] At the end of this long exposition Basil invites his hearers to ponder the greatness of the authority

[39] Ibid., 9: 408c. The authority (ἐξουσία) of discerning good from evil is attributed in *Reg. mor.* 80.15: 865A to one of the church members, the leader of the word, who in the body executes the function of the eye.

[40] *In ps.* 44.9: 408c.

[41] Ibid.

[42] *In ps.* 44.10: 409A; 11: 412c. On the theme of the church as bride of Christ in Origen see H. J. Vogt, *Das Kirchenverständnis des Origenes* (Cologne-Vienna, 1974), pp. 210-225.

[43] *In ps.* 44.10: 409A-B.

[44] Ibid., 10: 409A.

[45] Ibid., 10: 409c.

[46] Ibid., 11: 412c-D.

[47] Ibid., 12: 413B.

(ἐξουσία) of the church in constituting (καθιστάναι) and ordaining (χειρο-
τονέιν) princes all over the earth, that is, saints.[48] For them all the church,
the bride of Christ, is a mother, whom all people remember through their
confession of benefits and thanksgiving (ἐξομολόγησις).[49]

In the *Homilies on Psalm 45* and *59*, Basil applies to the church the Stoic
notion of the city, "an established community [σύστημα], administered [διοι-
κούμενον] according to law."[50] However, the church is a city only of a
special kind, that is, "fortified by the faith encompassing it," and a dwelling
"made joyful by the inflowing of the Holy Spirit."[51] The notion of the
Greek *polis* is applied both to the historical and eschatological community.[52]
The latter is in a certain sense identified with the "church of those who
[here on earth] have their conversation in heaven."[53]

The *Homily on Psalm 59* brings out also the idea that to the tradition of
the Christian church belong the books of the Old Testament which were actually written more with the purpose of serving the Christians ("those who
accepted the change") than the Jews.[54]

According to the *Homily on Psalm 28*, although between the two Testa-
ments there is a continuity of teaching, after the advent of Christ the church
is the sole "holy court" where God should be adored and worshipped.[55] In
the same homily the Jewish synagogue is called "parasynagogue"—illicit
assembly.[56]

The *Homily on Psalm 33* presents the idea of Christians as children
generated through apostolic preaching and ecclesiastical instructions; it

---

[48] Ibid., 12: 413c.

[49] Ibid., 12: 413D.

[50] *In ps.* 45.4: 421c-D; 59.4: 468B. On the sources of this definition see A. Harnack,
History of Dogma (New York, 1961), 2: 81-82 (Platonic idea from the *Republic* found in
Origen); also E. Hatch, *The Influence of Greek Ideas on Christianity* (New York, 1956),
p. 211, n. 5: "The Stoical definition of a *polis* was σύστημα καὶ πλῆθος ἀνθρώπων ὑπὸ νόμου
διοικούμενον." Cf. P. Scazzoso, *Reminiscenze della Polis platonica nel cenobio di s. Basilio*
(Milan, 1970).

[51] *In ps.* 59.4: 468B; 45.4: 421c.

[52] *In ps.* 45.4: 421B-c.

[53] Ibid., 4: 421c; 8: 428c-429A. As a parallel to these passages see *Reg. fus.* 5: 920B ff.,
and 8: 933D ff. See also in this connection our remark below, p. 19 about the moral rather
than institutional character of this "church in heaven."

[54] *In ps.* 59.2: 461B; see *In ps.* 1.2: 213A. On the idea of "change" in the sense of
progress from the imperfect to the perfect see *In ps.* 44.1-2: 388A ff.; *De fide*, 2: 681B; *Ep.*
223.3: Courtonne, 3: 12. On the concept of excommunication from the church referred to *In
ps.* 59.4: 468A, see *Ep.* 61: Courtonne, 1: 151-152.

[55] *In ps.* 28.3: 288A-c; cf. also *C. Eun.* 1.26: 569c.

[56] On the meaning of parasynagogue see *Ep.* 188, *c.* 1 discussed below, pp. 65-67.

speaks also of the bond of charity, peace and harmony binding together the stronger members to the weaker.[57]

The homilies on the *Hexaemeron*, delivered in a time of relative calm, probably 378, afford only incidental remarks. Their main concern is the "edification" of the hearers (the church) for whose spiritual benefit Basil presents an account of the origins of the universe based largely on the reading of the Genesis in the light of contemporary scientific ideas. More than popularizing philosophical theories, Basil's objective is to show that Moses' account of the origins of life in the universe is more trustworthy than that of all Greek philosophers. Already in the expositions of the Psalms we saw Basil crediting the church with the authority ($\dot{\varepsilon}\xi o\nu\sigma\dot{\iota}\alpha$) to discern ($\delta\iota\alpha\varkappa\rho\dot{\iota}\nu\varepsilon\iota\nu$) between what is good and viable and what is evil and objectionable. The same is claimed here with regard to scientific knowledge. Only the church, and consequently only a Christian as a result of being delivered from sin and ignorance, has a mind ($\nu o\tilde{\nu}\varsigma$) capable of knowing and deciding what cosmogonic account is genuine.

Many objections have been and perhaps could yet be raised regarding Basil's assumptions and treatment of science and its methods.[58] It should perhaps be remembered that science ($\dot{\varepsilon}\pi\iota\sigma\tau\dot{\eta}\mu\eta$) for him more than for anyone else was not a neutral field, nor an independent body, but part of a larger, more general and fundamental world view which implied the acceptance or rejection of an ultimate cause.[59] Because, as he understood them, the philosophical speculations of the Greek intellectuals led a great many of them to the negation of God, Basil, in his *Hexaemeron*, tried to discredit them on that score in the eyes of his audience.[60] Naturally the image of the church conveyed by such polemic is not one of openness and dialogue with the world of scientists, but one that is by and large determined by claims of "ideological" superiority.[61]

---

[57] *In ps.* 33.8: 369A-B. This same homily emphasizes the non-egalitarian character of Christian calling: "Just as the bones by their own firmness protect the tenderness of the flesh, so also in the church there are some who through their own constancy are able to carry the infirmities of the weak," etc. (ibid., 13: 384B-C; Way, p. 272). See also below, p. 29, n. 153. For a possible identification of the stronger members see *Hex.* 5.6: Giet, 304, and *Epistles* 28 and 29. Cf. *C. Eun.* 1.1: 500A.

[58] See in particular the study of Y. Courtonne, *Saint Basile et l'hellénisme* (Paris, 1934), and S. Giet's introduction to his edition of Basil's *Hexaemeron* (Paris, 1968), pp. 32 ff., esp. 43 ff.

[59] See Špidlik, *Sophiologie*, pp. 143 ff.

[60] See *Hex.* 1.3: Giet, 96 ff.; 11.8: Smets-Esbroeck, 246 f.

[61] This is, however, an historical judgment. Basil's objective as we mentioned was of a religious rather than sociological nature. On Basil's attitude towards Greek science see Cour-

C. THE CHURCH AS THE COMMUNITY OF COMPLETE CHRISTIANS
IN THE ASCETIC WRITINGS

To appreciate fully Basil's contribution to the understanding of the church and the functions of its leaders, it is important to preface the analysis of his ascetic writings with an historical note.[62]

Beginning with the accession to power of Julian in 361, the milieu of the church changed. Until that moment, Christian religion, despite internal difficulties and struggles, enjoyed some recognition and assistance from the state. Under the auspices of the emperors who regarded themselves not only as heads of the state but also as "external bishops" of the church, that is, the supreme lawgivers and defenders of Christian public and private interests, it was natural for Basil to feel comfortable in his retreat in Pontus.[63] The peaceful coexistence between church and state, which had occasionally been somewhat strained in the past, was forcefully interrupted by Julian and

---

tonne, *S. Basile et l'hellénisme*, and E. Amand de Mendieta, "The Official Attitude of Basil of Caesarea as a Christian Bishop towards Greek Philosophy and Science," in D. Baker, ed., *The Orthodox Churches and the West* (Oxford, 1976), pp. 25-49.

[62] Basil's *Corpus Asceticum* comprises the works listed foremost in his preface to the *Hypotyposis* (the text printed as spurious in PG 31, 1509-1513 has been vindicated as authentic by J. Gribomont, *Histoire du texte des Ascétiques de s. Basile* (Louvain, 1953), pp. 284-287; see there also, pp. 279-282, a critical edition of the Greek text). These works are: *De judicio, De fide, Moralia* and the *Great Asceticon*. However, it must be recognized that, in one way or another, all of Basil's writings bear the stamp of his ascetic training and background. Therefore in a study of his life and ideals connected with Christian asceticism one must also constantly refer to his sermons, letters and "dogmatic" writings. The existence of a previous edition of the *Great Asceticon* (known traditionally as the *Longer* and *Shorter Rules*) has been established only recently, thanks to the studies of F. Laun and J. Gribomont. It came to be known as the *Small Asceticon*. This early edition of Basil's *Asceticon* has been preserved only in two versions, the Latin of Rufinus from 397 (PL 103, 483-554), and in a less accessible Syriac translation from the sixth century. Both translations have been investigated and collated by Gribomont, *Histoire*, pp. 95-148. For reasons explained in the Chronological Table, I adopt the following chronology in the analysis of Basil's ascetic writings: *Small Asceticon*—between 365-369; *Great Asceticon*—370-376; *Moralia*—beginning with 360; final composition with the two prefaces; the *De judicio* and the *De fide*, from 376. The *Hypotyposis*—from 376.

[63] It is my contention that Basil became involved in the recruitment and organization of ascetic communities as a result, partially, of Julian's policies against the Christians and, partially, of emperor Valens' measures. Little consideration has been given until now in Basilian scholarship to the possible influence of these external factors on Basil's decision to switch from an isolated half-desert type of asceticism (Sarabaitism?) to one with closer ties with the church ostracized by the state. This change probably occurred during Basil's visit to Caesarea in 362, and his projects begun then were resumed on full scale on his return in 365. For the (Eastern) idea of the emperor as "always close to hand to his subjects," see P. Brown, *The World of Late Antiquity* (London, 1971), pp. 42-43.

was not to be restored completely until after the death of Basil in 379. In his solitude Basil must soon have become aware of the change. *Epistle 18* encourages two young Christians living in the imperial court to persevere in their convictions. By the time Basil made his appearance in Caesarea in 362, the proposals of the emperor-philosopher for revitalizing the ancestral religion had already been made public.[64] Julian's reform posed a menacing challenge to the church. His religion, more than a revival of old beliefs, was a curious but also updated blend of Neoplatonic and Christian elements. Julian indeed "wanted to smite the Galileans with their own weapons, wanted to build up an organization of pagan clergy on the Christian pattern, wanted to train his priests on principles and for tasks which he had learned among the Christians."[65]

Basil must have been impressed with the careful selection and high moral standards demanded of the new hierarchy by the philosophizing emperor. In one of his letters addressed to the High Priest Theodore, Julian was also stressing the importance of the social aspect—something hitherto unheard of among pagans:

> The Jews do not allow any of their own people to become beggars, and the Christians support not only their own but also our poor; but we leave ours unhelped. ... It is matters like this which have contributed most to the spread of Christianity: mercy to strangers, care for burying the dead, and the obvious honourableness of their conduct. ... And the people must learn to give part of their possessions to others; to the better placed—generously, to the indigent and the poor—sufficient to ward off distress; and, strange though it sounds, to give food and clothing to one's enemies is a pious duty, for we give to men as men, not to particular persons.[66]

Whether or not Basil was in Caesarea at the time of Julian's reprisal-visit to that city in September of 362, the confiscation of church property, the subordination of the clergy to the military authority, and the burden of heavy taxes imposed on all Christians of Caesarea by the emperor must

[64] *Epistles 84* and *89* of Julian, in which the emperor-philosopher sketches his plans to revive the old religion, were written before June of 362. "On June 17, 362, a law was promulgated which made the giving of instruction in school everywhere dependent on the permission of city authorities; and these were directed to test more the character of the applicants" (H. Lietzmann, *History of the Early Church* [Cleveland, 1961], 3: 274). If Eusebius was elected to succeed Dianius in June or July of 362 (see Maran, *Vita*, 8.4), Basil must have arrived at the summons of the dying Dianius either in May or June of the same year; see *Ep.* 51.2: Courtonne, 1: 133.

[65] Lietzmann, *History*, 3: 279.

[66] *Ep.* 89 quoted in Lietzmann, *History*, 3: 278-279.

have made clear to Basil, as to any one else, that in order to survive the
church needed a different kind of structure and arrangement that would
make its well-being less dependent on the state.[67] The strengthening of internal unity and the autonomy of the bishops in the administering of its affairs had to be given priority.[68] If at the time Basil had come up with concrete plans and tried a solution, he did not succeed in putting his projects
into practice. A conflict arose between him and the bishop Eusebius, and to
avoid the threat of an internal schism Basil retreated to Pontus.[69] The reign
of Julian, in any event, was short-lived.[70]

Whatever thoughts on the church and the functions of its leaders Basil
might have had during his exile in Pontus, we see him busily engaged in the
organization of ascetic communities. The corporate type of Christian life
had definitively prevailed in his mind over the individual one. From the
moment when in 365, with a visit of Valens imminent, Eusebius recalls him
to Caesarea, Basil will be seen as uncompromisingly committed to the
project of church reform on the pattern of the pre-Constantinian model or,
better yet, of the apostolic community of Jerusalem.

The desire to strengthen the internal organization, the distinctiveness and
self-sufficiency of the church as a society of its own is characteristic of
Basil's activities displayed during the period 365-378. It would be easy
perhaps simply to read his ascetic works from that period and draw conclusions from the material evidence.[71] The issue, however, becomes complicated from the moment when we firmly realize that Basil was above all
an ascetic. In the fourth century there were various existing models of perfect Christian life. However impartial we may try to be in the analysis of
Basil's writings concerned with his awareness of the church, conclusions
will largely depend upon whether we make of him a tributary of the desert
type of asceticism represented in its organized form by Pachomius, or of the

---

[67] I place Julian's visit to Caesarea in September of 362 because on September 7 was the
annual commemoration of the martyrdom of Eupsychius and Damas, who were executed by
order of the emperor during his stay in Cappadocia; see *Epp.* 100, 176 and 252, and Maran,
Vita, 8.5-6; L. Duchesne, *The Early History of the Christian Church* (London, 1912), 2:
265; Lietzmann, *History*, 3: 279-280 (I do not know on what evidence this author calls
Eupsychius a bishop, 3: 280).

[68] Julian's policies had certainly affected Gregory of Nazianzus. Besides his *Invectives
against Julian* from 363 (which were probably never pronounced in public), see *Orations 20,
42* and *43*. On the latter two see the important observation of Bernardi, *Prédication*,
pp. 257-258.

[69] See Greg. Naz., *Or.* 43.29.

[70] The emperor died on June 26, 363, and was succeeded by the pious Jovian.

[71] The same applies to his other works, see n. 62, above.

urban version practiced under the instigation of Eustathius of Sebaste in the northern provinces of Asia Minor. Since the question of Basil's indebtedness to either of these two representatives of Christian asceticism in the fourth century has been long debated, and although the opinion of modern scholars tends somewhat to favour Eustathius' influence on Basil, because of its undeniable import we have tried to reopen this question in two Appendices placed at the end of this work.[72] The following discussion of the church as a community of complete Christians presupposes some of the results reached in our two Appendices, and the reader, if in doubt, would be well advised to become acquainted with them first.

As we mentioned earlier, during the period commencing in 362 Basil became an uncompromising advocate of the ecclesial type of asceticism. This asceticism in his original intention was to be developed not on the margins of the local churches but as a sequel to the sacrament of baptism. All Christians, independently of sex, race, social condition and even age, were, within their limits, to practise the ascetic life.[73] Whereas the form could vary, the quality of the desire to become similar to God, so far as this is humanly possible, was to be the same.[74]

Basil's thought on the corporate character of Christian perfection is developed mainly in his *Asceticons*.[75] His recommendation of the corporate type of sanctity is based upon the premise "that all men by nature desire beautiful things, despite the fact that they differ as to what is supremely beautiful."[76] While some of the Gentiles (τῶν ἔξω) have declared that the

---

[72] See below, pp. 156 ff.

[73] That Basil's ascetic ideal is addressed to all, independently of sex, social condition, and also very largely of age, can be proved from *Interrog.* 6: 497D-498B; *Reg. fus.* 10.1: 944C ff.; 11: 948A-C; *Reg. mor.* 75.1: 856A; *Reg. fus.* 12: 948C ff.; 15.1-4: 952A-957A; *Reg. mor.* 73.1-6: 849D-853B; 76.1-2: 857A-B. The only remote condition seems to be baptism; see *Reg. fus.* 8.1: 936A and *Interrog.* 4: 498C, in the sense that catechumens, who in the local churches constituted the majority, would be excluded from Basil's "versions" of the church. That baptism was not an immediate condition can be inferred from Basil's account of his own ascetic renunciation in *Ep.* 223.2: Courtonne, 3: 10. Although regulations concerning the admission of slaves, married persons, and children appear only in the *Great Asceticon* it must be noted that the *Asceticons* are not systematic works but that their composition progressively developed as questions were raised; see *Scholion* 2, 3 and 4 in Gribomont, *Histoire*, pp. 152-154.

[74] See *De sp. s.* 2: Pruche, 252; *Reg. mor.* 80.8: 861D.

[75] We have in mind particularly the "systematic" part, the so-called "Longer Rules," in the *Small Asceticon, Interrogations* 1-11, and the *Reg. fus.* 1-54 of the *Great Asceticon*. While in all probability the titles of the shorter questions are original, that is, posited by the disciples of Basil, the headings of the longer ones were improperly added by the editors; see J. Gribomont, "Saint Basile," *Théologie de la vie monastique* (Paris, 1961), p. 104.

[76] See *Reg. fus.* 2.1: 909B; ibid.: 912A.

end is theoretical knowledge (ἐπιστήμη), others, practical activity (πρᾶξις), others, some profitable use (χρῆσθαι) of life and body, and others, simply pleasure (ἡδονή), Christianity transcends them all by placing man's end in "the blessed life in the world to come," which will consist in being "ruled by God." [77] "Up to this time," Basil observes, "nothing better than the latter idea [life under the rule of God] has been found in rational nature." [78]

Christian righteousness and holiness are identified by Basil with the observance of all divine commandments: "There is one rule and canon prescribed for our works, to fulfil God's commandments in a manner pleasing to Him." [79] The disposition (διάθεσις) of complete subordination to the divine rule is identified with the knowledge (γνῶσις) of God. [80] *Gnosis* in Basil's terminology is thus not the same as the abstract *epistēmē* of the Platonist philosophers. It is rather a religious intimacy and communion between man and God grounded on love. When Basil insists that all divine commandments ought to be implemented without distinction, his ideal of evangelical sanctity may be suspected of formalistic legalism. However, Basil expressly distinguishes between the character of the gospel and the Jewish law precisely on the score "that as the law forbids bad deeds, so the gospel forbids the very hidden sins of the soul," and so on. [81] It is here that we arrive at the core of Basil's ascetic teaching. Before stating that moral perfection consists in the implementation of all divine commandments, Basil makes clear that God's decrees act only as reminders and stimuli to man's inborn tendency to love. They do not force themselves upon man's faculty of self-determination from the outside but only activate and cultivate the *logos spermatikos* implanted in man from his first constitution. [82]

Love, Basil teaches, is such a moral action (κατόρθωμα) that, although it is only one, as regards power it accomplishes and comprehends every com-

---

[77] Cf. *In ps.* 48.1: 432A-B. That the expression τῶν ἔξω probably refers to the Gentile philosophers see J. Gribomont, "Le renoncement au monde dans l'idéal ascétique de saint Basile," *Irénikon* 31 (1958) 303. See also the excellent study of A. M. Malingrey, *"Philosophia". Etude d'un groupe de mots dans la littérature grecque, des Présocratiques au IVᵉ siècle après J.C.* (Paris, 1961), pp. 212-235 (the Cappadocians). The philosophical schools in question can be identified as follows: ἐπιστήμη—Platonists; πρᾶξις—Aristotle; χρῆσθαι—Stoics; ἡδονή—Epicureans.

[78] *In ps.* 48.1: 432B.

[79] *Reg. fus.* 5.3: 921C; Clarke, p. 160.

[80] Cf. *Hom.* 23.4: 597A which definition concords with the use of γνῶσις and its counterpart ἀγνωσία in the whole treatise *De judicio*, e.g., 3: 657A-B.

[81] *Reg. mor.* 43.1: 761C. See also ibid., 2: 761D; Clarke, p. 112: "That as the law makes a partial, so the gospel makes a complete demand as regards every good action," which confirms what was said above, pp. 15-16; see also *Reg. br.* 4: 1984C; 293, 1288C ff.

[82] See *Reg. fus.* 2.1: 908B-C; 909A-B.

mandment; hence all commandments issue in love.[83] This is an important conclusion that Basil reaches at the very beginning of his "systematic" part of the *Asceticon*. For the man seeking happiness and fulfillment there is one simple thing to be done: to let himself be moved by the love of God and of his neighbours. "For 'he that loveth me', saith the Lord, 'will keep my commandments'. And again: 'On these two commandments hang all the law and the prophets'."[84] Moreover, the Lord

> demanded as a proof [$\dot{\alpha}\pi\dot{o}\delta\epsilon\iota\xi\iota\nu$: syllogistic demonstration] that we are His disciples, not signs and marvellous works—and yet He bestowed the working of these too in the Holy Spirit—but what does He say? 'By this shall all men know that ye are my disciples, if ye have love one towards another.'[85]

The two commandments of love are so bound up together that the Lord

> transfers to Himself benefits conferred on one's neighbours. For He says: 'I was hungry and ye gave me to eat,' and so on. To which He adds: 'Inasmuch as ye did it to one of the least of these my brethren, ye did it unto me.'[86]

At this point, an inescapable conclusion imposes itself: If all commandments and virtues are indeed represented in love as their most genuine form and expression, *Christian perfection cannot be individual, but can flourish and achieve perfection only in a life of communion* ($\kappa o\iota\nu\omega\nu\iota\alpha$) *with God and one's neighbours.* We have thus reached the topic Basil deals with in the first chapter of his *Asceticons*: the corporate or ecclesial dimension of Christian perfection.[87]

Interrogations 1-3 of the *Small Asceticon* and the *Longer Questions 1-7* of the *Great Asceticon*, basically deal with the environmental problem, that is, with the ideal conditions for leading a life in conformity with the divine commandments. Two aspects are involved: (1) Should Christians converted to the gospel continue to live among those who hold in contempt the divine commandments ($o\dot{\iota}\ \ddot{\epsilon}\xi\omega\theta\epsilon\nu$)? (2) If not, should they live by themselves, in solitude, or should they come together with like-minded brethren ($\dot{o}\mu\dot{o}\varphi\rho o\nu o\iota$ $\dot{\alpha}\delta\epsilon\lambda\varphi o\iota$) and form communities of their own?[88] Both questions are very

---

[83] See *Reg. fus.* 2.1: 908D; Clarke, p. 153.

[84] Ibid.

[85] *Reg. fus.* 3.1: 917A-B; Clarke, p. 157.

[86] Ibid.

[87] For the sake of brevity I shall quote mainly from the expanded text of the *Great Asceticon* unless there is an important difference in content, in which case I shall also cite the text of the *Small Asceticon.*

[88] The first question is taken from *Reg. fus.* 6.1-2: 925A-928B; the second, from *Reg. fus.* 7.1-4: 928B-933C, and the corresponding *Interrog.* 2: 493B-494A and *Interrog.* 3: 494B-496B.

important from the ecclesial point of view despite the fact that some passages of Basil's ascetic works can be interpreted as favouring the constitution of particular ("monastic") communities within the universal community of the church.[89] In spite of such ambiguities, his *Asceticons* offer a valuable contribution for the understanding of the church as a community of baptized people trying to live a perfect life not only in the monastic seclusion but also in the middle of the world.

In referring to the subject treated in the first chapters of both *Asceticons* we called it an environmental problem. The fourth century was a time of numerous critical changes in the church's internal and external organization. When Basil insists in his treatises on the quality rather than the form of Christian life, and when he maintains that to be perfect it is not enough to follow some more convenient norms and ignore the rest, he is trying to protect the church's elements of distinctiveness, sacredness, and secrecy which so significantly, in his opinion, characterized early Christianity.[90] The fourth century saw crowds of people flocking into the church not for the sake of improving the spiritual character of their lives, but often for the mere convenience of becoming eligible for public offices and careers.[91] With the indiscriminately swelled ranks, the church's awareness of being a sacred community distinct from earthly society was in danger of disappearing. There was hardly any *disciplina arcani* left to keep church doctrines, rites and customs out of reach of the unworthy.[92] More as a solicitous pastor than a "monastic legislator," Basil, following a service in the church, evidences readiness to answer questions from those who are willing to inquire further "concerning that which belongs to sound faith and the true method of right conduct according to the gospel of our Lord Jesus

---

[89] See below, pp. 163 ff.; Gribomont, "Renoncement," pp. 300-302.

[90] On the church's elements of sacredness, distinctiveness, and secrecy see *Ep.* 28.1: Courtonne, 1: 66-67; *De sp. s.* 66: Pruche, 478 ff.; E. Amand de Mendieta, *The 'Unwritten' and 'Secret' Apostolic Traditions in the Theological Thought of St. Basil of Caesarea* (Edinburgh, 1965); Idem, "The Pair κήρυγμα and δόγμα in the Theological Thought of St. Basil of Caesarea," *JThS* 16 (1965) 129-142. However, I would be inclined to agree with the interpretation of the *De sp. s.* 66 given by G. Florovsky, "The Function of Tradition in the Ancient Church," *GOTR* 9 (1963) 181-200, despite Amand's reservations in "The Pair," p. 136.

[91] In Cappadocia many tried to join the ascetic communities only to avoid taxes and military service. If Basil managed to deter many from joining the church for trivial reasons, he probably did so by making almost compulsory acceptance of ascetic renunciation part of the baptismal renunciation. This is not, however, so clear from the *Asceticons* alone, nor from Basil's homilies. See on the latter Bernardi, *Prédication*, p. 396.

[92] Besides n. 90 see Lietzmann, *History*, 4: 98-99.

Christ" by means of which "the man of God is perfected."[93] If they are sincerely determined to redress their morals, to take up their cross as true disciples of the Lord and to deny themselves completely, he asks this elite not "to mix with those who are fearlessly and scornfully disposed towards the exact observance of the commandments."[94]

Life in the "world," that is, among people who despise the teaching of Christ, is described by Basil as full of overt and hidden dangers.[95] Basil does not advocate a physical separation or total withdrawal from this environment, at least not as a permanent measure. The concept of the *fuga mundi*, it has been noticed, does not occur in this context at all, and the description of Christians as having their "citizenship in heaven" appears to be more ethical than institutional in nature.[96] In a letter written from his Pontic retreat, where Basil retired to amend his way of life "long perverted by the intimacy with wicked people," he states:

> One way of escaping [μία φυγή] all this [that is the cares (μέριμναι) of life] is separation [χωρισμός] from the whole world. However, separation from the world [κόσμου ἀναχώρησις] not through bodily withdrawal from it [οὐ τὸ ἔξω αὐτοῦ γενέσθαι σωματικῶς], but through severance of the soul's sympathy with the body, so as to live without city, home, goods, society, possessions, means of life, business engagements, intercourse, human learning, that the heart may readily receive every impression of divine doctrine.[97]

It is obvious that what counts most is spiritual withdrawal from the environment of sinners and outsiders. However, as a temporary measure, seclusion from people and also withdrawal from the political community are recommended at the beginning of one's conversion to "philosophy"—the life according to the gospel.[98] Basil himself spent some time in the solitude of his estate. But, as his own letters show us, during his retreat Basil continued to be in touch with the world of friends, magistrates, public servants.[99] Whereas at one point he perhaps thought that he should cut off these relations too, later on he understood that quiet (ἡσυχία) lies not so much in physical separation as in freeing oneself from ties caused by a

---

[93] *Proem. in reg. br.*: 1080A; Clarke, p. 229.
[94] *Reg. fus.* 6.1: 925A; Clarke, p. 161; cf. ibid., 925C.
[95] For a definition of the "world" in the moral sense see *De sp. s.* 53: Pruche, 440 f.; see also n. 94.
[96] Cf. Gribomont, "Renoncement," pp. 295 and 300.
[97] *Ep.* 2.2: Rudberg, 158; cf. Jackson, p. 110; see also *Ep.* 223.2: Courtonne, 3: 10.
[98] Besides n. 97 see Gribomont, "Renoncement," pp. 305-306, and *Ep.* 210.1: Courtonne, 2: 190, ὅτε φεύγων τοὺς πολιτικοὺς θορύβους (γενέσθαι ἄπολιν in *Ep.* 2.2: Rudberg, 158).
[99] See *Epistles* 3-6, 9, 11-13, 15, 17-18, 20-21.

passionate attachment to life (τῶν δεσμῶν τῆς προσπαθείας τοῦ βίου), in the avoidance of distractions, and giving up of all unnecessary worldly cares (μέριμναι).[100] The criterion, however, for discerning and judging what things *in concreto* should be avoided is a very subjective one: it is anything that, in one's opinion, seems to interfere with the way of piety (εὐσέβεια) and the strictness of the gospel.[101]

Undoubtedly Basil advocates the necessity of abandoning the world in order to serve God adequately, not the world as such—for our anxieties will pursue us everywhere—but the world conceived as the society of outsiders-sinners (οἱ ἔξωθεν), people hostile to the teaching and the spirit of Christ.[102]

Next Basil speaks in his *Asceticons* against withdrawing from the company of the like-minded, that is, from those who share sound views on the commandments and on the gospel.[103] Many in the fourth century, affected adversely by the evils of the world and of the church, fled to the desert. Basil categorically rejects such a solution as unchristian (unscriptural) and inhuman. Instead, Basil wishes his converts to come together, to live together (συζῆν) as closely as possible in one body, with Christ as the head and the Holy Spirit as the soul.[104]

W. K. L. Clarke had already noticed that the doctrine contained in the *Longer Rule 7* on the disadvantages of eremitic life and benefits of community life can be applied "equally well to a Christian life in the world."[105] There can be no doubt that Basil meant something more than a convent when he spoke of the benefits of sharing (κοινωνεῖν) spiritual gifts (charismata) and material possessions with others. He assuredly intended his new church to be patterned on the model of the first Christian community of Jerusalem, whose members "were together and had all things in common."[106] We shall, then, summarize Basil's teaching from his *Longer*

---

[100] See *Reg. fus.* 5.1-3: 920A-924D, esp. 921A.

[101] Cf. Gribomont, "Renoncement," pp. 300-301.

[102] Cf. *Ep.* 2.1-2: Rudberg, 156 ff.

[103] Cf. *Reg. fus.* 7: 928B ff.; *Interrog.* 3: 494B ff.

[104] Besides *Reg. fus.* 7.2: 929C see *De jud.*, 3: 660A.

[105] *Saint Basil the Great. A Study in Monasticism* (Cambridge, 1913), p. 86, n. 2. Unfortunately this author often fails to draw the pertinent conclusions from many of his remarkable insights. For instance, on pp. 112-113 of the same work Clarke skillfully demonstrates that the term μιγάς in Gregory of Nazianzus is used to describe the ascetic life lived in the world. However, he never follows up this accurate observation.

[106] Text from Acts 2.44 quoted in *Reg. fus.* 7.4: 933C. There do not seem to be substantial changes between the exposition in the *Reg. fus.* 7 and the *Interrog.* 3 regarding our subject. The only discrepancy I noticed is that Rufinus' text speaks also of prayer as drawing benefit from the communal life; see 495C. However, in the *Great Asceticon* there seems to be a certain insinuation, but no more than that, as to the benefits of living in the same place.

Rule 7.[107] Concomitantly, we shall adduce parallel passages from Basil's other writings in order to see whether his doctrine on the corporate type of Christian life is applicable to all members in the church.

Basil's arguments in favour of communal Christianity are contained in the following general principles:

(1) No man is individually self-sufficient (αὐτάρκης). By nature he needs the assistance of other fellow members in providing for his bodily needs.[108]

(2) The *logos* of Christian love does not allow each man to look to his own good exclusively. "For 'love', we read, 'seeketh not its own'."[109]

(3) It is harmful to the soul when men have no one to rebuke them for their faults.[110]

(4) The solitary life is idle and fruitless for it allows only a partial implementation of the commandments.[111]

(5) "All of us who have been received in one hope of our calling are one body having Christ as head, and we are severally members of one another. But if we are not joined together harmoniously in the close links of one body in the Holy Spirit, but each of us chooses solitude, not serving the common welfare in a way well-pleasing to God but fulfilling private desires, how, when we are thus separated and divided off, can we preserve the mutual relation and service of the limbs one to another, or their subjection to our head, which is Christ?"[112]

(6) A charisma is a gift of the Holy Spirit given and accepted for the benefit of others.[113] No person can possess all the charismata. But "when a number live together," a man enjoys not only his own charisma, but he multiplies it "by imparting it to others, and reaps the fruits of other men's charismata as if they were his own."[114]

(7) Life in the company of many provides a good protection against the plots of the enemy, and the presence of others is a good means for the correction of one's own faults.[115]

---

[107] A rather "monastic" analysis of this interrogation can be found in E. Amand de Mendieta, *L'ascèse monastique de saint Basile* (Maredsous, 1949), pp. 118-128; see also Clarke, *Monasticism*, pp. 85-86.

[108] Cf. *Reg. fus.* 7.1: 928c-d. The concept of "insufficiency" is also expressed in *Ep.* 97: Courtonne, 1: 210. See also *Ep.* 203.3: Courtonne, 2: 170.

[109] *Reg. fus.* 7.1: 929a.

[110] Ibid.

[111] Ibid.: 929b.

[112] Ibid., 2: 929c; Clarke, p. 164.

[113] *Interrog.* 3: 495a: "quae [charismata] singula non tam pro se unusquisque quam pro aliis suscipit a Spiritu sancto."

[114] *Reg. fus.* 7.2: 932b; Clarke, p. 165.

[115] Ibid., 3: 932b-c.

(8) In a structure that allows no personal relations it is impossible to practice many of the Christian virtues such as humility, mercy or long-suffering. Scripture provides only the theory of perfection ; theory without practice is void.[116]

It was perhaps only natural that in the course of later institutional developments such an exposition of the advantages of the communal life, strongly motivated by scriptural and philosophical arguments, should be almost exclusively applied by many Christians to monastic institutes. Basil, in such a view, would be speaking here not to all Christians but only to those who have decided to practice not only the commandments but also the so-called evangelical precepts. Such an attempt to limit the scope of Basil's projected reform of the contemporary church to one small portion of it should, however, be dismissed as ill-founded and anachronistic.[117]

As we observed earlier, throughout his works Basil never employs a special name to designate his close followers. His disciples, even those ad-dressed in the shorter interrogations of the *Great Asceticon*, are active mem-bers of the local church. Through them Basil expects to revive the ideal of the first apostolic community, whose members were "of one heart and one soul," and had all things in common with no one seeking what is his own but only what is for the good of others.[118] The communal life in Basil's ter-minology is the "apostolic life"; it is Christian life grounded on and nur-tured by love; it is in other words "faith working through love."[119] As the *Moralia*, the manual for ascetics living in the world, puts it,

> the *logos* wishes Christians to be: as disciples of Christ, conformed only to the pattern of what they see in Him, or hear from Him; ... as members of Christ, who are perfect in the working of all the commandments of the Lord, or equipped with the charismata of the Holy Spirit according to the worthiness of the head, which is Christ; ... as light in the world, so that both they them-selves are not receptive of evil and enlighten those who approach them to a knowledge of the truth, and these either become what they should be or reveal what they are; as salt in the world, so that they who communicate with them [κοινωνοῦντας] are renewed in the spirit unto incorruptibility.[120]

Between his churches as communities of perfect Christians and the world

---

[116] Cf. ibid., 4: 933A.

[117] For more on this see below, pp. 161-165.

[118] On the frequent use of Acts 2.44 and 4.32, see Amand de Mendieta, *Ascèse*, p. 129, n. 88.

[119] Cf. *Ep.* 295: Courtonne, 3: 169-170. Cf. also *Reg. mor.* 80.22: 868c: "What is the ethos of a Christian? Faith working through love."

[120] *Reg. mor.* 80.1, 4, 9-10: 860c-864A; Clarke, pp. 127-128.

of οἱ ἔξωθεν Basil does not think any friendship (φιλία) possible, for no one can be a friend of the wicked and undiscerning (τῶν πονηρῶν καὶ ἀμαθῶν).[121] He does, however, admit a beneficial relationship with a view to winning the wicked to the church.[122]

As we mentioned earlier, in his long exposition of the benefits resulting for the individual from the adoption of a communal standard of life, Basil had also tried to deprive the eremitic experience of reasonable foundation by declaring it to be inhuman and unscriptural. Previously he had identified the requirement to abandon the world with the demand to flee and resist the company of outsiders not physically, but so far as friendship was concerned. His further appeal to constitute new fellowships of perfect Christians alongside the officially supported societies of the οἱ ἔξωθεν was aimed at the formation of a new nucleus of authentic practitioners of the gospel, whose conversation would be in heaven, from where the light of the gospel would diffuse to all.

Basil's plea to Christians to adopt a corporate concept of sanctity acquires further moment if considered in its historical context. Fourth-century churches were mostly found in the cities or near populated areas. Many Christians perhaps, in view of the scarcely edifying urban life, would have preferred to spend their time after baptism in some quiet spot, far from those centres of corruption and loose morality. Basil himself, after suffering a similar crisis of Christian identity, realized that ἡσυχία, spiritual peace, and ἀπάθεια, freedom from sins, was to be found not through "bodily separation" from the world "but in the severance of the soul's sympathy with the body."[123] Through his action, he thus prevented the questionable Egyptian experiment of Christians deserting the churches from repeating itself in Asia Minor.

D. THE HOLY SPIRIT AND LIFE IN THE BROTHERHOOD:
THE BASILIAN BROTHERHOOD AS THE BODY OF CHRIST

The term ἀδελφότης is indiscriminately applied by Basil to both the ascetic community and the local church.[124] Basil's cenobia were clearly

---

[121] See In ps. 44.2: 392c. Compare Cicero, De officiis 1.17, 53-58: Miller, 56-60.

[122] See Reg. mor. 80.9-10: 864A; 18.6: 732c-D, and also below, pp. 74-75.

[123] See Ep. 2.2 analyzed above, pp. 19 f.

[124] See on the ascetic community, Epp. 223.5: Courtonne, 3: 14; 257.2: ibid., 100; and the Great Asceticon, passim. As applied to the church, see Epp. 133: Courtonne, 2: 47; 135.2: ibid., 50; 226.2: ibid., 3: 25; 255: ibid., 96. See also Didascalia Apostolorum and Firmilian's, among Cyprian's, Epistle 175.25: CSEL 3.2. Cf. also 1 Pet 5.9. However,

structured on the pattern of the first community of Jerusalem—the ideal
church, according to Basil, in which all things were common, whose members were united by the same faith and brotherly love, "all in common
seeking in the one Holy Spirit the will of the one Lord Jesus Christ." [125]
These communities of perfect Christians patterned on the model church of
Jerusalem were designed to serve as models for the contemporary local
churches. [126] Since we shall continually speak of the Holy Spirit as being for
Basil the main architect of the church, we here propose to outline first the
notion of charisma in Basil's writings, notably in the *Moralia* and the *De
Spiritu Sancto*, and second the idea of the Christian life as a life in the body
of Christ characterized by the presence and riches of the Holy Spirit. Our
intent is to indicate briefly that the Basilian brotherhoods—the ascetic communities and ideally all the local churches—are organic unities, whose life
and functioning depends directly upon the charismatic operation of the
Holy Spirit.

i. *What is Charisma?*

From time to time throughout this chapter we have heard Basil speak of
the charismata and the charismatic structure of the church. We must now
consider more closely the significance of this term in his theological
vocabulary, especially in view of its frequent occurrence in the *Moralia* and
the *De Spiritu Sancto*. As Basil seems to derive his notion of charisma from
Paul, we shall first outline Paul's concept inasmuch as he is the first to introduce this term into the Christian theological vocabulary. [127]

---

beginning with the fourth century it is commonly restricted to the ascetic communities; see
Greg. Nys., *Vit. Macr.* 16: Maraval, 194 and n. 1, ibid., references to Gregory of Nazianzus,
Macarius, and Jerome.

[125] *De jud.*, 4: 660c-d; Clarke, p. 81.

[126] L. Vischer, *Basilius der Grosse* (Basel, 1953), p. 49, whose position Gribomont,
"Renoncement," p. 474, endorses, has tried to reverse the statement of P. Humbertclaude by
saying that Basil endeavoured to reform the local churches on the pattern of his cenobia, and
not vice versa. It seems, however, that the most accurate statement to make is that Basil first
built (or re-built) his ascetic communities on the pattern of the model church of Jerusalem,
and that he then proceeded to apply that model to the contemporary churches: thus
(a) church of Jerusalem; (b) ascetic community embodying that model; (c) the local church
extending and perpetuating it. The interest in the model community of Jerusalem has been
constantly present in the mind of many church reformers, from the early centuries through
Basil and Augustine to the Middle Ages. In the absence of an overall study the reader may
consult the works of A. Vööbus, *History of Asceticism in the Syrian Orient...* (Louvain,
1958, 1960), and P. C. Bori, *La chiesa primitiva* (Brescia, 1974).

[127] The following exposition of Paul's teaching on charismata is based largely on the
works of E. Käsemann, "Ministry and Community in the New Testament," in *Essays on*

Although the reality signified by the word 'charisma' is familiar to other New Testament writers, Paul is the first to give it a precise theological significance.[128] The basic notion of charisma can be found in Romans 6.23: "The charisma of God is eternal life in Christ Jesus our Lord." "Other charismata only exist because of the existence of this one charisma to which they are all related, and they only exist where the gift of eternal life is manifested in the eschatologically inaugurated dominion of Christ."[129] In our opinion, the key passage to study in considering Paul's notion of charisma is 2 Corinthians 13.13, where the apostle uses the expression, $ἡ$ $κοινωνία$ $τοῦ$ $Πνεύματος$. As it stands, this text admits of two equally possible renderings, "The participation [fellowship] *of* the Holy Spirit," or, "The participation [fellowship] *in* the Holy Spirit."[130] This is precisely what charisma is: It is a participation or communion both in the objective and subjective sense; that is, it is a fellowship *of* and *in* the Holy Spirit.

Charisma points first towards the event of man's participation in the eschatological riches imparted by the death and resurrection of Jesus Christ. In this latter sense it is referred to by Paul also by the terms $κλῆσις$ and $φανέρωσις$ $τοῦ$ $Πνεύματος$ (cf. 1 Cor 12.7). In the second place or rather concomitantly with the first sense, charisma is a participation in the fate and sufferings of others. Paul identifies it with the *diakonia*, the service which Christians render to their fellowmen (1 Cor 12.4 ff.). The term that comprehends all these aspects of charisma is $κλῆσις$ $τοῦ$ $Θεοῦ$, the calling from God addressed to each person individually to participate in his life through his Son in the Holy Spirit and to render the necessary services to our neighbours (Rom 11.29; 1 Cor 7.7, 17 ff.).

Charisma essentially is a *koinonia* in and of the Holy Spirit through which Christians are called by the Risen Lord to serve his cause by serving their neighbours. The Pauline concept of charisma encompasses the whole range of human actions which under the influence and guidance of the Holy Spirit are performed for the specific purpose of proclaiming the lordship of

---

New Testament Themes (London, 1964), pp. 63-94; Idem, "Worship in Everyday Life: a note on Romans 13," in *New Testament Questions of Today* (London, 1969), pp. 188-195; E. Schweizer, *Church Order in the New Testament* (London, 1961); Idem, *Jesus* (Richmond, Va., 1971); J. D. G. Dunn, *Jesus and the Spirit* (London, 1975). See also the articles "Charisma" (by H. Conzelmann) and "Pneuma" (by E. Schweizer) in *TDNT* and the homonymous entries in *PGL*.

[128] See Käsemann, "Ministry," p. 64.

[129] Käsemann, "Ministry," p. 64.

[130] For a discussion of these possibilities see L. S. Thornton, *The Common Life in the Body of Christ* (London, 1963), pp. 66 ff., and J. D. G. Dunn, p. 261.

Christ and edifying his church. Reacting against the Enthusiasts of Corinth, the apostle reminds them that they should not restrict this notion exclusively to the supernatural and miraculous phenomena such as ecstasies and glossolalia (1 Cor 12.22 ff.). As the Antichrist can also produce signs, wonders and powers (see Mt 24.24; Mk 13.22 and 2 Thess 2.9), the possession of the former is not yet a guarantee of participation in eternal life. Conversely, Paul points out that such inconspicuous and ordinary tasks as tending the sick or providing physical welfare for the poor *can be* charismata of the Spirit *if* accompanied by faith in the lordship of Christ and the intention to edify his community, the church. In other words, the true measure of charisma is the way in which, in and for the Lord, an existing set of natural circumstances is transformed by the new obedience to the Risen Lord. My previous condition of life becomes charisma as soon as in baptism the Spirit transforms and takes possession of me. From that moment on nothing is secular or unclean for me as a Christian anymore, but everything becomes holy and purified as long as I use it to proclaim the lordship of Christ and to build up his church.[131] It is in virtue of this comprehensive conception that Paul could speak of marriage, of virginity, of widowhood, of the condition of being slave or free, male or female, etc., as charismata, that is, possible callings and services.[132] As Käsemann observes :

> Charisma is no longer the distinguishing mark of elect individuals but that which is the common endowment of all who call upon the name of the Lord, or, to use the phraseology of the primitive Christian tradition as we have it in Acts 2.17 ff., a demonstration of the fact that the Spirit of God has been poured out on all flesh.[133]

In summing up Paul's teaching on charismata, the same author writes:

> Paul's teaching on the subject of charismata constitutes the proof, first, that he made no basic distinction between justification and sanctification and did not understand justification in a merely declaratory sense; further, that he binds justification by faith tightly to baptism, so that it is not permissible to drive a wedge into his gospel, separating the juridical from the sacramental

---

[131] See Käsemann, "Ministry," p. 72. The term "new obedience" for the post-Easter faith is also taken from him; see also Idem, "Worship," p. 194, where it is demonstrated that for Paul there was no difference between the private and public realm.

[132] See for the biblical references Käsemann, "Ministry," p. 69; *contra*, Dunn, *Jesus*, pp. 206 f.

[133] "Ministry," pp. 73-74.

approach; and finally, that he considers faith to be actually constituted by the new obedience.[134]

In view of Basil's use of the term charisma in other contexts, we should add also Paul's application of this term in the description of the "social" relations among the Christians as members of the church, the body of Christ. First, in his teaching on charismata, Paul rules out any ecclesiastical egalitarianism.

> God does not repeat himself when he acts, and there can be no mass production of grace. There is differentiation in the divine generosity, whether in the order of creation or of redemption. Equality is not for Paul a principle of Church order.[135]

It is within such contexts that we often hear Paul saying, "To each his own" (Rom 12.3; 1 Cor 3.5; 11.18; 12.7).

> Within the ranks of the community there are to be found both strong and weak, aristocrat and proletarian, wise and foolish, cultured and uncultured. No one, according to 1 Cor 12.21, may say to his brother 'I have no need of you.' Over them all stands the sign $\kappa\alpha\theta\dot{\omega}\varsigma$ $\beta o\acute{u}\lambda\varepsilon\tau\alpha\iota$ or $\mathring{\eta}\theta\acute{\varepsilon}\lambda\eta\sigma\varepsilon\nu$ (1 Cor 12.11, 18); this expresses the sovereignty of the divine grace and omnipotence, which is both liberal and liberating, which puts an end to worry and envy by giving individually to every man.[136]

The second watchword coined by Paul in the context of his doctrine on the charismata is, "For one another" (1 Cor 12.23).

"The third watchword designed to stifle self-will is to be found in Rom 12.10, Phil 2.3, 1 Peter 5.5 and with special force in Eph 5.21. It runs, 'Submit yourselves to each other in the fear of Christ'."[137] The humble subordination in love to one's neighbour by rendering him a service, without thereby exercising an act of authority is the truly Christian way of witnessing to the power of the one who "did not count equality with God a thing to be grasped, but emptied himself, taking the form of a servant. ... And being found in human form he humbled himself and became obedient unto death, even death on the cross" (Phil 2.6-8).

Did Basil, who was familiar with all these passages, understand Paul in the very way we perceive him today? If Paul had indeed contended that there is no opposition between body and spirit, and that the bodily and

---

[134] Ibid., p. 75.
[135] Ibid., p. 76.
[136] Ibid.
[137] Ibid., pp. 77-78.

material are the sphere of operation of the *Pneuma* (the Power and Grace of the Risen Lord),[138] at least on this point Basil along with other early writers seems to be in closer agreement with the Platonist than the Pauline tradition. His homily entitled, "Take Heed of Yourself," it is true, incorporates all life occupations and stations under the rubric of charismata.[139] Also, his understanding is that each charisma or calling expresses itself in a specific praxis. At the conclusion of the homily Basil pays a high tribute to the body (σῶμα) as the place where divine wisdom, love, generosity, goodness and beauty reveal themselves.[140] But elsewhere, in a quite thoroughgoing manner, he almost completely surrenders to the philosophical dictum that the body is a tomb (σῶμα σῆμα).[141] On the other hand, Basil expands the Pauline notion of charisma to include earthly goods as well.[142] Not only the sharing of spiritual endowments produces the unity in the Body of Christ, but also the *koinonia* in the material possessions contributes to edifying the Christian fellowship. It is precisely in such a perspective that the opposition between spirit and matter is resolved through the realization that nothing material is intrinsically evil.[143] On the contrary, Basil admits, through an act of "dedication" anything can be converted into an instrument (ὄργανον) of love and virtue.[144]

After these preliminary comparisons between the thinking of Paul and Basil let us now take a closer look at Basil's notion of charisma. Although nowhere in his writings do we find what we might call a technical definition of the term, it is clear that the two Pauline criteria for validating charismata—the confession of the lordship of Christ and the edification of the church—have found ample expression in his writings. The confession of Christ, however, does not necessarily assume a dogmatic form. It is understood rather as a *gnosis* of God, that is, as the unconditional observance of all divine commandments.[145] This is the most telling proof authenticating all kinds of claims to charismata.[146] The other variable of this motif is the

---

[138] Cf. Käsemann, "Worship," p. 191; "Ministry," pp. 67 f.

[139] *Hom.* 3.4: Rudberg, 29 f.; *Hom.* 9.5: 340B; *In ps.* 29.1: 308A.

[140] *Hom.* 3.8: Rudberg, 36-37; *Hex.* 10.1, 2, 6: Smets-Esbroeck, 166 ff., 178 ff.

[141] This is already indicated, guardedly though, in *Hom.* 3.3: Rudberg, 26 ff.; see Amand de Mendieta, *Ascèse*, pp. 191 ff.

[142] Before Basil this meaning is found only in the *Didache* 1.5; see *Hom.* 11.5: 384A ff.

[143] See *Reg. br.* 92: 1145c f.; *Hom.* 11.5: 381c ff.

[144] Ibid., and *Reg. fus.* 9.1: 941B ff.; *Reg. mor.* 48.2: 768D ff.

[145] See *Reg. mor.* 7.1: 712B; *Hom.* 23.4: 597A.

[146] *Reg. br.* 225: 1232B ff. and n. 145, above. The interpretation of this rule in Amand de Mendieta, *Ascèse*, p. 143 seems to us less correct. It is evident that throughout his writings, notably the *Moralia*, Basil is faced with the uncontrollable demands for freedom of

renunciation of one's own self-will through complete surrender to the authority of the Holy Scriptures.[147]

The "edification of the church" as a criterion for testing and discerning the spirits is also often found in Basil.[148] Sometimes it assumes the form, known also to Paul, of the search for the "common good" of others.[149] This in its turn entails the renunciation of self-love and even private property.[150]

We have already indicated that under the rubric of charisma Basil places all natural goods and services. Nowhere is this better attested perhaps than in the *Moralia*. Any condition or status in life is suitable to proclaim the "death of Christ" in our bodies and to take part in the victorious advance of the gospel through various parts of the world.[151]

His more detailed treatment of the individual charismata Basil precedes with a summary description of the nature of charisma:

> Since the charismata of the Spirit are different, and neither is one able to receive all nor all the same, each should abide with sobriety and gratitude in the charisma given to him, and all should be harmonious with one another in the love of Christ, as members in a body. So that he who is inferior in charismata should not despair of himself in comparison with him that excels, nor should the greater despise the less. For those who are divided and at variance with one another deserve to perish.[152]

Strongly emphasized here is the non-egalitarian principle, on the one hand,[153] and the unitary character of the action of the Spirit, on the other. Charismata are the grounds of Christian unity, eschatological peace and deep love because they stem from the one and same Holy Spirit who is their only cause and source. At the same time charismata manifest the manifold

---

the Messalians, the Enthusiasts of the fourth century; see the sources on their teaching in M. Aubineau, *Grégoire de Nysse, Traité de la Virginité* (Paris, 1967), pp. 534-536; cf. esp. p. 534, "they regard the zeal for the works of the commandments detrimental to their souls." See also J. Gribomont, "Les Règles Morales de s. Basile et le Nouveau Testament," *SP* 2 (Berlin, 1957) 416-426.

[147] The expression, "Submit to each other," is also strongly attested in Basil's writings; see briefly *Reg. br.* 1: 1081c, and Špidlik, *Sophiologie*, pp. 74 ff.

[148] See the references given below, pp. 90 ff.

[149] See *Reg. fus.* 7.2: 932A; *Ep.* 135.1: Courtonne, 2: 50; *Hom.* 11.5: 381D-384A.

[150] See *Ep.* 236.7: Courtonne, 3: 54-55; *Hom.* 6.7: 267B ff.; also Špidlik, *Sophiologie*, pp. 149 ff.

[151] See in general *Hom.* 5.2: 241A; *In ps.* 1.3: 217A; *Hom.* 3.4: Rudberg, 29-30, and also the inclusion of the various life-situations in the *Moralia*; see *Reg. mor.* 70-79 preceded by the *Reg. mor.* 60 quoted next.

[152] *Reg. mor.* 60.1: 793A-B; Clarke, p. 117 (rev.).

[153] See also *Reg. br.* 235: 1240c, and *In ps.* 33.13 cited above, n. 57.

and variegated character of the Bride of Christ.[154] This unity in diversity
and diversity in unity is explained by the idea of the Holy Spirit acting as a
whole in parts:

> In relation to the distribution of charismata, the Spirit is to be conceived as a
> whole in parts. For we all are 'members one of another, having different
> charismata according to the grace of God that is given us' (Rom 12.5-6).
> Wherefore 'the eye cannot say to the hand, I have no need of thee; nor again
> the head to the feet, I have no need of you' (1 Cor 12.21), but all together
> complete the body of Christ in the unity of the Spirit, and render to one
> another the needful aid that comes of the charismata. 'But God hath set the
> members in the body, every one of them, as it hath pleased Him' (cf. 1 Cor
> 12.18, 11). But 'the members have the same care for one another' (1 Cor
> 12.25) according to the spiritual communion of their inborn sympathy [κατὰ
> τὴν πνευματικὴν κοινωνίαν τῆς συμπαθείας αὐτοῖς ὑπαρχούσης]. ... And as parts
> in the whole so are we individually in the Spirit, because we all 'were baptized
> in one body into one spirit' (cf. 1 Cor 12.13).[155]

Because of the dialectical nature of charismata moderation and restraint
(σωφροσύνη) should accompany their use and exercise.[156]

The extent to which Basil admitted the principle of charismatic ordering
in his communities is difficult to determine simply by reading his works. A
more thorough study will almost certainly show that the ministerial structure of his brotherhoods was rather loose, flexible, and open, allowing considerably more freedom for the charismatic manifestations than one would
be ready or willing to admit. The *Shorter Interrogation 114* is a case in
point: the commands of anyone who has passed the test of the Scriptures—
a criterion similar to the one for the validation of all charismata—should be
obeyed as if they had the same authority as the will of God (1160A ff.).
Anyone who has unselfishly dedicated himself to his brothers "in the love
of Christ" (*Reg. br.* 146: 1177D) is capable of contributing through his individual charismata to the edification of the body of Christ as long as he
does not arbitrarily volunteer his services but offers them in response to the
needs of others.

ii. *Life in the Spirit*

While the Egyptian Christians, desirous of working out their salvation
and sanctification, were advised to abandon through physical withdrawal

---

[154] See *In ps.* 44.9: 408c.
[155] *De sp. s.* 61: Pruche, 468 f. See also *De jud.*, 3: 660A; *Reg. fus.* 7.2: 929c.
[156] See *Reg. mor.* 60 quoted above.

the world of human relations and to seek in the wilderness the ideal environment for their vocation, Basil, dealing with the same subject, proposes what he terms a "paradoxical" statement: the "ambiance" ($\chi\acute{\omega}\rho\alpha$) of Christian sanctification and worship is not to be found in any physical or geographical location but essentially consists in living and in being in the Holy Spirit who is the $\chi\acute{\omega}\rho\alpha$ of those being sanctified.[157] The withdrawal of passions and the subsequent quiet ($\acute{\eta}\sigma\nu\chi\acute{\iota}\alpha$) are precisely intended to facilitate this contact and even the entry of the soul into the "ambiance" called the Holy Spirit.[158]

Baptism is the means by which every single member is introduced into the life in the Holy Spirit.[159] Through this sacrament of Christian regeneration humans not only bury themselves with Christ and die to sin, but they are also positively enabled to become "that very thing" of which they were born anew, that is to say, they receive from the Spirit the power to become assimilated to God:

> Shining upon those that are cleansed from every spot, the Spirit makes them spiritual [$\pi\nu\varepsilon\nu\mu\alpha\tau\iota\kappa\circ\acute{\nu}\varsigma$] by fellowship [$\kappa\circ\iota\nu\omega\nu\acute{\iota}\alpha$] with Himself. Just as when a sunbeam falls on bright and transparent bodies, they themselves become brilliant too, and shed forth a fresh brightness from themselves, so souls wherein the Spirit dwells, illuminated by the Spirit, themselves become spiritual, and send forth their grace to others. Hence come foreknowledge of the future, understanding of mysteries, apprehension of what is hidden, distribution of charismata, heavenly citizenship, a place in the chorus of angels, joy without end, abiding in God, being made like to God, and, what is most desirable, being made God [$\theta\varepsilon\grave{o}\nu$ $\gamma\varepsilon\nu\acute{\varepsilon}\sigma\theta\alpha\iota$].[160]

In virtue of this deifying principle apportioned to every single member of the body of Christ, the church is referred to by Basil as the place of the fellowship ($\kappa\circ\iota\nu\omega\nu\acute{\iota}\alpha$) in and of the Holy Spirit.[161] In it humans communicate with each other by sharing their material and spiritual goods and through the mutual (social) exchange of services.[162]

---

[157] *De sp. s.* 62: Pruche, 470. $X\acute{\omega}\rho\alpha$ could also be translated "the position" or "proper place" of a person in life.

[158] "Now the Spirit is not brought into intimate association [$\circ\grave{\iota}\kappa\varepsilon\acute{\iota}\omega\sigma\iota\varsigma$] with the soul by local approximation. ... This approximation results from the withdrawal of passions, which, coming afterwards on the soul from its friendship to the flesh, have alienated it from its close friendship to God" (*De sp. s.* 23: Pruche, 326; Jackson, p. 15).

[159] See *De sp. s.* 61: Pruche, 470; *Reg. mor.* 80.22: 868D-869B.

[160] *De sp. s.* 23: Pruche, 328; Jackson, pp. 15-16 (rev.). Cf. also *Reg. mor.* 20.1-2: 736D ff.

[161] *Ep.* 90.1: Courtonne, 1: 195.

[162] On the social function of charismata see *Reg. br.* 253: 1252B-C; also the fine interpretation of the *Moral Rule* 58 by Amand de Mendieta, *Ascèse*, p. 139, n. 125; see also

As Basil is explicit, on the one hand, that the members of his brotherhoods are people filled with the Spirit and his endowments, so he is very firm, on the other, in asserting the organic unity of his communities as the body of Christ. To the question "Ought one in the brotherhood to obey what is said by every one?" Basil replies:

> The answer to this question is fraught with considerable difficulty. In the first place the question indicates disorder when it mentions things said by every one, for the apostle says: 'Let the prophets speak by twos and threes and let the others discern' (1 Cor 14.29). And the same writer in dividing charismata has assigned the proper rank (order) of each of the speakers. ... And by his example of the members of the body he shows clearly that the lot of the speaker is to speak in turns [ἐν μέρει εἶναι τὸ μέρος τοῦ λαλοῦντος].[163]

Basil then proceeds to explain the structure of the brotherhood basically as consisting of those entrusted with the charisma of leadership and those entrusted with the charisma of obedience.[164]

The Holy Spirit, as it is not difficult to illustrate from Basil's works, is present not only in each member of the community. His lifegiving and sanctifying presence and operation, besides being universal and comprising all intelligent beings, are apparent particularly in the mysteries of the church—the sacraments of baptism and confirmation, the inspired writings of the Old and New Testament, the proclamations (κηρύγματα) of the church; that is, homilies, ordinances, decisions made by spiritual men, instructions, the exchange of letters and visits, consultations and spiritual advice, as well as in meetings for the purpose of edifying the faith and in the prayers of the church.[165]

---

below, p. 119 and n. 74. B. Bobrinskoy, "Liturgie et ecclésiologie trinitaire de s. Basile," *VC* 89 (1969) 16 ff., has interpreted the words ἡ κοινωνία τοῦ Πνεύματος, which Basil obviously derives from 2 Cor 13.13, in the sense of a communion and participation in the Holy Spirit modelled on the eucharistic communion. Although some such meaning is possible according to Thornton, *The Common Life*, pp. 71 ff., if it is adopted "it must not be understood in a sense which excludes the other alternative," that is, "the human fellowship which the Holy Spirit brought into existence, the social entity which has the Holy Spirit for its creative author or fountain-source" (ibid., pp. 74 and 69; for such a sense in Basil see *In ps.* 48.1: 433A-D. Cf. S. Giet, *Les idées et l'action sociales de s. Basile* [Paris, 1941], p. 173). Cf. also Dunn, *Jesus*, pp. 260 f.: "shared experience."

[163] *Reg. br.* 303: 1296D-1297A.

[164] Ibid.: 1297B-C; see *Reg. br.* 235: 1240C-D. Besides the two mentioned charismata, Basil acknowledges the existence of others; see Amand de Mendieta, *Ascèse*, pp. 139 and 142-144. It should be noted that Basil is far from advocating an indiscriminate or blind obedience on the part of the subjects. In *Reg. br.* 303: 1297B-C the subjects are given the same rights to "test the spirits" as the hearers of the word in *Reg. mor.* 72.1-2: 845D ff.

[165] On the sanctification of angels by the Holy Spirit see the study of A. Heising, "Der Hl. Geist und die Heiligung der Engel in der Pneumatologie des Basilius von Caesarea,"

E. THE BROTHERHOOD OF CHURCHES

If Basil often appealed to the need for order and decency within his ascetic brotherhoods, in doing so he was far from basing his claims on conciliar decisions or "rules" drawn up by himself or others to that effect.[166] The only commandment of vital importance and urgency for Basil was the commandment of love, often referred to as the first fruit and charisma of the Holy Spirit.[167] As we shall see in more detail in Chapter Four the *logos* of love should not only bind the Christian communities together internally, but it should also compel each individual community to seek intercourse and communion with the others. Thus, in place of a hierarchical system, we find in Basil an order of brotherhood intended to regulate not only individual but also intercommunal relations.

Basil's design provided that the ascetic communities be the prime model in this. In the *Longer Rule 35* Basil first advocates the welding together (συγχροτεῖσθαι) of several brotherhoods existing in the same parish (χώμη).[168] The rule invoked is the apostolic command, "Not looking each to his own things, but each also to the things of the others" (Phil 2.4). Basil explains:

> For I reckon this cannot be carried out in separation, when each section takes care for its fellow denizens, but thought for the others is outside its ken, which, as I said, is clearly opposed to the apostolic command. And the saints in the Acts bear witness to this frequently, of whom it is written in one place: 'The multitude of them that believed were of one heart and soul' (Acts 4.32), and in another place, 'All that believed were together, and had all things common' (Acts 2.44). So it is obvious that there was no division among them all, nor did each live under his own authority, but all had one and the same

---

ZKTh 87 (1965) 257-308. On the "inspiration" of the Bible see the dissertation of B. B. Wawryk, *Doctrina Sancti Basilii Magni de inspiratione Sacrae Scripturae* (Rome, 1943). On the presence of the Spirit in other ecclesiastical actions see *Reg. mor.* 80.22: 868D; 20.2: 736D; *Ep.* 188, *c.* 1: Courtonne, 2: 123; *In ps.* 44.3: 396A; *Epp.* 229.1: Courtonne, 3: 33-34; 92.3: ibid., 1: 202-203; 207.4: ibid., 2: 187; and in general see the studies of J. Verhees, "Pneuma, Erfahrung und Erleuchtung in der Theologie des Basilius des Grossen," *Ostkirchliche Studien* 25 (1976) 43-59, and "Die Bedeutung der Tranzendenz des Pneuma bei Basilius," ibid., 285-302.

[166] The title "Longer" and "Shorter Rules" given in some MSS to the questions-answers of Basil's *Asceticons* is illegitimate not only because of its being interpolated but also because in replying to the questions Basil acts less as a legislator than as a spiritual adviser.

[167] See *In ps.* 32.1: 324C; *Epp.* 65: Courtonne, 1: 155; 133: ibid., 2: 47; 172: ibid., 107; 204.1: ibid., 173. Cf. *In ps.* 33.13: 384C.

[168] Less aptly Maran and Clarke translate συγχροτεῖσθαι by "construi" and "formed," respectively; see PG 31, 1003A and Clarke, *Ascetic Works,* p. 201.

care—and that too although the total number was five thousand, and with such a number one would think perhaps there were no few obstacles to union. But where men living in a single parish are found so inferior in numbers to those, what in reason allows them to remain separated from one another? [169]

But Basil is not satisfied with this first step of union among local brotherhoods. The same reasons of convenience and of better provision for the private needs of the individuals compel him to formulate a more far-reaching wish:

> Would that it were possible, that not only those in the same parish were thus united, but that a number of brotherhoods existing in different places might be built up into a community under the single care of those who are able without partiality and wisely to manage the affairs of all in the unity of the spirit and the bond of peace! [170]

That Basil sought the implementation of the same apostolic pattern of union and brotherhood for all the churches spread throughout the *oikoumene* is easy to gather from his correspondence and the *De Spiritu Sancto*. As I shall deal more extensively with this subject in the fourth chapter, it should suffice here to provide additional evidence indicating Basil's interest in seeing all churches amalgamated into one universal brotherhood. It can hardly be said that Basil considered the church as a monad.[171] Time and again throughout his writings he shows a consciousness of the church as a brotherhood of all believers in Christ: "All believers in Christ are one people; all Christ's people, although He is hailed from many regions, are one church."[172] As we shall see in Chapter Four, the concrete circumstances in which Basil lived were far from ideal for the realization of a union of all Christians. The scene, particularly east of Illyricum, dominated by endless theological squabbles, personal rivalries and partisanship, rather resembled a storm at sea, "as when at sea many ships sailing together are all dashed one against the other by the violence of the waves, and shipwreck arises in some cases from the sea being furiously agitated from without, in others from the disorder of the sailors hindering and crowding one another."[173] Some bishops, if they were not in open warfare with their neighbours, tried to ignore them and live in confinement in

---

[169] *Reg. fus.* 35.3: 1008A-B; Clarke, pp. 203-204.
[170] Ibid.: 1008B; Clarke, p. 204.
[171] See ch. 4, B, i: "Intrinsic Limitations of the Local Church."
[172] *Ep.* 161.1: Courtonne, 2: 93; Jackson, p. 214.
[173] *Ep.* 82: Courtonne, 1: 184; Jackson, p. 172. The last words clearly refer to the internal difficulties.

their own cities. Basil, although fully conscious of his personal sins which he considered to be the major obstacle to friendship and to achieving ecclesiastical unity, often made an appeal to more transcendental ties—the bond of love, of one Lord, one faith, one hope—as the only valid motives to be taken into account in the formation of a universal brotherhood of churches.[174] To the bishops of Pontus unsettled by the Eustathian propaganda about his orthodoxy, Basil wrote in an expostulatory letter:

> Nothing, brethren, separates us from each other, but deliberate estrangement. We have one Lord, one faith, the same hope. ... For we are assured, that though you are not present in body, yet by the aid of prayer, you will do us much benefit in those most critical times. It is neither decorous before men, nor pleasing to God, that you should employ such words which not even the Gentiles who know no God have employed. Even they, as we hear, though the country they live in be self-sufficient for all things, yet, on account of the uncertainty of the future, make much of alliances with each other, and seek mutual intercourse as being advantageous to them.[175]

It was not only the uncertainty of the situation under a hostile government that compelled Basil to seek the establishment and reinforcement of the brotherhood among Christian communities spread throughout the world, but the principle that no Christian or individual community can adequately take care of oneself or itself while ignoring the interests of others. "General disaster involves individual ruin."[176] Wherefore "'whether one member suffereth, all the members suffer with it' (1 Cor 12.26), for 'there should be no schisms in the body, but the members should have the same care for one another' (1 Cor 12.25), according to the spiritual fellowship of their inborn sympathy, and being moved, no doubt, by the one indwelling Spirit."[177] But as we said earlier the situation was far from ideal for an enduring conciliation of the spirits on whom weighed heavily the consequences of the long war in which many churches became involved following the Council of Nicaea:

> We are confined now each in his own city, and everyone looks at his neighbour with distrust. What more is to be said but that our love has grown cold?

---

[174] In his study, *Basilius der Grosse*, L. Vischer draws attention to the frequency with which Basil makes reference to personal sins as possible obstacles to the achievement of church's union; see e.g. *Epp.* 59.1: Courtonne, 1: 147; 124: ibid., 2: 29-30; 266.2: ibid., 3: 135; 204.4: ibid., 2: 175; 203.1: ibid., 168.

[175] *Ep.* 203.3: Courtonne, 2: 170; Jackson, p. 242.

[176] *Ep.* 136.2: Courtonne, 2: 52.

[177] Conflation of *De sp. s.* 61: Pruche, 470; Jackson, p. 39 and *De jud.*, 3: 657D-660A; Clarke, p. 80.

Yet it is through [love] alone that, according to our Lord, His disciples are distinguished.[178]

The love of many has grown cold throughout, brotherly concord is destroyed, the very name of unity is ignored, brotherly admonitions are heard no more; ... but mutual hatred has blazed so high among fellow clansmen that they are more delighted at a neighbour's fall than their own success. ... And to such depth is this evil rooted among us that we have become more brutish than the brutes; they do at least herd with their fellows, but our most savage warfare is with our own people.[179]

However, before considering in more detail Basil's far-reaching scheme to constitute all churches into one universal brotherhood, we should first study his functions and those of other church leaders in their particular communities. These essentially can be reduced to two: defence of orthodoxy and proclamation of the word of God.

---

[178] *Ep.* 191: Courtonne, 2: 145.
[179] *De sp. s.* 78: Pruche, 526-528. See *De jud.* 3: 657c.

2

The Charisma of Church Leadership

To appreciate properly Basil's understanding of the presence and exercise of leadership and care (προστασία) in the church, we should be aware of the historical circumstances which provided the immediate background for his position. Part of the concrete milieu in which Basil acted has been described in the first chapter.[1] Again we should abide by Basil's own perception and account of the situation, but not without measuring his witness against the general historical context.

In the foregoing chapter we saw that probably as a result of the change of policy towards the church that took effect under Emperor Julian and later on under Valens, Basil, with other Christians, took refuge in the asceticism which emerged as a force in opposition to the secularized and Arianized church.[2] It is not our purpose here to study in greater depth the question of the relationship between church and empire during the reign of Valens, nor to undertake a more comprehensive investigation into this problem so far as Basil's writings are concerned.[3] In this present chapter, devoted to the question of church leadership, we propose instead to begin with a few summary remarks concerning Basil's attitude toward the civil power in so far as this is evidenced in his life and in his works.

---

[1] See especially pp. 12 ff., and also ch. 4.

[2] On the persecution of the ascetics at the hand of Arians, see *Ep.* 257: Courtonne, 3: 98-99. On monasticism in general as a protest against Arianism in the fourth century, cf. Hilary of Poitiers, *Ad Constantium Augustum* 1.6: PL 10, 560B-561C; Idem, *Fragmenta historica* 2.3: PL 10, 633C-634C; and 3.9: 665A-B; Gregory of Nazianzus, *Oration* 43.46: PG 36, 556B-C; Idem, *Oratio contra Arianos* 3: PG 36, 217A-C.

[3] Some indications on the relationship between church and empire during Basil's time can be found in G. F. Reilly, *Imperium and Sacerdotium according to St. Basil the Great* (Washington, 1945). The situation of Christians between 361-378 was not always and everywhere the same. There were many magistrates and civil servants under Julian and Valens who were either orthodox or who favoured the orthodox; see *Epp.* 18, 106, and 225. Valens himself seemed to have respected Basil.

The question of Basil's attitude toward the civil authorities is closely related to that of his social origin. Although there is still no agreement among the scholars on this score,[4] in practice we find him relating very successfully to all types of civil servants, and what is perhaps more important, we see Basil trying to establish during his lifetime a close cooperation between the *Imperium* and *Sacerdotium*. The latter is probably nowhere more prominent than in the construction of the Great Hospital (the *Ptochotrophium*: Poor-House) of Caesarea. This work, although not unique in its kind,[5] was the direct result of Basil's involvement in the programme of relief undertaken during the winter of famine and drought of 368/369. Already then, according to Gregory of Nazianzus, Basil

> assembled in one place those afflicted by the famine. ... He collected through contributions all kinds of food helpful for relieving famine. ... He ministered to the bodies and the souls of the needy, combining marks of respect with the necessary refreshment, thus affording them relief in two ways.[6]

The description of the hospital given in a letter of apology to the governor of Cappadocia acquaints us with the broad scope of Basil's social action.[7] The construction was intended to serve the needs of all, the natives and the foreigners, the elderly and the young, the sick as well as the illiterate. The area occupied by the *Ptochotrophium* was very extensive and it comprised a variety of buildings—the church, the residence of the bishop and his associates, the various schools, hospices and places of training in the most varied occupations.[8] As Gregory put it, Basil built a whole "Brand New City," that is, a town of its own which was destined to survive its founder for centuries to come.[9]

---

[4] The opinions of W. M. Ramsay, E. von Ivanka (both favouring Basil's descendancy from a Persian-Iranian country aristocracy), B. Treucker (supporting Basil's senatorial origin), and S. Giet (municipal aristocracy) are discussed and assessed in T. A. Kopecek, "Social Class of the Cappadocian Fathers," *CH* 42 (1973) 453 ff. However, I think that Basil descended from a family of *possessores* (πλούσιοι) who, at least on his father's side, had no part in the contemporary political life. On these *homines novi* of the later Roman Empire see R. Teja, *Organización económica y social de Capadocia en el siglo IV, según los Padres Capadocios* (Salamanca, 1974), pp. 79-96, 187-188; see also below, p. 104, n. 9.

[5] See below, p. 162, n. 19 for the antecedent Eustathian models.

[6] *Or.* 43.35: PG 36, 544c ff.; McCauley, p. 58.

[7] Referred to is *Epistle 94* to the governor Elias.

[8] *Ep.* 94: Courtonne, 1: 204 ff.

[9] W. M. Ramsay, *The Church in the Roman Empire A.D. 170* (New York, 1893), p. 264, remarks that "the 'New City' of Basil seems to have caused the gradual concentration of the entire population of Caesarea round the ecclesiastical centre, and the abandonment of the old city. Modern Kayseri is situated between one and two miles from the site of the Graeco-Roman city." See, however, G. Bernardakis, "Notes sur la topographie de Césarée de Cappadoce," *EO* 11 (1908) 22-27.

But what interests us most here is Basil's conception of a single human order as composed of both the spiritual (ecclesiastical) and material (civil) realms. The place that the discussion of the ministry of civil rulers occupies in the *Moralia* is significant.[10] Along with other forms of Christian calling and serving it belongs in the realm of the charismatic, of the concrete manifestation of the universally caring rule of divine providence.

> Though Basil has at no time stated that a particular ruler or type of government is from God, he does profess with St. Paul, that there is no power but from God and that every soul should be subject to higher powers, for he that resists the power, resists the ordinance of God.[11]

Basil saw no danger to the church's well-being and functioning from the civil ordinances, provided that the latter did not interfere or conflict with the divine commandments; that is, if they were capable of withstanding the same test invoked for the validation of all other charismata.[12] It is obvious that in his attitude toward the *Imperium* Basil falls into the long tradition which takes its beginning from Paul's teaching contained in Romans 13.[13] Thus, while he avoids any kind of imperial cult, Basil, on the other hand, does not hesitate to assure of his prayers the various receivers of his letters: the magistrates, generals, governors and soldiers ministering in the government of the Arianizing Emperor Valens. Nor does Basil at any time incite Christians to civil disobedience despite the flagrant injustice of some of the civil laws.[14]

We could perhaps explain Basil's positive evaluation of the civil order by appealing to his conviction that every man is a social (political) being.[15] This instinct of gregariousness naturally leads humans to seek the company of others and to associate with each other. But more than anything else it is the *experience* of one's own helplessness and insufficiency to discharge adequately the duties of life which compels Basil to conclude in favour of

[10] *Reg. mor.* 79: 860A f. The context for the whole section 70-80 concerned with the varied forms of Christian ministration is provided by *Reg. mor.* 60 which deals with the notion of Christian charisma.

[11] Reilly, *Imperium*, p. 27.

[12] See *Reg. mor.* 79.2: 860B and above, p. 28. Cf. the use of "calling" in *Epistle 83* with *Epistle 161.1*.

[13] For an interpretation of Romans 13 see E. Käsemann in *NT Questions of Today* (London, 1969), pp. 196-216; for the subsequent period see W. Parsons, "The Influence of Romans 13 on Pre-Augustinian Christian Political Thought," *Theological Studies* 1 (1940) 337-364.

[14] Cf. *Epistles 225, 72, 74, 85.*

[15] For this point see briefly *Reg. fus.* 2, and below, pp. 114 ff.

man's corporate tendency. "Man is not a solitary but a sociable being," and this also at the level of natural communication. We must clarify that of the experience of inadequacy Basil seems to show only an indirect awareness in the examples he often adduces to persuade other Christians to unite with each other.[16]

Although, it is true that Basil accepted the principle that the civil order is compatible with the Christian well-being, on the other hand we also find in him some indications which clearly point toward an order increasingly dominated by the authority of the Christian church. Basil not only felt that as a churchman and spiritual father of the people entrusted to his care he had more rights over their souls than their natural parents, but also by embracing and promoting asceticism he had a hand in the creation of a community of people capable of providing for all their needs independently of the state. Basil's brotherhood, as we have mentioned several times, was deliberately patterned on the pre-Constantinian model of the first community of Jerusalem, and for it Basil sought not only exemptions from taxes and the military service but also he tried to make its members directly accountable not to the secular but the ecclesiastical leaders.[17] As we pointed out at the beginning of this chapter, asceticism in the fourth century was the most articulated power which grew in opposition to the state (and in some cases, to the church), compromised by its allegiance to a questionable form of Christianity, the Arianizing party. It was thus more as an ascetic than a bishop that Basil showed courage and determination with regard to Modestus, the prefect of the emperor who tried to intimidate and force him to sign the formulary of Rimini. The phrases, "No one has ever spoken with such boldness to me," and Basil's reply, "Perhaps you have never met a bishop before," are no doubt Gregory's compositions[18] but they nevertheless accurately convey the impression left on the reader by the perusal of Basil's letters. While showing deference to civil servants and avoiding direct confrontation with the secular power Basil was far from either displaying blind subservience to the will of civil authorities, or offering only a passive resistance to their mistaken rulings. Quite the contrary, the leader of Caesarea knew also how to be on the counteroffensive. His promptness in acting in a time of emergency during the famine of 368/369 and his con-

---

[16] Cf. below, p. 117, n. 64.

[17] See *Epp.* 104, 142, 225, 284, and *Reg. br.* 187. On the economic consequences for the church of Basil's "communism" or rather "communalism," see J. Gribomont, "Un aristocrate révolutionnaire, évêque et moine: s. Basile," *Aug* 17 (1977) 189 f.

[18] See below, p. 57, and also p. 55 for Gregory's intent in writing *Oration 43.*

struction of the Great Hospital were not only living protests against the inertia of the government but constituted also significant milestones in securing for the church major independence from the state.

It should be apparent to the reader that Basil's position vis-à-vis the civil authorities was not always coherent and consistent with his more general principles. The difficult period of history in which he lived and the urge to serve the present hour in the most adequate manner seem to account best for his somewhat incomplete and conflicting views on the subject.

A. The Question of Leadership in the Church

According to Basil, the church at the empirical level is a body (σῶμα) composed of individual members.[19] Each member of the community is assigned a particular charisma.[20] The church's life and growth ("edification") are ensured through the mutual cooperation of its members in the exercise and participation of the individual charismata.[21]

The Pauline analogy of the church as a charismatic body leads Basil to envisage the ecclesiastical community as an organic structure.[22] Holding first place among the members of a body is mutual harmony, love and unity. The ὁμολογία of human and especially of Christian unity is linked in Basil with the "confession" of the need for interdependence and fellowship. In a letter to the senate of Tyana, after the partition of Cappadocia, Basil wrote:

[19] See *Ep.* 243.1: Courtonne, 3: 68; *In ps.* 29.1: 308A; *In ps.* 44.5: 397D. The title "regional," "local," or "particular" is not found in Basil. See *Ep.* 227: Courtonne, 3: 30 for the title mother church. There is, however, in Basil a strong consciousness of the church's presence in various regions and territories of the *oikoumene*; see *Epp.* 161.1: Courtonne, 2: 93; 204.7: ibid., 179 f.; 133: ibid., 47.

[20] See *Reg. mor.* 60.1: 793A-B; *Reg. fus.* 7.2: 932A.

[21] See *Reg. fus.* 7.2: 932A-B.

[22] See *Reg. fus.* 24: 981D-984A. Throughout this chapter I shall often use section 24-54 of the *Great Asceticon*, which constitutes a kind of "manual for the use of community officers," and in which the attributes and qualities of the ascetic προεστώς are discussed. At this stage of the evolution of Basilian foundations, the ascetic προστασία is in all likelihood an office, a "charismatic function," parallel to that of the leadership exercised in the local churches by the local bishops. The treatment of the προστασία in chapters 24 and following can be applied therefore to any Christian leader, but especially to an ecclesiastical one. Not only does the terminology agree (the same name for the community and the church which throughout are called ἀδελφότης, and the same titles of προεστώς-προεστῶτες for both the ascetic and ecclesiastical leader), but also the qualities required in both leaders are the same; see e.g. *Reg. fus.* 43.1: 1028A-B and *Ep.* 190.1: Courtonne, 2: 141; *Reg. fus.* 24: 981D-984A and *Ep.* 222: Courtonne, 3: 7; *Proem. in reg. br.*: 1080A and *Ep.* 199: Courtonne, 2: 154; *Reg. fus.* 25.2: 985A-B and *Ep.* 161.2: Courtonne, 2: 93-94. See also above, p. 24, n. 126.

Truly, from our own bodily constitution, the Lord has taught us the necessity of fellowship [κοινωνία]. When I look to these my limbs and see that no one of them is self-sufficient [αὐτάρκης], how can I reckon myself competent to discharge the duties of life? One foot could not walk securely without the support of the other; one eye could not see well, were it not for the alliance of the other and for its being able to look at objects in conjunction with it. Hearing is most exact when sound is received through both channels, and the grasp is made firmer by the fellowship of the fingers. In a word, of all that is done by nature and by the will, I see nothing done without the concord of fellow forces.[23]

Also in the letter to the bishops of Pontus, Basil declared:

Let not this consideration influence you: 'We dwell on the sea, we are exempt from the sufferings of the generality, we need no succour from others; so what is the good to us of foreign communion [κοινωνία]?' For the same Lord Who divided the islands from the continent by the sea, bound the island Christians to those of the continent by love. Nothing, brethren, separates us from each other, but deliberate estrangement. We have one Lord, one faith, the same hope. ... The hands need each other; the feet steady each other. The eyes possess their clear apprehension from agreement. We, for our part, confess [ὁμολογοῦμεν] our own weakness, and we seek your fellow feeling [σύμπνοιαν].[24]

Second, bodily unity and interdependence implies diversity, and in the body of the church is involved the acknowledgment (ὁμολογία) of the various functions proper to each member. No one member of the community can have all the charismata, as no one limb of the body can on its own fulfil all the duties incumbent upon it.[25]

Third, the "confession" of both unity in diversity and diversity in unity of a body issues naturally in the acknowledgment of a hierarchical structure.

Since the charismata of the Spirit are different, and neither is one able to receive all, nor all the same charismata, each should abide with sobriety [σωφρόνως] and gratitude in the charisma given to him, and all should be harmonious with one another in the love of Christ, as members in a body.[26]

The survival of a community such as the church is here made dependent upon the preservation of the natural order (τάγμα). In this sense, when in

---

[23] *Ep.* 97: Courtonne, 1: 210-211; Jackson, p. 181.

[24] *Ep.* 203.3: Courtonne, 2: 170; Jackson, p. 242; cf. also *Epp.* 243.1: ibid., 3: 68; 266.2: ibid., 135.

[25] See *Epp.* 243.1 and 203.3: Courtonne, loc. cit. and n. 26, below.

[26] *Reg. mor.* 60.1: 793A-B; Clarke, p. 117 (rev.).

the *Longer Rule 24* Basil is asked about the manner of the Christian life together (μετ' ἀλλήλων διαγωγή), his reply is: "Since the apostle says: 'Let all things be done decently and in order,' we reckon this to be a decent and orderly manner of life among the society of the faithful [τῶν πιστῶν συνάφεια], in which the *logos* of the members of the body is preserved."[27] This physical *logos* of the orderly structure points to some of the consequences for a discussion of church leadership. Let us therefore attempt to draw out some of the implications for Basil of a recognition of the validity of this natural principle applied to the church community.

In the first place, the "confession" of an order in the body implies the ὁμολογία of Christ's supreme lordship in the church community. Wondering what and whence was the cause of the great evil of the division and dissension that plagued the church of his day, Basil chanced upon a passage from the Book of the Judges where it was written: "In those days there was no king in Israel" (Judg 11.25).

> So having remembered this, I considered this also about the present situation, which indeed is perhaps fearful and strange to speak of, but is most true if you look into the matter—that perhaps even now, because of the neglect of the one great true and only King and God of all, such great dissension and strife take place among Churchmen, each man deserting the teaching of our Lord Jesus Christ and arbitrarily claiming the right to arguments and definitions of his own, and wishing to rule over against the Lord rather than be ruled by Him. ... For if those who obey one command and have one king are characterized by good order and agreement, then all discord and division is a sign that there is no one to rule. In the same fashion such disagreement as regards both the commandments of the Lord and one another, if found in our midst, lays us open to the accusation that we have either deserted our true King, ... or else have denied Him.[28]

This text shows two things. First, Christ is not created king by the people who follow him. His royal kingship is a divine attribute and property which can be deserted or denied, but not annulled. Second, the order in the church is dependent upon the recognition (ὁμολογία) of Christ as its only true Lord and true head. The latter point Basil further expands in the following paragraph of the *De judicio*. This ὁμολογία of Christ as the Lord and the head of Christianity is not a theoretical exercise but a very concrete duty. Only those who through practical conduct preserve among themselves the spirit of harmony, peace, and meekness on the one hand, and avoid

---

[27] *Reg. fus.* 24: 981D-984A; Clarke, pp. 190-191.
[28] *De jud.*, 2: 656A-C; Clarke, p. 79.

division, strife, and jealousy on the other, are true members of Christ's body and are assuredly ruled by him.[29] In other words, the only valid test by which a member of the church can be said to belong to Christ is through the observance of all his commandments: "My sheep hear my voice, and I know them, and they follow me" (Jn 10.27).[30] According to Basil, it is of no avail to make appeal, as some ascetics of his day would do, to some special endowments, illuminations or even to the charismata of the Spirit because "though a man may seem to confess the Lord and hear His words, yet if he disobeys His commandments he is condemned, although he may be allowed by a divine concession to possess spiritual charismata."[31]

In the second place, the ὁμολογία of Christ's supreme lordship entails the imitation by the other members of the obedient conduct he observed during his earthly sojourn. Basil lays great emphasis on the practical implications of Christ's Incarnation. Christ took on himself the "sojourn in the flesh for the very purpose that, by patterns of duty, He might regulate our life" (ἵνα καὶ τοῖς ὑποδείγμασι τῶν πρακτέων ῥυθμίσῃ τὸν βίον ἡμῶν).[32] Of all virtues Christ exhibited as exemplar the primary are love and obedience, or rather, loving submission to the Father in all respects. Here we reach the point in which Basil's consciousness of the Christian order implies much more than the direct subjection to Christ's commandments.

There can be no denying that the will of God is to be sought and found foremost in Scripture. Nothing whatsoever should ever be done or said by a Christian without (ἄνευ) or outside (ἐκτός) the testimony of the inspired Scripture.[33] Thus things stand as far as the written testimony goes.

> But as for those things passed over in silence [σεσιωπημένων] the apostle Paul gave us a rule [κάνονα] when he said: 'All things are lawful to me but all things edify not. Let no man seek his own, but each his neighbour's good' (1 Cor 10.23). So that it is absolutely necessary, either to be subject to God according to His commandment, or to others because of His commandment. For it is written: 'Subjecting yourselves one to another in the fear of Christ' (Eph 5.21). And the Lord says: 'He that wisheth to be great among you let him be

[29] See De jud., 3: 660A.
[30] Quoted in Hom. 23.4: 597A. See also the whole context in which the recognition of the royal kingship of Christ is stressed with a view of achieving Christian unity.
[31] Reg. mor. 7.1: 712B; Clarke, p. 103 (rev.). On the Messalian form of illuminism, see the study of I. Hausherr, "L'erreur fondamentale et la logique du Messalianisme," OCP 1 (1935) 328-360. Their presence in Pontus and Cappadocia is attested by Gregory of Nyssa, De virginitate 23.3: PG 46, 409; Aubineau, p. 536. See also in Aubineau's edition the literature quoted.
[32] Ep. 203.1: Courtonne, 2: 167; Jackson, p. 241. Cf. also De sp. s. 35: Pruche, 364.
[33] See Reg. br. 1: 1080C-1081C; Reg. mor. 80.22: 868C; cf. also Reg. mor. 26.1: 744C.

last of all and servant of all' (Mk 9.34)—alienated that is from his own wishes, imitating the Lord Himself Who says: 'I am come down from heaven not to do mine will, but the will of my Father which sent me' (Jn 6.38).[34]

The corporate and social aspect of Christ's teaching and doing—of his gospel and commandments—are brought out in the *Longer Interrogation 7* which discusses the communal (charismatic) character of the Christian vocation. Love and other social virtues, Basil declares, can only be fulfilled and have significance in a life led in continuous communion with others. But leaving aside consideration of this undoubtedly important question which has partially been dealt with elsewhere, let us try here to uncover the manner in which, in addition to the practical "confession" of the lordship of Christ and to his testimony recorded in the Scriptures, Basil advocates the necessity for humans of a human leader (προεστώς).[35]

First, Basil is led to the conclusion that people need to be led by people by reason of the charismatic structure of the church. In the book *On the Holy Spirit* Basil asks:

> Is it not plain and incontestable that the ordering of the church is effected through the Spirit? For He gave, it is said, 'in the church, first apostles, second prophets, third teachers, then miracles, then charismata of healing, helps, governments, diversities of tongues' (1 Cor 12.28). And this order is ordained according to the distribution of the gifts of the Spirit.[36]

---

[34] *Reg. br.* 1: 1081B-C; Clarke, pp. 230-231; cf. *Reg. mor.* 26.2: 745A; *De sp. s.* 66: Pruche, 480, 484.

[35] There can hardly be any doubt that Basil was a biblicist in root and branch. Without speaking of the direct quotations which abound on every page of his works, Basil's thinking and style were heavily influenced and permeated by the biblical *Weltanschauung*. In practice Basil adheres to the principle that every word and action of a Christian should be warranted and confirmed by the authority of the Scripture, that anything that disagrees with the explicit teaching of the Bible should be avoided as sinful, and that in consequence the highest criterion of what is good, beautiful and right is the testimony of the inspired sayings of Christ, the apostles and the prophets (see the sources quoted in n. 33). Despite the fact, however, that this biblicism of Basil's seems to have prevailed in an ever increasing manner during the last years of his life, there was from the outset the situation described in chapter 30 of the book *On the Holy Spirit*. As a result of a long period of domestic squabbles, Scripture was declared "powerless" to mediate between the opposing parties, the apostolic traditions unable to suggest terms of arbitration (*De sp. s.* 77: Pruche, 524). Thus in seeking a solution for the chaotic situation, Basil appealed not only to the Scriptures and the past authorities (although he quoted them frequently, see e.g. *De sp. s.* 71 ff., and *passim*) but he also tried from the beginning to find a living "human" authority such as Athanasius (cf. *Epp.* 66, 67, 69) and the "ecumenical" synod (cf. *Epp.* 70, 263), which would act as arbiters in the dispute. These convictions stemmed in Basil from his consciousness of the corporate nature of humankind (see *Reg. fus.* 2-7) and of the Christian calling (see above, pp. 15 ff.).

[36] *De sp. s.* 39 : Pruche, 386; Jackson, p. 25 (rev.).

The latter proposition is explained in the *Shorter Interrogation 235*. According to the division of charismata, two orders (τάγματα) can be detected in the Christian "brotherhood" (ἀδελφότης): the order of those entrusted with the charisma of leadership and care (προστασία), and of those whose function is "to defer and obey."[37] As Basil sees it, this disposition is not for the burden of the souls "aspiring towards heaven" but for their safeguard and protection. Because of the many dangers, "souls grafted by faith into the church" God surrounds not only with the authority of his precepts and the guard of angels but also for their full benefit he has planted, "so to say, props [χάρακας], in establishing in his church apostles, prophets, teachers."[38]

More explicitly still, in the same charismatic vein, Basil discerns in the bodylike constitution of the church the functions of eyes and lips, fulfilled by the ecclesiastical προεστώς. After having stated that a decent and orderly manner of life among the faithful takes place, "in which the *logos* of the members of the body is preserved," Basil continues: "So that one has the power of the eye, being entrusted with the general oversight [ἐπιμέλειαν], both approving what has been done, and foreseeing and arranging what is to be done; and another the power of the ear or hand in respect of hearing or doing what is necessary—and so on."[39] The authority (ἐξουσία) of approving, foreseeing and arranging define well the functions of the human leader in a post-Biblical community. In this sense, the presbyters who ruled the church of Chalcis in the absence of the local bishop are referred to as "leaders and guides [οἱ καθηγούμενοι] toward the good, whom others follow in accord [μετὰ συμπνοίας]."[40] They are called not only eyes but also heads of the community.[41]

Second, the other way in which Basil arrives at the concept of a church community "hierarchically" structured is derived from the Stoic notion of city (πόλις).[42] This evokes the idea of a church not only based on the rules

---

[37] *Reg. br.* 235: 1240c. On the difference in rank as based exclusively on the different and unequal distribution of the charismata see *Reg. mor.* 60: 793A-B.

[38] *Hex.* 5.6: Giet, 304; see also *Epp.* 227: Courtonne, 3: 30-31; 28.1: ibid., 1: 66-67.

[39] *Reg. fus.* 24: 984A; Clarke, p. 191. Cf. *In ps.* 33.11: 376c.

[40] *Ep.* 222: Courtonne, 3: 7.

[41] As a matter of fact, the text quoted in n. 40 is the only one where the leaders' functions are compared to that of the head in the body. However, I do not agree with J. Gribomont, "Obéissance et évangile," *VSSt* 21 (1952) 206, who, speaking of the ascetic προεστώς, affirms that "Basile ne songe pas à lui attribuer l'organe du commandement; la tête, c'est Christ." See also T. Špidlik, *La sophiologie de saint Basile* (Rome, 1961), pp. 167 ff. Christ is the exclusive head only in the sense that he is the only organ of the body to receive the προσκύνησις; see *In ps.* 44.10: 409c.

[42] See *In ps.* 45.4: 421c-D; 59.4: 468B. Cf. above, p. 10, n. 52.

of the gospel and on the charismatic dispensation but also subject to human regulations. This concept in Basil is closely associated with the notion of a living tradition (παράδοσις) as integral part of Christian existence.[43]

B. THE GENERAL ATTRIBUTES OF THE CHRISTIAN LEADER

The most common name that Basil gives to the highest ranked member in the church is that of προεστώς.[44] The term episkopos designates the single head of a church community. When the bishop was in exile, as was often the case during the reign of Valens, his functions were performed by a group of presbyters.[45] Thus the name προεστώς-προεστῶτες could signify either the single bishop, or a college of presbyters acting on his behalf or in his name. Also, as we saw earlier, this designation is often applied to the heads of the ascetic communities.[46] In order to be exercised, the charisma of leadership and care[47] had to be recognized (ἐγκριθέντα), in the case of the ascetic προεστώς by the leaders of the neighbouring brotherhoods, in the case of the ecclesiastical head by the neighbouring bishops and the members of the local church.[48] Here I shall describe, where possible in Basil's own

---

[43] On the Basilian notion of tradition, see Špidlík, Sophiologie, pp. 172-186; G. Florovsky, "The Function of Tradition in the Ancient Church," GOTR 9 (1963) 181-200.

[44] The term προεστώς occurs only seven times in the Small Asceticon (see Gribomont, "Obéissance," p. 203), and nearly fifty times in the Great Asceticon (see Clarke, Ascetic Works, p. 39, n. 10). It is applied in Basil's works equally to the ascetic and ecclesiastical leaders. See, on the latter, In ps. 28.2: 284A-B; Ep. 184: Courtonne, 2: 118; De jud., 1: 653B; Reg. fus. 15.4: 956B. On the historical and theological significance of the title προεστώς see P. J. Fedwick, "The Function of the προεστώς in the Earliest Christian κοινωνία," in Recherches de théologie ancienne et médiévale (forthcoming); see also B. Reicke, προΐστημι in TDNT 6: 700 f.; PGL s.v.; J. D. G. Dunn, Jesus and the Spirit (London, 1975), pp. 250 ff. Προεστώς occurs in Basil as an absolute participle only and is ordinarily used to denote the act rather than the office of "leading," "presiding," and, by extension, of "protecting," "caring for."

[45] As for instance in Antioch (the Meletian church); see Ep. 253: Courtonne, 3: 94; (Samosata), Epp. 182: ibid., 2: 117; 219: ibid., 3: 1 ff.; (Tarsus), Ep. 113: ibid., 2: 16 f.; (Chalcis), Ep. 222: ibid., 3: 6 ff. Cf. G. L. Prestige, St. Basil and Apollinaris (London, 1956), p. 15.

[46] See above, nn. 44, 35, and 22.

[47] Cf. n. 44, above.

[48] Rather than a concept of "election" there is in Basil the concept of "recognition," "acknowledgment" (ἔγκρισις). It is not because a person has been chosen as leader that he may exercise that ministry, but on the contrary, because God has given him the charisma, the possibility is given to him, through the church, of exercising it (see Reg. fus. 43.2: 1029A; Epp. 161.1-2: Courtonne, 2: 92 ff.; 197.1: ibid., 149 f.). While at the beginning the assumption was that the whole church should participate in the "election" of its bishop (see Epp. 28, 29, and 61), in other documents this decision seems to rest more and more with the clergy alone (see Epp. 227-230). The leaders, it is implied, decide who is to lead the people,

words, the attributes of the Christian προεστώς (the ecclesiastical and ascetic alike), as found in all of his writings.

According to Basil, the Christian προεστώς is a vessel (σκεῦος: "instrument") of divine election whom the Lord himself calls and chooses in a manner similar to that of the kings, prophets, and apostles.[49] "Since now [in the New Testament] all who have placed their hopes in Christ are one people and those who belong to Christ are one church,"[50] the leader's calling often takes him to exercise the ministerial functions beyond the boundaries of his native country. As an instrument, he is chosen and used by the Lord for the ministry (λειτουργία) of the saints and the sacred things.[51] He is charged with the care of (ἐπιμέλεια) and the pastoral solicitude of (φροντίς) Christ's flock.[52] To him is entrusted the ministry of the altar and the dispensation (οἰκονομία) of the sacred mysteries.[53]

Like the apostles, the προεστώς is sent (ἀπεστάλη) by Christ not to follow others, but to guide and teach (καθηγέομαι) those who are on the way to salvation.[54] He is called to take men captive for the Lord and to correct the infirmities of the people.[55] To the leader is entrusted the charisma of teaching, interpretation, and the ministry of the word.[56] Through the leader-

---

and the people are expected to show deference and submission to their decision ἐν συμφωνίᾳ τῆς γνώμης (Ep. 229.1: Courtonne, 3: 34). The circumstance, however, warranting this procedure is a very elusive one. Its legality is based on an a priori assumption that the πνευματικοί always act under the guidance and inspiration of the Holy Spirit. With the ordination of the two Gregorys Basil proceeded rather arbitrarily (see briefly S. Giet, *Sasimes. Une méprise de s. Basile* [Paris, 1941]). The whole incident could be summed up in one sentence: after the partition of Cappadocia, Basil needed leaders; not finding them, he created them! Amphilochius was probably still reeling under the impact of Gregory of Nazianzus' glamourized defection; thus in *Epistle 161* Basil spares no words to convince Amphilochius that his eventual flight or refusal would be a direct challenge to the express will of God. To make the picture look more gloomy we could add that Basil's own appointment to succeed Eusebius in 370 was the work of one man (Gregory the Older) and to a considerable extent of Basil himself. On some requirements of the candidates see ch. 3.A; see also in this connection *Epp.* 290: Courtonne, 3: 161 f.; 28.2: ibid., 1: 69. Moral qualities seemed to have prevailed, thus even a neophyte could qualify for the ministry (see *Ep.* 217: Courtonne, 2: 209).

[49] *Epp.* 161.1: Courtonne, 2: 93; 197.1: ibid., 150; cf. *Ep.* 188, c. 1: ibid., 123-124. On the σκεῦος see *Hom.* 3.4, quoted above, p. 8.

[50] *Ep.* 161.1: Courtonne, 2: 93; cf. *In ps.* 59.2: 464B-C.

[51] *Ep.* 161.1: Courtonne, 2: 93; cf. *Ep.* 188, c. 1: ibid., 123.

[52] *Epp.* 197.1: Courtonne, 2: 150; 156.2: ibid., 2: 83.

[53] *Ep.* 222: Courtonne, 3: 7; *De fide,* 1: 677A; cf. *Epp.* 93: Courtonne, 1: 204; 226.2: ibid., 3: 25; 251.3: ibid., 91.

[54] *Ep.* 161.2: Courtonne, 2: 93.

[55] *Epp.* 161.1: Courtonne, 2: 93; 197.1: ibid., 150; 200: ibid., 165.

[56] *Proem. in reg. br.*: 1080A; *De fide,* 1: 677A; *Reg. br.* 235: 1240C; *Reg. mor.* 70-71: 816D ff. *Ep.* 199: Courtonne, 2: 154. See also *Ep.* 28.2: Courtonne, 1: 68.

ship of the word, he builds and shapes the Christian community; in it he executes the functions of head, eyes and lips.[57] He is the voice of the church; its *coryphaeus*; the guardian of the institutions and ordinances of the fathers.[58] By word and example he is the guide of the Christians who are in pursuit of the good.[59] Under his leadership and care Christians are protected from the blows of the heretics and outsiders.[60] He is a pillar and support of the truth, a stay of the faith in Christ.[61] He is a pastor and spiritual father; although he is not allowed to add anything of his own, through his conduct and activity he is capable of building or altering the church.[62] Through his conduct more than through his words, he is a canon of conduct for his subjects.[63]

The προεστώς is the centre of ecclesiastical and Christian communion (κοινωνία): (1) through prayers and the eucharist; (2) by letters and visits.[64] To him is entrusted the οἰκονομία—the distribution of consecrated properties and possessions to the poor, as his duty is to care not only for the spiritual but also for the bodily needs of his subjects.[65] He is responsible for the discipline and good order in the Christian communities. He admonishes the offenders, first privately, then in the presence of others ("the church"), and if necessary, he excludes from the Christian community unworthy members.[66] Without its leader—dead or banished—the church becomes orphaned.[67]

---

[57] *Ep.* 28.2: Courtonne, 1: 68 (ἐκκλησιάζων used about the Holy Spirit *In ps.* 48.1: 433A); *Ep.* 222: Courtonne, 3: 7; *In ps.* 44.5: 397c.

[58] *Epp.* 28.2: Courtonne, 1: 68; 29: ibid., 71; 28.1: ibid., 66.

[59] *Reg. fus.* 43.1: 1028B; *Epp.* 150.4: Rudberg, 200; 222: Courtonne, 3: 7.

[60] *Ep.* 28.2: Courtonne, 1: 68; see *Epp.* 29: Courtonne, 1: 71; 219.2: ibid., 3: 3 ("the members of the church are united by his leadership as by one soul"; cf. the same about the Holy Spirit in *De jud.*, 3: 660A).

[61] *Epp.* 28.1: Courtonne, 1: 66; 29: ibid., 71; 222: ibid., 3: 7. Both statements occur in 1 Tim 3.15 with reference to the church as a whole. Applied to the leader, they should, however, be qualified in view of what is said in *Ep.* 257.2: Courtonne, 3: 99, and below, p. 69, n. 149.

[62] *Epp.* 62: Courtonne, 1: 153; 28.3: ibid., 70; 28.2: ibid., 68; 222: ibid., 3: 7; 227: ibid., 29-30; 28.1: ibid., 1: 66. Cf. *Epp.* 200: Courtonne, 2: 165; 190.1: ibid., 141-142; *Reg. fus.* 43.1: 1028B; *In ps.* 33.8: 369B; also *De fide*, 1: 677A; *Ep.* 159.2: Courtonne, 2: 86.

[63] *Reg. fus.* 25.2: 985A-C; 43.1-2: 1028A-1029B; *Ep.* 150.4: Rudberg, 200.

[64] *Epp.* 191: Courtonne, 2: 144-145; 204.7: ibid., 179-180; 65: ibid., 1: 155; 91: ibid., 197; 99.1: ibid., 214; 93: ibid., 204; 224.2: ibid., 3: 19; 203.1: ibid., 167-168.

[65] *Ep.* 150.3: Rudberg, 199; *Reg. br.* 187: 1208B-C; *Epp.* 92.2: Courtonne, 1: 200; 31: ibid., 73; *Reg. fus.* 31: 993B-C; *Reg. mor.* 70.21: 833B.

[66] *Epp.* 200: Courtonne, 2: 164-165; 53-55: ibid., 1: 137-142; *Ep.* 288: Courtonne, 3: 158; *Reg. fus.* 28.1: 988C-D; *Epp.* 289: Courtonne, 3: 159; 61: ibid., 1: 151-152.

[67] *Epp.* 28.2: Courtonne, 1: 68; 183: ibid., 2: 118.

Although he is invested with a dignity (ἀξίωμα) and primacy (προεδρία), the Christian προεστώς should remember that "the care of many entails the service of many."[68]

> The προεστώς then, mindful of the apostle's injunction, 'Be thou an example to them that believe,' (1 Tim 4.12) must make his life a clear example of every commandment of the Lord so as to leave the taught no chance of thinking that the commandment of the Lord is impossible or may be despised. First of all then—which truly comes first—humility must be so practised by him in the love of Christ that even when he is silent the example of his deeds may stand out more strongly than any word as a means of teaching. For if this is the standard of Christianity, the imitation of Christ according to the measure of His Incarnation as is appropriate to the calling of each, those who are entrusted with the guidance of the many ought by their own mediation to lead on the weaker to the imitation of Christ, as the blessed Paul says, 'Be ye imitators of me, even as I also am of Christ' (1 Cor 11.1).[69]

C. The Ecclesiastical Leader
as Defender of Orthodoxy

Essentially there are two main duties of the ecclesiastical leaders implied in the images of eyes and lips that Basil has applied to these members of the ecclesiastical body. One is to discern events, plan them, and keep constant watch on their development. To this effect Basil wrote to the community of Chalcis: "Day and night I pray the King of the ages to preserve the people in the integrity of their faith, and for them to preserve the clergy, like a head unharmed at the top, exercising its own watchful forethought for every portion of the body underneath."[70] In the *Longer Interrogation 24* the statement is made that the function of the eye is to test what has been done (γεγενημένων), to foresee and arrange what will be done (γενησομένων).[71] In plain words, it is implied that the duty of the leader as the eye of the body is to bear responsibility for the growth ("edification") of the church's life of faith. In the second place, through the metaphor of the lips it is suggested

---

[68] *Reg. fus.* 30: 992D-993A.
[69] *Reg. fus.* 43.1: 1028B-C; Clarke, p. 216.
[70] *Ep.* 222: Courtonne, 3: 7; Jackson, p. 262.
[71] *Reg. fus.* 24: 984A; Clarke, p. 191. In this connection should be noted the rationale that Basil uses for the existence of some kind of order in the church. It rests not so much on an act of divine (historical) institution (besides its charismatic origin) as on natural convenience and necessity; that is, even if the church order is postulated by "common sense" (see *De jud.*, 2-3: 656B ff.; *Reg. br.* 235: 1240C; *Ep.* 203.3: Courtonne, 2: 170; cf. *De sp. s.* 51: Pruche, 426 ff.; also Giet, *Idées*, pp. 34 ff., 152 ff., and esp. 173 ff.

that the duty of the προεστώς in the community is to communicate with his flock and to show it the road of moral goodness and salvation: in other words, to confront it with teaching about the commandments of God. Of this second duty of preaching and interpreting the word of God we shall speak in the next chapter. Here we shall focus on the first responsibility of the ecclesiastical leader, which consists in protecting and defending the Christian faith.

According to Basil, the main accusation brought against the orthodox leaders by the heretics before the authorities was that the heads of the local communities were solicitous in keeping the ecclesiastical traditions. "One charge is now severely avenged," writes Basil to the Western episcopate, "the solicitous guarding of the traditions of the Fathers."[72] And then he adds: "Shepherds are persecuted that their flocks may be scattered."[73] Such an explicit reference to the responsibilities of the individual leaders for the preservation of the Christian identity in their communities raises the following question: What is, in Basil's ecclesial awareness, the role attributed to the individual local leader in the defence and protection of the orthodox faith? There is no doubt that every Christian by virtue of his baptism is committed to the preservation of the deposit of the faith. All the people of Neocaesarea are reminded not to leave to their neighbours the common interests of all (τῶν κοινῶν ἐπιμέλειαν).[74] However, since Basil early rejected the concept of individualistic faith, the responsibility to defend and support the believing community seems to be increasingly concentrated in the hands of the local leaders. Of the "collegial" character of the episcopal institution and of the common endeavour to defend the orthodox churches we shall speak in the last chapter. Here our immediate concern is to see if in such an assumption of a collective effort on the part of all Christian leaders it is insisted also that each individual member of that body take every precaution necessary to protect the integrity of the church's spiritual heritage. With a view to finding an answer to that question, we shall analyze some of the letters Basil wrote either on the occasion of local events, or which were expressly intended for the individual heads of a given Christian community.

When in 371 Musonius the bishop of Neocaesarea died, Basil was unable to pay final homage to his deceased colleague personally. In a letter ad-

---

[72] *Ep.* 243.2: Courtonne, 3: 69.

[73] Ibid.

[74] *Ep.* 28.3: Courtonne, 1: 69. See further on the subject of common responsibility pp. 85 f., 87 f., below; for John Chrysostom see A. M. Ritter, *Charisma im Verständnis des Joannes Chrysostomos und seiner Zeit* (Göttingen, 1972), p. 199.

dressed to the people, Basil calls to mind the illustrious exploits of their leader.[75] Above all, great emphasis is laid on the achievements of Musonius in matters of faith and doctrine. Musonius is personally credited with the fact that Neocaesarea remained loyal to orthodoxy. Musonius indeed, Basil emphasizes, has been "an enemy of innovation, exhibiting in himself the ancient fashion of the church, and making the state of the church put under him conform to the ancient constitution, as to a sacred model, so that all who lived with him seemed to live in the society of them that used to shine like lights in the world two hundred years ago and more."[76] On account of this Basil calls Musonius "an ornament of the churches, a pillar and support of the truth, a stay of the faith of Christ, a protector of his friends, a stout foe of his opponents, a guardian of the principles of his Fathers."[77] Thanks to such qualities of its pastor, the church of Neocaesarea remained remarkably consistent with the apostolic principle transmitted through the preaching of Gregory Thaumaturgus and his worthy successors.[78]

The other quality which emerges from *Epistle 28* and other of Basil's letters and contemporary documents is that of the προεστώς as a patron of the church entrusted to his care. In almost identical terms as those Basil uses to portray Musonius, Gregory of Nazianzus describes Basil as the ideal bishop in his *Oration 43*.[79] The ideal leader was not only to protect the faith of the community but he also was expected to protect all civil rights of the members of his church. J. Bernardi pointedly observes: "In such circumstances one understands why people were anxious to have rich and influential men as their leaders."[80] Musonius is in fact presented in his panegyric not only as "a pillar and support of the truth, a stay of the faith of Christ," but also as "first [ἔξαρχος] among the nobles [τῶν ἐν τέλει], a patron [προστάτης] of

---

[75] The literary genre of *Epistle 28* and *29* should be noticed. They belong to what is called ἐπιτάφιος λόγος (funeral oration) in epistolary form. Thus in their analysis we have to omit personal references and take into account only those elements that are of a universal application so far as the episcopal functions are concerned.

[76] *Ep.* 28.1: Courtonne, 1: 66; Jackson, p. 132.

[77] Ibid.

[78] See *Epp.* 204.2: Courtonne, 2: 173-174; 28.1: ibid., 1: 67. It should be noted that according to Basil Christian doctrine and tradition are not passed on by a series of uninterrupted successions in office, although their integrity is insured through the watchfulness of the bearers of such office; rather they are transmitted by being spoken and heard (see *Epp.* 223.3: Courtonne, 3: 12; 204.6: ibid., 2: 178; 229.1: ibid., 3: 34; *De sp. s.* 79: Pruche, 528).

[79] For the claim that, more than a biographical sketch, Gregory intended to portray in his panegyric the image of an ideal bishop, see J. Bernardi, *La prédication des Pères cappadociens* (Paris, 1968), p. 238.

[80] Ibid., p. 242. See also Kopecek, "Social Class."

the people, a support [τροφεύς; a provider of food] of the needy."[81] This patronage concerned equally the protection of the rights of the individuals as those of the community at large.[82]

Finally, it must be observed that the role of the local leader could not possibly be of such paramount importance unless it were because he enjoyed within his community and in the execution of his duties a certain sovereignty and autonomy. Of this again we have some indications in Basil's correspondence. To Count Terentius, despite the urgency to proceed as soon as possible with the reunification of the divided churches, Basil insists:

> Nevertheless, there is one point which I should like to have pressed on your excellency, that you and all who like you care for the truth, and honour the combatant in the cause of true religion, ought to wait for the lead to be taken in bringing about this union and peace by the foremost authorities [προστάτας] in the church, whom I count as pillars and foundations of the truth and of the church.[83]

Similarly *Epistle 156* emphasizes that even if someone—Basil included— were endowed with charismatic gifts (πνευματικοῖς χαρίσμασι) of prevailing over the rival parties in Antioch, such an attempt should not be carried out "without the cooperation of the bishop, on whom principally falls the care of the church" (ᾦ ἡ φροντὶς ἀνῆκε προηγουμένως τῆς ἐκκλησίας).[84] To protect effectively this principle of autonomy Basil sided with the traditional view that there could not be more than one bishop-leader in a city.[85] Hence the priority given in his unionistic efforts to have first settled the schism of

---

[81] *Ep.* 28.2: Courtonne, 1: 68. Some parallels from *Oration 43* can be found in Bernardi, *Prédication*, pp. 243 ff. Cf. Kopecek, "Social Class," p. 460, for the translation of οἱ ἐν τέλει as "city curials." According to A. R. Hands, *Charities and Social Aid in Greece and Rome* (London, 1968), p. 60, "the term *tropheus* is simply one of the less common titles (*euergetes* is the most common) invented with almost unlimited ingenuity for benefactors in the Hellenistic age." See also ibid., n. 62 for other references.

[82] See Bernardi, ibid., and the comprehensive look at Basil's social activity on behalf of his province and of those oppressed in Giet, *Idées*, pp. 356 ff., and Teja, *Organización*, pp. 119 ff., 196 ff.

[83] *Ep.* 214.4: Courtonne, 2: 206; Jackson, p. 254.

[84] *Ep.* 156.2: Courtonne, 2: 83; Jackson, p. 254.

[85] See on this subject E. Hatch, *The Organization of the Early Christian Churches* (New York, 1972), pp. 102-104. The chorepiscopi of Cappadocia, who must have numbered about fifteen (and not fifty as Gregory of Nazianzus would have us believe), constituted no threat to the singleness of the occupant of the see of Caesarea; rather they emphasized his preeminence. On the chorepiscopi see G. Bardy, *La théologie de l'Eglise de s. Irénée au concile de Nicée* (Paris, 1947), pp. 258-266; A. H. M. Jones, *The Later Roman Empire 284-602* (Oxford, 1964), 2: 879, with nn. 13-14, and B. Jackson, p. 156, n. 2.

Antioch where two orthodox bishops, Meletius and Paulinus, contended the see.[86]

Since the autonomy and competence of a bishop were such that he could "shape" (διαμορφόω) a church after his own pattern of conduct and belief, the search for suitable candidates became crucial. The shortage of good candidates for church leadership prompted Basil in some cases to withhold nominations to some smaller sees and also to act occasionally as an "exarch."[87] His conduct is in a sense explained in a letter to Amphilochius. After recognizing that a better and more expedient administration of the churches could result from an increased number of bishops, Basil observes:

> But it is not easy to find fit men. While, then, we are desirous of having the credit that comes of a number [πλῆθος], and cause God's church to be more effectively administered by more officers, let us be careful lest we unwittingly bring the word into contempt on account of the unsatisfactory character of the men who are called to office, and accustom the laity to indifference.

Then he adds:

> You yourself know well that the conduct of the governed is commonly of a piece with that of those who are set over them [προεστῶτες].[88]

In the enunciation of these "unitarian" principles we can see originating an agonizing dilemma for the future Christian generations. On the one hand, an effective leader needed to be in constant touch with his people; as their spiritual father and shepherd he needed to know his flock "by name," take personal care of their individual problems. Thus a community of small size where he could be known and easily available to every member was more suitable. On the other hand, because of the shortage of such people of high moral standards who could teach their flock more by example than words, Basil was personally led either to take under his direct control many such small communities, or to place them under the oversight of one authority (the churches of Isauria under the supervision of Amphilochius). In this way, by merging smaller churches into one and by centralizing the ecclesiastical authority in the hands of one person the pastoral care was im-

---

[86] Besides its obvious merits, the principle of autonomy contained some unintentional side-effects, as can be inferred from the case history of the churches of Sebaste, Neocaesarea, Antioch, and others: "Cujus regio, ejus religio"!

[87] On complaints about lack of suitable candidates for church ministries, see *Epp.* 239.1: Courtonne, 3: 59; 190.1: ibid., 2: 141. On the general situation described by Gregory of Nazianzus, see Bernardi, *Prédication*, pp. 238 ff.

[88] *Ep.* 190.1: Courtonne, 2: 141-142; Jackson, p. 232; cf. *Reg. fus.* 43.1: 1028B; *De sp. s.* 77: Pruche, 526.

paired, although it seemed to benefit from the removal of many "single-handed principates" that threatened the quality of church's faith and life.[89] But in spite of some of its merits, this Basilian solution was an endorsement and a further, albeit indirect, contribution to the consolidation in the church of other types of self-contained unities, authentic empires, the patriarchates and the centralized religious orders.

D. BASIL AS DEFENDER OF THE FAITH IN CAESAREA

Because Basil is not a systematic writer, and because his treatment of church leaders as guardians of the faith is incomplete, it seems convenient to study more closely his own conduct as the leader of the church of Caesarea. This should enable us to appreciate his ideas more fully. In attempting to portray Basil as an ideal ecclesiastical leader, we have been preceded by Gregory of Nazianzus. Concerning the latter's funeral discourse on Basil, J. Bernardi has observed:

> In delineating the portrait of Basil, in reconstructing the salient features of his career, it is the image of a great bishop, and, to a great extent, of the ideal bishop that Gregory proposes to his listeners; for them and for us he recreates a page of religious history, and he contributes to an understanding of the relations of a bishop with his church.[90]

Also, Basil's works from before and during his episcopate yield many valuable indications as to his attitude regarding the defense of orthodoxy.[91]

As early as 359, Basil came into direct contact with some of the problems facing the church. However, neither his appearance in the Council of Constantinople in January of 360, nor his apology against Eunomius from *ca.* 364, earned for him as much notoriety as the events in which he became directly involved in 365. On the general mood prevailing in

---

[89] The same centralizing tendency appears in Basil's *Great Asceticon* regarding cenobitic institutions; see *Reg. fus.* 35.3: 1008B.

[90] *Prédication*, p. 238. The use of Gregory's rhetorical work—*Oration 43*—is warranted in a historical study of Basil's pastoral conduct, among others, through comparison of his narrative with Basil's own records. Even a cursory glance in our case has yielded the following parallels: *Or.* 43.47: PG 36, 557A: *Ep.* 203.1: Courtonne, 2: 168; *Or..* 43.41: PG 36, 552A: *Ep.* 65: Courtonne, 1: 55; cf. *Ep.* 67: ibid., 159. Although Gregory does not recount the events in strictly chronological order, his portrait of Basil can be taken as quite accurate.

[91] There is little difference in the account of Gregory of Basil's activities before and during the episcopate, as Basil since 365 practically "led the one [that is, Eusebius] who then led the people": *Or.* 43.33: 541A.

Caesarea on the eve of Valen's first visit to that city, Gregory reports: "Great, then, was the struggle in prospect. The ardor of the multitude was not wanting, but their battle line was weak for lack of a champion and one trained to fight for them with the power of the Word and the Spirit."[92] The newly appointed bishop, Eusebius, lacked theological training and experience, and on Gregory's advice he decided to recall Basil from Pontus. Gregory reports that Basil "had no sooner seen me on my mission, for the struggle was common to us both as defenders of the faith, than he yielded at once to my plea. ... At once he departed with me from Pontus and was filled with zeal in defence of truth in danger, offering himself as a willing ally in the fight and dedicating himself to his mother, the church."[93] As a first step in preparing the Christians of Caesarea for the imminent danger, Basil conducted an internal reform. Gregory recalls:

> He removed all the obstacles and stumbling blocks in our way and all that had given encouragement to those attacking us. He gained in one quarter, held his ground in another, and drove back the attack in a third. He became to some a strong wall and rampart, to others an axe breaking the rock to pieces, or a fire among the thorns.[94]

But the most convincing victory over a government compromised by and in connivance with heresy was obtained by Basil in 371-372. Valens was determined this time to make up for his previous defeat. He had decided to crush through threats and intimidation the opposition of the leader of Caesarea, the only one still refusing to submit to his policies. Basil, however, rejected decisively and with dignity both the tempting propositions and the most violent threats with which the emperor tried to subdue him. Basil's imperturbability and presence of spirit during the protracted colloquy with the prefect Modestus evoked from this magistrate expressions of the most sincere respect and admiration. "No one up to this day has ever spoken in such a manner and with such boldness to me," said the prefect, seeing all his attempts to overcome Basil fruitless. "Perhaps you never met a bishop before," replied Basil. Then he added:

> For in other respects, prefect, we are reasonable and more submissive than anyone else, for so our law prescribes. We do not show ourselves supercilious to such high authority or even to any ordinary person. But when God's in-

---

[92] *Or.* 43.31: 537D-540A; McCauley, p. 54.
[93] Ibid.
[94] Ibid., 32: 540B; McCauley, p. 55.

terests are endangered or at stake, we count the rest as nothing, and look to these alone. Fire and sword and wild beasts and tongs that tear the flesh are a source of delight to us rather than of terror. Therefore, go on with your insults and your threats, do whatever you will, make the most of your authority. Let the emperor hear this, also, that you will never prevail on us or persuade us to make a covenant with impiety, even though you utter threats still more violent.[95]

In this confrontation between Basil and Modestus is contained perhaps the best exemplification of the conduct of a bishop, which Basil outlined to Amphilochius following the latter's ordination:

Play the man, and be strong, and walk before the people whom the Most High has entrusted to your hand. Like a skillful pilot, rise in mind above every wave lifted by heretical blasts; keep the boat from being whelmed by the salt and bitter billows of false doctrine.[96]

Basil was an authentic leader of his community, and this is one of the qualities Gregory most tries to emphasize in his eulogy. Even after Basil's death Gregory could have repeated regarding the church of Caesarea what Basil said about the Neocaesareans after Musonius' departure:

For, so far as I know, you alone, or, at all events, you and but very few others, in the midst of such a storm and whirlwind of affairs, were able under his guidance to live your lives unshaken by the waves. You were never reached by the heretics' buffeting blasts, which bring shipwreck and drowning on unstable souls.[97]

E. THE TWO METHODS OF DEFENCE

"Those who engaged in hand-to-hand conflicts he overthrew at close range by word of mouth. Those who engaged at a distance he struck with arrows of ink."[98] There is ample evidence in Basil's works to support the use of this double method in the defence of orthodoxy. Basil's writings are a testimony to his personal contribution to the cause of orthodoxy in a moment of stress and uncertainty. I shall discuss in more detail the value and uses of the written word in Appendix E. Here I propose to concentrate on Basil's apologetic method in its oral form. To that effect I shall sample

---

[95] Ibid., 50: 560D-561B; McCauley, p. 69 (rev.).
[96] *Ep.* 161.2: Courtonne, 2: 93; Jackson, p. 214.
[97] *Ep.* 28.1: Courtonne, 1: 67; Jackson, p. 132. Cf. also *De fide*, 2: 680C-D.
[98] *Or.* 43.43: 553A; McCauley, p. 64.

some of his homilies which, despite the changes they underwent while being edited for publication, still preserve the flavour of an original eye-to-eye confrontation. The homiletic style which Basil is chiefly credited with introducing into Christian preaching, is characterized and enlivened by the use of rhetorical questions. There is a constant dialogue (ὁμιλία) between the preacher and his audience. In his dogmatic homilies Basil brings in the objections of his opponents, in particular those of the anti-trinitarian theologians. Though the interpellants are not identified by name, it is not difficult to pin down their backgrounds, as Basil for the most part couches their objections in their own vocabulary. They are, as the title of a homily makes clear, the Sabellians, the Arians and the Anomoeans.[99] To these should be added the Pneumatomachi, the Manichaeans, the Gnostics and the Montanists.[100] Like the *Asceticons*, Basil's homilies convey the experience of a live dialogue and confrontation, and thus they provide the best clue for the study of his apologetic method in its oral form. As most of his homilies follow an analogous pattern of development, I shall sample one homily in which the use of Basil's method of combating the heresies is most conspicuously represented.

Homily 16, on the words "In the beginning," provides a good illustration of Basil's method of handling a face-to-face confrontation with his trinitarian opponents.[101] Basil is aware that the first chapter of the gospel according to St. John has been an object of admiration and even of appropriation on the part of several heathen philosophers. But his immediate concern is to prepare every new member of his community with adequate means to confront the Arian's sophisms. Basil knows that the members of his congregation lack sufficient knowledge of theological subjects and that they can be easily deceived by their opponents. For his part, as a truly enlightened leader, thoroughly acquainted with the secrets of human and divine wisdom, Basil supplies them with the weapons to combat the erroneous teachings. What does he advise them to do?

> Hold fast to the text, and you will suffer no harm from men of evil arts [κακοτέχνων]. Suppose your opponent argues, 'If He was begotten, He was not'; you retort, 'He was in the beginning.' But, he will go on, 'Before He was begotten, in what way was He?' Do not give up the words 'He was.' Do not

---

[99] See *Hom.* 24: "Against the Sabellians, Arians and Anomoeans."

[100] See *De sp. s.*, *passim*, on the Pneumatomachi; *Hex.* 2.4: Giet, 154 (here also the Marcionites are mentioned); *Ep.* 188, c. 1: Courtonne, 2: 122; *Hom.* 9 (against the Manichaeans).

[101] *Hom.* 16: 472ʙ ff. delivered before catechumens, cf. ibid.: 481ᴄ.

abandon the words 'In the beginning.' The highest beginning point is beyond comprehension; what is outside beginning is beyond discovery. Do not let any one deceive you by the fact that the phrase has more than one meaning. There are in this world many beginnings of many things, yet there is one beginning which is beyond them all. ... Never give up the 'was' and you will never give any room for vile blasphemy to slip in. Mariners laugh at the storm, when they are riding upon two anchors. So will you laugh to scorn this vile agitation which is being driven on the world by the blasts of wickedness, and tosses the faith of many to and fro, if only you will keep your soul moored safely in the security of these words.[102]

Had not Basil used this highly dialectical method of argumentation in live disputes with the heretics, how could he have used it in a catechetical oration intended for the catechumens? The viability of dialectics as an apologetic method is not only supported by the analysis of Basil's works but also by the external testimony of Gregory of Nazianzus, which may properly be referred to in this regard:

Who was like him in philosophy, that truly sublime science which soars aloft, whether one consider the practical and speculative side, or that which deals with logical demonstrations and oppositions and with controversies, namely, dialectics? In this, he so excelled that it would have been easier for those who disputed with him to extricate themselves from labyrinths than to escape the meshes of arguments he wove whenever he had need.[103]

To withstand effectively the theological arguments of Arians (and others), which often were constructed on narrowly logical premises, it was pastorally advisable that Christians also be familiar with this type of weaponry. However, such display of dialectical craftiness in the hands of a Christian was never to go beyond certain limits. It was only to be a means of demonstrating the inanity of all human reasoning vis-à-vis the inscrutable mystery of God, and why not of nature as well?[104]

Typically enough, in *Homily 23* the pursuit of the adversary ends with a plea to accept an "ascetic" (practical) interpretation of the Christian message:

To know God is to keep His commandments. Surely you do not mean, then, that the essence of God should be investigated thoroughly? Or supramundane things searched out? Or the invisible objects pondered over? 'I know mine

---

[102] *Hom.* 16.1: 473ʙ-476ᴄ. Part of the translation is owed to B. Jackson, p. lx.
[103] *Or.* 43.23: 528ᴀ; McCauley, p. 47. See also *De fide*, 1-2 677ʙ-680ᴅ, esp. 680ʙ-ᴅ.
[104] Some examples of *a fortiori* argumentation can be seen in *Hom.* 24.6-7: 613ᴀ-616ʙ; *Epp.* 234 and 235.

and mine know me.' It should be enough for you to know that there is a good shepherd who gave His soul for His sheep. The knowledge of God is comprised within these limits. How big God is, what His limits are, and of what essence He is, such questions as these are dangerous on the part of the interrogator; they are as unanswerable on the part of the interrogated. Consequently they should be taken care of with silence [σιωπή].[105]

The recommendation of "silence" in the last paragraph as a means of countering probes into the divine mysteries by means of philosophical questions should not be regarded as incidental. In fact it constituted part of the theology and church politics Basil adopted with regard to those who were undecided because of the silence of the Bible and the Council of Nicaea on the question of the ὁμοούσιος of the Holy Spirit.[106] For the longest time Basil believed that through "silence" (σιωπή) and "prudent handling" (οἰκονομία), that is, by studiously abstaining from speaking openly of the Spirit's deity, he could win over to orthodoxy the Pneumatomachi, headed by his former teacher and friend, Eustathius of Sebaste.[107] Only after his "silence" was repeatedly interpreted as complicity in the Pneumatomachian position, which was more and more compromised by a progressive denial not only of the divinity but also of the non-creatureliness of the Holy Spirit, did Basil gradually abandon his policy of reticence.[108]

F. Relations of the Ecclesiastical Leader with Non-Orthodox Christians

In this chapter concerned with the ecclesiastical leader as guardian of orthodoxy, in addition to dealing with his pastoral responsibilities to protect and defend the deposit of the faith, we must also investigate his role in the relationship between orthodox and nonorthodox groups of Christians. The

---

[105] *Hom.* 23.4: 597A.

[106] On "silence" as a Basilian *locus theologicus* see H. Dörries, *De Spiritu Sancto. Der Beitrag des Basilius zum Abschluss des Trinitarischen Dogmas* (Göttingen, 1956), pp. 121 ff., and pp. 181 ff.; as a political device, see H. von Campenhausen, *The Fathers of the Greek Church* (New York, 1959), pp. 94-95.

[107] As a characteristic illustration of Basil's position on the τρόπος τῆς ὑπάρξεως of the Holy Spirit see his *Hom.* 24. After speaking openly that the Father is "ingenerate" and the Son "generate," Basil is not ashamed of inculcating reticence as to the "manner of coming to be" of the Holy Spirit: Εἰ δὲ πολλὰ ἀγνοεῖς, καὶ μυριοπλάσια τῶν ἐγνωσμένων ἐστὶ τὰ ἀγνοούμενα, τί οὐχὶ μετὰ πάντων καὶ περὶ τοῦ τρόπου τῆς ὑπάρξεως τοῦ ἁγίου Πνεύματος τὴν ἀκίνδυνον ἄγνοιαν ἀνεπαισχύντως ὁμολογεῖς ; (6: 613A).

[108] The definitive breach with Eustathius did not occur until 375 with the publication of the "open" letter 223 and the *De Spiritu Sancto*; see *De sp. s.*, 79: Pruche, 528. For more on Basil's "prudent handling" see below, p. 63.

previous pages have disclosed to us in the teaching and in the example of Basil the qualities of the ecclesiastical leader as defender and champion of the faith. Regarding Basil's role and character as a church politician H. von Campenhausen has written:

> Basil's true greatness becomes apparent only when he is studied in the context of the conflicts of his age and his role is properly understood. As an ecclesiastical politician Basil did not display the rocklike strength of Athanasius; as a theologian he did not possess the harmony and universality of his younger brother, Gregory of Nyssa; as a monk he did not possess the subtle refinement of some of the later mystics. But these things must not be interpreted as signs of natural incapacity or a weakness in his character. On the contrary, it was his very devotion to the needs of the hour, the necessity of adapting himself to the difficulties of his situation, which compelled him constantly to vary his tactics and made it impossible for him to develop his rich talents in peace or follow the bent of his spirit as he wished. He found his work as an ecclesiastical politician so difficult because he was not only wiser and more farseeing but also more profound and more honest than most of his colleagues.[109]

However, despite the overall accuracy of this judgment, the primary role that Basil himself attained in the church does not seem to pertain so much to the domain of ecclesiastic politics as to that of enlightened Christian leadership. "Devotion to the needs of the hour" and adaptability to changing circumstances are not necessarily virtues unless motivated and accompanied by a spirit of genuine love and sincerity. Eustathius of Sebaste was a celebrated case in the fourth century of an "ecclesiastic chameleon," of a shrewd tactician who knew how to manipulate people and dogmatic formulae in order to achieve his personal aims.[110] Basil, although his disciple and friend, had to terminate all relationships with him because he could not agree with Eustathius' deceitful conduct.[111]

If there was an historical dimension to which Basil tried to attune himself in all sincerity of heart and mind, this must have been the finitude and limited character of individual human nature. Early in his career Basil proclaimed the universal principle of human solidarity as the only possible

---

[109] *Greek Fathers*, p. 97.

[110] A good summary of Basil's views on Eustathius can be found in B. Jackson, p. xxvii. See also there the sources, esp. *Epistle 130* and *244*. In this connection one should also consult the "rehabilitating" study of F. Loofs cited with other sources on Eustathius below, p. 160, n. 8.

[111] With respect to Eustathius Basil not only displayed a certain naïveté, but also in comparison with his teacher Basil was less of a politician.

response to the naturally contingent situation. "Who does not know that man is a tame and sociable being, and not a solitary and fierce one? For nothing is so characteristic of our nature as to associate with one another, to need one another, and to love our kind." [112] "None of us is self-sufficient even as regards bodily needs, but we need one another's help in getting necessities." [113] Translated into Christian terminology, this meant that man's salvation and survival depends upon love and communion ($\varkappa o \iota \nu \omega \nu \iota \alpha$: "sharing") with God and with his neighbours.

It must not have taken long for Basil to realize that the once peculiarly Christian characteristic of love ($\dot{\alpha} \gamma \dot{\alpha} \pi \eta$) was absent from the church of his day. "Our love has grown cold," we hear Basil complaining often throughout his works. [114] Violent and uncontrollable theological disputes, accusations and counter-accusations, reciprocal suspicions, in a word, a state of warfare on the domestic scene replaced the atmosphere of love that once reigned among the Christians throughout the *oikoumene*. [115] Faith was no longer uniting but separating Christians, and, what was worse, Christians were persecuting Christians on account of the faith. [116]

> For it is an evil time, a time when some trip up their neighbour's heels, some stamp on a man when he is down, and others clap their hands with joy, but there is not one to feel for the fallen and hold out a helping hand, although according to the ancient law he is not uncondemned, who passes by even his enemy's beast of burden fallen under his load. This is not the state of things now. Why not? The love of many has grown cold; brotherly admonitions are heard no more, nowhere is there Christian pity, nowhere falls the tear of sympathy. Now there is no one to receive 'the weak of faith,' but mutual hatred has blazed so high among fellow clansmen that they are more delighted at a neighbour's fall than at their own success. [117]

Was Basil's reaction to the situation confined to mere complaints? Gregory of Nazianzus relates that when Basil saw the church of God

> in a miserable plight and torn asunder into an infinity of doctrines and errors, ... he did not think it enough to lament misfortune in silence and

---

[112] *Reg. fus.* 3.1: 917A; Clarke, p. 157.

[113] *Reg. fus.* 7.1: 928c; Clarke, p. 163.

[114] The quotation referring to Mt 24.12 occurs often in Basil's writings; cf. *Epp.* 141.2: Courtonne, 2: 64; 191: ibid., 145; 164.2: ibid., 99; *De sp. s.* 78: Pruche, 526; *Hom.* 8.2: 309B, etc. It is always applied to the love of neighbours.

[115] See *Ep.* 191: Courtonne, 2: 145.

[116] See *Ep.* 257.1: Courtonne, 3: 98-99.

[117] *De sp. s.* 78: Pruche, 526 f.; Jackson, p. 50.

merely lift up his hands to God to implore deliverance from the pressing evils, himself remaining asleep. Rather he thought he was bound to render aid and to make some personal contribution.[118]

The problem of Christian reunification in the fourth century was approached and dealt with in different ways by different people. With regard to the "weak of faith" Basil from the beginning adopted a stance of goodwill and understanding. His rather liberal views on ecclesiastical communion with and reception of alienated members into the church were cause for no little apprehension on the part of many, even of his closest friends. Basil's conciliatory approach was particularly noticeable with respect to the Pneumatomachi, a new sect which refused to attribute the titles of *homoousion* and "God" to the hypostasis of the Holy Spirit. A monk who heard Basil preaching one day in Caesarea publicly accused Basil of heresy because he did not hear him talking with the same explicitness about the divinity of the Spirit as he did in relation to that of the Father and the Son.[119] Even two years after Basil's death the question of his orthodoxy because of friendly relations with people suspected of heresy must still have been in the air, since part of Gregory's eulogy is devoted to the rehabilitation of his friend from that stigma.[120] Not only Gregory but the great champion of Nicaea, Athanasius of Alexandria, had to defend Basil when the monks of Caesarea threatened to withdraw from his communion if he did not become more precise in his teachings about the Holy Spirit.[121]

While Gregory and Athanasius tried to explain Basil's singular attitude by appealing to the notion of *oikonomia*, meaning "prudent handling," some modern scholars have turned to the distinction between the concepts of *kerygma* and *dogma* in order to account for the same facts.[122] Our main concern here lies not so much in the history per se of Basil's relations with Eustathius of Sebaste, the Pneumatomachi and other left-wing groups of Christians, as in the motives in general that stood behind his adoption of friendly policies toward the nonorthodox. Consequently we should try to uncover the grounds, other than those mentioned by his contemporaries and modern scholarship, on which Basil tried to base his conduct of friendship

[118] *Or.* 43.41: 549D-552B; McCauley, pp. 62-63.

[119] See Gregory of Nazianzus, *Ep.* 58: Gallay, 75-76.

[120] See *Or.* 43.68-69.

[121] See *Epistola ad Palladium* (from the end of 371 or beginning of 372): PG 26, 1168C-D.

[122] See on the latter Dörries, *De Spiritu Sancto*, pp. 23-28, and E. Amand de Mendieta, "The Pair 'Kerygma' and 'Dogma' in the Theological Thought of St. Basil of Caesarea," *JThS* 16 (1965) 129-142.

with people who lived outside his own church. For that purpose let us determine first of all his own understanding of heresy and schism. This should allow us to see in a better perspective the whole issue of church intercommunion as exemplified in Basil's teaching and conduct.

G. HERESY-SCHISM-PARASYNAGOGUE

In a letter to Amphilochius of Iconium, following some undesignated ancient authorities, Basil distinguishes three modes in which there can take place a separation of a baptized person from the orthodox community.[123] These three modes affecting Christian unity were said to be heresy, schism and parasynagogue, depending on whether a disagreement (διαφορά) fell on actual faith in God, on church discipline or on ecclesiastical rulings.

(i) Heresy. From antiquity heretics were understood to be people "who were altogether broken off [παντελῶς ἀπερρηγμένους] and alienated [ἀπηλλοτριωμένους] in matters relating to the actual faith."[124] Faith and love are according to Basil the constitutive element of church unity.[125] The element of consent and agreement (συγκατάθεσις) in the definition of faith makes the church a σύμπνοια, that is, a harmonious body animated by the breath of the one indwelling and lifegiving Spirit, the church's only soul.[126] To have faith is to have the Holy Spirit operating in one's soul. The breaking off from the church is a breaking off from the Spirit.[127] Heresy is a διαφορά, a discrepancy on vital issues and the negation of the unity of God, of the church and of the human brotherhood.[128] As causes of separation (χωρισμός; ἀλλοτρίωσις) Basil mentions pride and arrogance (μεγαλοφροσύνη) and a mania for novelty, each vice originating in the human faculty of free choice (προαίρεσις).[129] Thus because it was an act of deliberate choice, heresy was punishable and not tolerated in the churches. Its authors were cautioned first; then if they refused to obey, they were excommunicated

---

[123] See *Ep.* 188, c. 1: Courtonne, 2: 121. On the identification of τοῖς ἐξ ἀρχῆς see the erudite note 39 of the Benedictines in PG 32, 666.

[124] *Ep.* 188, c. 1: Courtonne, 2: 121; Jackson, p. 223.

[125] See *Ep.* 203.3: Courtonne, 2: 170. For a more comprehensive view on the subject, see below, pp. 125 ff.

[126] See in the following order: *De fide*, 1: 677D; *Ep.* 203.3: Courtonne, 2: 170; *De jud.*, 3: 660A.

[127] See *Ep.* 188, c. 1: Courtonne, 2: 122-123.

[128] Cf. *Ep.* 188, c. 1: Courtonne, 2: 123, with *Ep.* 203.3: ibid., 170. Cf. also *In ps.* 48.1: 433C.

[129] See *Ep.* 188, c. 1: Courtonne, 2: 123 and *Ep.* 203.3: ibid., 170; *In ps.* 48.7: 449A; *De sp. s.* 16: Pruche, 298; *Ep.* 52.1: Courtonne, 1: 134 (αὐθάδεια).

from the churches, as an exposed heresy was believed to cause less harm than a camouflaged one.[130]

(ii). Schism. The term σχίσμα in Basil has a variety of meanings. The ancient authorities defined schism as a disagreement (διαφορά) among church members concerning ecclesiastical questions capable of mutual solution.[131] In schism elements concurred that were more of a disciplinary than a doctrinal nature. Often personal reasons were involved.[132] In *Homily 23* Basil cites a difference of opinion regarding the Lord's sayings as an example of division (σχίσμα).[133] These and similar reasons were not of such a serious nature as to warrant a lasting feud among members of church communities. Nonetheless, to hear Basil speak, trivial reasons often stood at the root of not a few divisions among Christians. One such classical example was Antioch.[134]

(iii) Parasynagogue. "Rival" or "counter-assemblies" were called "gatherings set up by insubordinate presbyters or bishops and by uninstructed people [τὰς συνάξεις τὰς παρὰ τῶν ἀνυποτάκτων πρεσβυτέρων ἢ ἐπισκόπων καὶ παρὰ τῶν ἀπαιδεύτων λαῶν γινομένας). As, for instance, if someone who has been apprehended in error [πταίσματι: 'fault,' 'sin'] has been hindered from ministerial functions [ἐπέσχεθε τῆς λειτουργίας] and has not submitted to the canons, but has arrogated to himself the presidency and the ministerial functions [τὴν προεδρίαν καὶ τὴν λειτουργίαν] and some persons abandon the catholic church and join him, this is parasynagogue."[135]

From this description parasynagogue would appear mainly as a case of misconduct on the part of certain members of the Christian community. No false teaching or creedal matter would, at least initially, be involved. In describing the impropriety of those who originate rival assemblies Basil uses the term ἀνυπότακτος, the opposite of εὐταξία, the good order and discipline of the church.[136] The other term ἀπαίδευτος can mean anything from "uneducated," "uninstructed," "ignorant," to "boorish" or "coarse." More important to notice is the context within which the Basilian description of the parasynagogue occurs. The order (κανών) in violation of which the

[130] See *C. Eun.* 1.2: 504B. On the sick limb and the need to amputate it, see *Reg. br.* 84: 1141C; 281: 1280B; 57: 1121A-B; *Reg. fus.* 28.1: 988C-D.

[131] *Ep.* 188, c. 1: Courtonne, 2: 121.

[132] See *Ep.* 69.2: Courtonne, 1: 164.

[133] See *Hom.* 23.4: 596C.

[134] Although the dispute between the two rival factions of Meletius and Paulinus was ostensibly no more than a schism (see *Ep.* 156.1: Courtonne, 2: 82), later on Basil will try to put Paulinus on the list of heretics; see *Ep.* 263.5: Courtonne, 3: 125.

[135] *Ep.* 188, c. 1: Courtonne, 2: 121.

[136] See *In ps.* 44.11: 412D; *Ep.* 161.1: Courtonne, 2: 93.

unruly Christians set up their assemblies is not so much the juridical, canonical one, as the liturgical one.[137] The words καὶ παρὰ τῶν λαῶν need not necessarily be understood "[presbyters or bishops] along with the laymen" but they should be taken as implying *also* the laity or, better yet, the Christian people in general as the authors of rival assemblies. In fact, from fourth-century documents we learn that besides insubordinate clergy there were also groups of supercilious ascetics—one such group being the Eustathians—who would assemble for worship outside and even in spite of the established churches, often in private homes or in the open. Against such improper, as it was thought, practices we have the canons 6 and 20 of the Council of Gangra and Basil's *Shorter Interrogation 310.*[138]

Because in *Epistle 188* Basil is not speaking of ecclesiastical discipline in general but of the infraction of the liturgical order, each parasynagogue or constitution of a rival assembly implies the breach of ecclesiastical unity. Already the Council of Nicaea in canon 5 spoke of breaches of church unity caused by unruly clergy. The words ἀποσυνάγωγος γίγνομαι taken probably from the Gospel of John 9.22 mean "to be cast, put out of the synagogue" and have the same meaning as the phrase ἀκοινώνητος γίγνομαι, "to become excommunicated." Although without speaking expressly of excommunication, Basil seems to indicate quite unmistakably that parasynagogues are cases leading their authors in that direction. As we saw earlier, prayers and liturgy (especially the eucharistic one) are for Basil means of ecclesiastical communion and unity, and whoever abandons or despises them is putting himself out of the catholic community.[139] He becomes excommunicated, not necessarily in the juridical term, but in the sense of no longer partaking of the eucharist of the ecumenical church, in which alone abides the Holy Spirit.

The motive or reason for establishing a rival assembly is also indicated by Basil. According to him, parasynagogues are acts of revenge (ἐκδίκησις) on the part of those who refuse to accept in full or in part the body of ecclesiastical laws and customs (κανόνες). In *Epistle 188* it is the rejection of canonical punishment for past misdeeds, in *Epistle 265* the Apollinarians, refused on account of their dire Christological speculations, are said to be

---

[137] Both the eucharistic and the penitential liturgy are dealt with in *Epistle 188, c.* 1. See also there on baptism, confirmation, and the notions of σύναξις, λειτουργία and προεδρία.

[138] The canons of Gangra are discussed below, p. 158. See also Basil's *In ps.* 28.3: 288A-B, and the pseudo-Basilian homily on the same Psalm in PG 30, 73A. For canon 5 of the Council of Nicaea discussed next see C. J. Hefele - H. Leclercq, *Histoire des conciles* (Paris, 1907), 1: 548 ff.

[139] See above, p. 49, and below, pp. 120 f.

trying to avenge (ἐκδικεῖν) themselves by setting up their own hierarchies in places controlled by the catholics: "Men are sent by him [scil. Apollinaris] to the churches governed by the orthodox to tear them asunder and to claim to themselves revengefully particular rival assemblies" (τὸ σχίσαι καὶ ἰδίαν παρασυναγωγὴν ἐκδικῆσαι).[140]

In light of this brief analysis of the Basilian notion of the parasynagogue it can be said that for him the term "parasynagogue" has at least three meanings. It means unlawful gatherings arranged by catholic ministers under suspension, or indisciplined Christians in general, or ministers divided on matters of belief. Because of the latter meaning, the concepts of heresy-schism-parasynagogue in a certain manner overlap, as in the Christian order, faith, worship, and praxis constitute an indivisible unity.

H. HERETICS

Until now we have tried to determine the concepts that express the various modes in which total or partial separation of an orthodox believer from the church community could happen. We have seen that for Basil total rupture from the living body of the church took place only as a result of a completely different manner of understanding the Christian faith in God. Only after an individual was repeatedly warned because of this and he refused to obey did heresy or sect originate.

Schism involved a mere discrepancy of opinion. As Basil himself acknowledges, at stake were differences regarding solvable matters which could easily be settled if only there were a little good will on both sides. Probably there were no penalties with regard to people falling into this category, unless there intervened some aggravating circumstance such as contumacy.[141] The same can be said about the parasynagogue in the first two senses. Therefore in this section devoted to the relations of the orthodox leader with heterodox people or groups, we shall confine ourselves to the heretics only.

In fact, it was the heretics who constituted the most serious pastoral problem for the church in the fourth century. In his works Basil time and again complains about the havoc and devastation brought about in many places, especially in the Eastern provinces, as a consequence of the rapid proliferation and spread of erroneous opinions opposed to the sound

---

[140] *Ep.* 265.2: Courtonne, 3: 129.
[141] See the sources cited above, n. 129.

teaching of the Scripture and the traditions of the Fathers. Then, as now, the question was: Should there be applied against such people only the extreme measures of ecclesiastical condemnation and excommunication, or should the orthodox leaders exercise some pastoral care on their behalf? Let us examine this question more closely. First let us try to determine even more accurately the concept of heresy; then let us try to explain Basil's attitude—theoretical and practical—with respect to people not belonging to the orthodox communion; finally we shall try to determine the motives that inspired his conduct of condescension and friendliness toward all such people.

From his early childhood Basil lived the experience of a church divided and torn apart. Until the end, however, Basil was profoundly convinced that he belonged to the only true church of Christ. "Up to this day," he writes in an open letter of 375, "by the grace of Him Who has called me in His holy calling to the knowledge of Himself, I know of no doctrine opposed to the sound teaching having sunk into my heart; nor was my soul ever polluted by the ill-famed heresy of Arius."[142] In another writing, although acknowledging a certain progress in his faith, Basil is aware of never having suffered any radical change in this respect.

> The concept about God which I had received as a boy from my blessed mother and my grandmother Macrina I have ever held with increased conviction. On my coming to ripe years of reason I did not shift my opinion from one to another, but carried out the principles delivered to me by my parents. Just as the seed when it grows is first tiny and then gets bigger but always preserves its identity, not changed in kind though gradually perfected in growth, so I reckon the same doctrine to have grown in my case through gradually advancing stages.[143]

This certainty of belonging to the true church of God, Basil evinced from the circumstance that he received from his grandmother Macrina "the words of the blessed Gregory; which, as far as memory had preserved down to her day, she cherished herself [ὅσα πρὸς αὐτὴν ἀκολουθίᾳ μνήμης διασωθέντα αὐτῇ τε ἐφύλασσε], while she fashioned and formed me, while yet a child, upon the doctrines of piety [τοῖς τῆς εὐσεβείας δόγμασιν]."[144]

---

[142] Ep. 204.6: Courtonne, 2: 178-179; Jackson, p. 245.

[143] Ep. 223.3: Courtonne, 3: 12-13; Jackson, pp. 263-264.

[144] Ep. 204.6: Courtonne, 2: 178; Jackson, p. 245. Not only did Basil greatly esteem the teaching of Gregory Thaumaturgus handed down to him through Macrina (see ibid. and De sp. s., 74), but in everything he sought to conform his views with those of the great apostle of Neocaesarea; see for the legitimacy of this claim K. Holl, quoted above, p. 3, n. 10.

However, since Gregory Thaumaturgus has little or next to nothing extant in writing, Basil, often suspected and accused of heresy, could not simply appeal to this tradition; he had to make use of other criteria to prove his orthodoxy. Often in his writings mention is made of three such criteria: the inspired Scriptures, the Council of Nicaea and the "multitude of bishops throughout the *oikoumene*" with whom he was in communion.[145] None of these tests had validity separately. They were interchangeable in the sense that frequently only one was explicitly invoked but always with the understanding that the others were referred to as well.[146] These four criteria of orthodoxy were comprised in the concept of the church as the living tradition.[147] Its carrier could be any one of the "spiritual men" (οἱ πνευματικοί).[148] However, this role is more and more relegated in Basil's ecclesial consciousness to the ecclesiastical leader, that is, the bishop in most cases, but not in the Ignatian sense ("where the bishop is, there is the church"), but only "with the provision that he [the bishop] be in accord and communion with the whole church."[149]

In light of these data, it is easy to answer the following question: Who is a heretic? Already earlier Basil had given a summary answer: A heretic is one who dissents from the others on matters of belief. Now we are in a position to specify further this concept by saying that, according to Basil, a heretic is an individual whose faith is lacking one of these ingredients: he is in disaccord with the teaching of the Scriptures and the tradition; or he does not agree with the definition of Nicaea; or finally, a heretic is any one who

[145] On the Scriptures as a test of orthodoxy see *Reg. mor.* 72.12: 845D-848B; *De jud.*, 1: 653A. Basil's adhesion to the Council of Nicaea was more qualified: see *Epp.* 114: Courtonne, 2: 18-19; 52.1: ibid., 1: 134-135. On the multitude (πλῆθος) of bishops with whom he communicated as a sign of orthodoxy, see *Ep.* 204.7: Courtonne, 2: 179 f. Basil, as was said before, gave a qualified assent to the Council of Nicaea as he supported the addition of a clause to the Nicene symbol with the mention of the non-creaturehood of the Holy Spirit; see *Epp.* 113: Courtonne, 2: 17; 125.3: ibid., 33-34; 140.2: ibid., 62; 258.2: ibid., 3: 102. On the traditional sources of this datum see H. Dehnhard, *Das Problem der Abhängigkeit des Basilius von Plotin* (Berlin, 1964), pp. 20 ff. Moreover, Basil was in favour of a distinction between the terms "hypostasis-ousia" which the Council considered as synonyms; see *Epp.* 125.1: Courtonne, 2: 30 ff.; 214.4: ibid., 205 f.

[146] The reason being that the heretics also claimed support for their teachings in the Scriptures and the Council of Nicaea; see *De sp. s.* 25: Pruche, 334; *Ep.* 125.1: Courtonne, 2: 31 f.

[147] See on this subject the excellent remarks of Špidlik, *Sophiologie*, pp. 172-186.

[148] See *Ep.* 229.1: Courtonne, 3: 34, and Špidlik, *Sophiologie*, pp. 182-183.

[149] Špidlik, ibid., p. 185; *Ep.* 257.2: Courtonne, 3: 99 f., quoted below, p. 76, n. 175. See also above, p. 4, nn. 17-18.

professes a faith different from the "unanimous agreement" (σύμπνοια: "conspiratio") of the whole church.[150]

As we have mentioned earlier, in the church of the fourth century heresies were commonplace. Their rise and spread were facilitated by a combination of factors: hasty and "opportunistic" conversions, bishops with insufficient theological training, confused formulation of symbols of faith, support of the secular arm (especially in the regions controlled by Valens), internal feuds and animosities among ambitious men, etc.[151] The effects were often devastating. The heretics made easy conquests among poorly instructed people who at the beginning were unable to distinguish them from the orthodox teachers. What was worse, as Basil often points out, is that many set their orthodox confessions at naught "not through fear of fire, or sword, or cross, or scourge, or wheel, or rack, but merely by being led astray by the sophistry and seductions of the Pneumatomachi."[152] The last named heresy of the "spirit-fighters," which denied the divinity and consubstantiality of the Holy Spirit, was the one that caused the most concern to Basil.[153] Among its chiefs was his old friend and master, Eustathius of Sebaste. From the pastoral standpoint, however, every heresy created a difficult problem for communal life. Persons convicted of heresy undoubtedly set a bad example for the rest of the members of the church. For this reason it was necessary to proceed as soon as possible to their expulsion from the local community, as these sick limbs could not but cause harm to the organs which were still healthy.[154] But our immediate concern here is to see whether, according to the conduct and teaching of Basil, the

---

[150] An example of the first was Apollinarius of Laodicaea; see *Ep.* 263.4: Courtonne, 3: 124; the Pneumatomachi (they rejected the tradition), see *De sp. s.* 16: Pruche, 300; cf. ibid., 66: Pruche, 478 ff. Marcellus was an instance of the second case; see *Ep.* 125.1: Courtonne, 2: 31; also Eustathius, see *Ep.* 226.3: Courtonne, 3: 26 f. The term σύμπνοια is used by Basil to designate the "spiritual, dynamic, and joyful accord" among the members of the church or the ascetic community. The term, of Stoic origin, is derived from the description of the organs of the body which because of one soul "breathe together"; cf. *Epp.* 97: Courtonne, 1: 211; 203.3: ibid., 2: 170. See the texts assembled in L. Vischer, *Basilius der Grosse* (Basel, 1953), p. 54, and the study of J. Daniélou, "'Conspiratio' chez Grégoire de Nysse," *L'homme devant Dieu. Mélanges H. de Lubac* (Paris: Aubier, 1963), 1: 295-308.

[151] Cf. Bernardi, *Prédication*, pp. 367-370.

[152] *De sp. s.* 27: Pruche, 340 f.; Jackson, p. 17.

[153] An account of this heresy can be found in B. Pruche, *Basile de Césarée, Traité du Saint-Esprit* (Paris, 1968), pp. 72-77, and J. N. D. Kelly, *Early Christian Doctrines* (London, 1968), pp. 259 ff. See also the Index in PG, s.v. "Pneumatomachi," "Spiritus Sanctus."

[154] See *Ep.* 263.2: Courtonne, 3: 122 and n. 130, above.

responsibility of a bishop or a general church leader should be limited only, as it were, to the task of pruning.

On the relations of orthodox Christians with the heretics Basil has several texts. Some refer to intercourse of bishops with their colleagues who have fallen prey to heresies; others deal with the relations of the bishops with laymen become heretics; and others are concerned with the relations between the orthodox faithful and the nonorthodox. The solution proposed by Basil will therefore vary according to the particular circumstances.

The ascetics in general were forbidden to associate with those who fell into errors concerning morals (ἐν τοῖς ἠθικοῖς σφαλλομένων), and more forcibly yet, with those who held depraved opinions (κακοδοξούντων) about God.[155] A similar recommendation is made to the deaconesses, the daughters of Terentius.[156] With profound regret, but not without a certain feeling of pride, Basil reports in a letter that most orthodox in the East prefer rather to abandon "the houses of prayer" and hold "congregations of their own in the wilderness" than have anything to do with the heretics. His description of this resort is pathetic: "Women, boys, old men, and those who are in other ways infirm, remain in the open air, in heavy rain, in the snow, the gales and the frost of winter as well as in summer under the blazing heat of the sun. All this they are suffering," Basil explains, "because they refuse to have anything to do with the wicked leaven of Arius."[157]

There is no doubt therefore that in principle there was enforced a certain line of noncommunication and an attitude of considerable intransigence between the orthodox and nonorthodox. There was perhaps even some logic to this policy of intransigence, so that Basil did his best to comply with the decisions of his predecessors. However, in practice, although not rejecting such rulings *en bloc*, Basil seems to have adhered not to the letter but to the spirit of Christian charity that inspired them. In *Epistle 188*, which was quoted earlier, after having explained to his pupil Amphilochius *per longum et latum*, what heresy, schism and parasynagogue were, Basil confesses: "I am aware that I have received into episcopal rank Izois and Saturninus from the Encratite following. I am precluded therefore from separating from the

---

[155] See *Reg. br.* 20: 1096D-1097A; *Ep.* 262.2: Courtonne, 3: 120. However, in *Reg. br.* 124 Basil allows them to greet the heretics and pagans, a novelty unheard of in antiquity according to E. Leggio, *L'ascetica di s. Basilio* (Turin, 1934), pp. 219-222. Contrast P. Brown, *The World of Late Antiquity* (London, 1971), pp. 103-106.

[156] See *Ep.* 105: Courtonne, 2: 7.

[157] *Ep.* 242.2: Courtonne, 3: 66-67; Jackson, p. 283.

church those who have been united to their company, inasmuch as, through my acceptance of the bishops, I have promulgated a kind of canon of communion with them." [158] Again, in spite of the fact that some ancient authorities rejected the baptism of heretics altogether because this practice erred against faith, Basil is inclined under certain circumstances to accept it as valid. [159] His rationale? "For I am under some apprehension lest, in our wish to discourage them from baptizing, we may, through the severity of our decision, be a hindrance to those who are being saved." [160] He also seems to have for a long time acknowledged the validity of the episcopal ordinations performed by heretics. In *Epistle 240*, when announcing the change of his position—"I do not recognize as bishop, I would not count among Christ's clergy, a man who has been promoted to leadership by polluted hands, to the destruction of the faith"—Basil realizes that his stance now is something new for him. To the presbyters of Nicopolis he says: "This is my judgment. If you have any part with me, you will doubtless think as I do." [161] The more intransigent position, we should note, was taken after the breach with Eustathius of Sebaste. But until then Basil maintained friendly relations particularly with regard to Eustathius, the leader of those Homoeousians who were known as Pneumatomachi; these relations were for many, even for some of his closest friends, true cause for apprehension, suspicion, anger, threats of withdrawal from his communion, and even public accusations of heresy. [162]

Is there any explanation for Basil's earlier broad-minded attitude of friendship and communion toward people of different religious persuasions? As was mentioned earlier, to explain Basil's non-use of the name God with regard to the Spirit, Athanasius and Gregory resorted to the concept of the *oikonomia*—prudent handling—while some modern scholars have tried to bring in the distinction between *kerygma* and *dogma* in order to account for the same fact. [163] However, it would seem that neither theory, and par-

---

[158] *Ep.* 188, c. 1: Courtonne, 2: 124; Jackson, p. 225.
[159] See the Benedictines' n. 37 in PG 32, 665D.
[160] *Ep.* 188, c. 1: Courtonne, 123; Jackson, p. 225.
[161] *Ep.* 240.3: Courtonne, 3: 64.
[162] See pp. 63 f.
[163] See above, nn. 118, 120-122. For some of the other modern opinions see B. Pruche, "Autour du *Traité du Saint-Esprit* de s. Basile de Césarée," *RSR* 52 (1964) 204-232; Idem, "*Dogma* et *kerygma* dans le *Traité sur le Saint-Esprit* de s. Basile de Césarée," *SP* 9 (Berlin, 1966) 257-262; J. Gribomont, "Esoterisme et tradition dans le *Traité du Saint-Esprit* de s. Basile," *Oecumenica* 2 (1967) 22-56; Idem, "Intransigencia e irenismo en san Basilio. Introducción al *De Spiritu Sancto*," *Estudios trinitarios* 9 (1975) 227-243; and S. de Boer, "Paradosis, dogma en kerygma naar de opvatting van Basilius de Grote," *NTT* 24 (1970) 333-372.

ticularly the second, can be generalized. They probably can account for some facts but they can hardly be invoked to explain Basil's prolonged relations with many people suspected of heresy: (1) If the *homoousion* of the Son was for Basil a *kerygma* in the sense suggested by H. Dörries and E. Amand de Mendieta, why did Basil avoid using it regularly? (2) In *Epistle 214* the Nicene definition is referred to as *dogma* not *kerygma*, which indicates that Basil's terminology is inconsistent in itself and thus we cannot base on philological analysis of single words any conclusions as to his general behaviour.[164]

Instead of seeking confirmation in Basil's works for preconceived theories, I propose to look for his understanding of the two key concepts involved, faith and church unity. I believe that his doctrine regarding these two topics can be summarized in six propositions.

(1) Unity of faith is not incompatible with the multiformity of its expressions.[165]

(2) The propositions on faith are based on only partial knowledge of the mystery of God. Thus they sometimes vary and must be accommodated to various times and circumstances.[166]

(3) The minimum and not the maximum of theological precision should be postulated in relations with and reception of people joining the church.[167]

---

[164] See *Ep.* 214.3: Courtonne, 2: 204. It is, however, from *Ep.* 263.1: ibid., 3: 121 that the interchangeability of both terms appears more clearly. One should not forget that despite its incomparable value, the treatise *On the Holy Spirit* was written in the middle of a fierce polemic between Basil and his former friends, the Eustathians. In the heat of the argument, Basil has undoubtedly forced the meaning of several terms in order to prove his point. On the antecedents of the distinction between *kerygma* and *dogma*, see *De sp. s.*, 65: Pruche, 478.

[165] As an example of this awareness in Basil one can consider the *De fide*. See the "private" creed inserted there: 685A ff. What counted was not the wording but the meaning attached to the words. Thus Basil progressively will substitute the ill-fated *homoousion* (this term is absent from the *De fide*) with other more acceptable terms like ὅμοιος κατ' οὐσίαν (see *Ep.* 9.3: Courtonne, 1: 39), ὁμότιμος (see Pruche, *Traité*, pp. 100 ff.).

[166] See *De fide*, 2: 681c; ibid., 1-2: 677B-680D.

[167] See *Ep.* 113: Courtonne, 2: 16. This I believe was also the reason why Basil did not require the confession of the divinity of the Spirit in an explicit form. He was satisfied with the negative proposition that the Spirit is not a creature. The following words should be noted especially: "Let us then seek no more than this, but propose to all brethren who are willing to join us, the Nicene Creed. If they assent to that, let us further require that the Holy Spirit ought not be called a creature, nor any of those who say so be received into communion. I do not think that we ought to insist upon anything beyond this. *For I am convinced that by longer communication and mutual experience without strife, if anything more requires to be added by way of explanation, the Lord Who worketh all things together for good of them that love Him, will grant it*" (*Ep.* 113: Courtonne, 2: 17; Jackson, pp. 189-190).

(4) Faith being difficult to assess, anxious thought must be taken before excluding from or denying a member communion.[168]

(5) Ecclesiastical communion, the external sign of church unity, is an expression of brotherly love and solicitude through common participation in the prayers, the sacraments, in the sharing of spiritual and material goods, and through exchange of letters.[169]

(6) Although friendship (φιλία) as such is probably to be excluded, some kind of care (ἐπιμέλεια) particularly in the epistolary form and by way of encounters with people alien to the orthodox faith ought to be encouraged.[170]

That Basil did not act on the spur of the moment when accommodating himself to the people who were "weak in faith" can be proved from the fact that when his method was questioned and opposed by enemies, colleagues, and friends he continued to believe firmly in the validity of his approach. He must have believed then that his method was sound because rooted on scriptural and theological premises. Otherwise Basil could not be himself; in his actions he would be alienated from the sound heritage he had received from his family. Thus I prefer to account for his broad-minded attitude

---

[168] Cf. *Ep.* 223.6: Courtonne, 3: 15-16; Jackson, p. 265: "Much anxious thought must be taken, and many sleepless nights must be passed, and with many tears must the truth be sought from God, by Him who is on the point of cutting off from a brother's friendship. Even the rulers of this world, when they are on the point of sentencing some evil doer to death, draw the veil aside, and call in experts for the examination of the case, and consume considerable time in weighing the severity of the law against the common fault of humanity, and with many a sigh and many a lament for the stern necessity of the case, proclaim before all the people that they are obeying the law from necessity, and not passing sentence to gratify their own wishes. How much greater care and diligence, how much more counsel, ought to be taken by one who is on the point of breaking off from long established friendship with a brother!" See also *Ep.* 204.5: Courtonne, 2: 176 ff.

[169] See above, p. 49 the explanation of church communion.

[170] That φιλία, "affectionate regard," "friendship on an equal to equal basis" should be excluded in the relations with those who do not share the orthodox faith has been seen above, pp. 23 f. That ἐπιμέλεια, that is, basically "a charitable disposition" expressed in greetings and epistolary form should be maintained is indicated in *Reg. mor.* 70.35: 844B; *Reg. br.* 124: 1165C-D, and notably *Ep.* 128.3: Courtonne, 2: 39; Jackson, p. 197: "Not that I think it is absolutely our duty to cut ourselves off from those who do not receive the faith, but rather to show care (ἐπιμέλειαν) for them in accordance with the old law of love, and to write to them with one consent, giving them all exhortation with pity, and to propose to them the faith of the Fathers, and invite them to union. If we succeed we should be united in communion with them; if we fail we must be content with one another." See also *Epistle 263* discussed below, pp. 111 ff.; also pp. 96 f. That Basil, unlike Gregory of Nazianzus, preferred to express the idea of friendship through the Scriptural term *agapē* rather than the Hellenistic *philia*, see K. Treu, "*Philia* und *agapē*. Zur Terminologie der Freundschaft bei Basilius und Gregor van Nazianz," *Studii classice* 3 (1961) 421-427.

toward people of different convictions on the assumption of a deeper and far-sighted understanding of faith and church unity. "Since God the Creator ordained that we need one another, as it is written, we ought to be linked with one another. But apart from this the *logos* of the love of Christ does not allow us to look each at his own good. For 'love' we read 'seeketh not its own' (1 Cor 13.5)."[171] Where could motives of self-interest, revenge, ambition, etc. be more insidiously found intertwined with God's salvific designs than in an institution committed to "draw the devil's prey from the deep into the light?"[172] Thus, though deeply preoccupied with the purity of the church's faith, Basil, instead of being a hair-splitter and perfectionist, preferred "to make himself weak with the weak" in order to be of "no hindrance to those who are being saved."[173]

When viewed in such a broad perspective—broader than the one afforded by the abstract notions of "economy," "kerygma" and "dogma"—Basil's pastoral activity as an ecclesiastical leader appears removed from any narrow self-interest or partisan approach.

> Whereas others never progressed beyond the theology of their school, never saw beyond their party interests and purely material considerations, Basil had always kept in view the whole life of the Church. He suffered from the narrow-mindedness and lack of spiritual insight of his fellow-bishops far more than those who were too otherworldly, too sensitive, or too complacent to enter the fray themselves.[174]

Basil was sure that by giving priority to the extension of church membership (the πλῆθος) he was not overlooking or impairing the quality of the church's life as long as love (ἀγάπη) and nothing else was the leit-motiv of his actions.[175]

---

[171] *Reg. fus.* 7.1: 928D-929A.

[172] *Ep.* 161.1: Courtonne, 2: 93. See also his remark about the situation in the churches in *Ep.* 92.2: Courtonne, 1: 201; Jackson, p. 178: "And now the very vindication of orthodoxy is looked upon in some quarters as an opportunity for mutual attack: and men conceal their private ill-will and pretend that their hostility is all for the sake of the truth."

[173] See in the following order: *Ep.* 114: Courtonne, 2: 18; Athanasius, *Epistola ad Palladium* (applying to Basil 1 Cor 9.22): PG 26, 1168C: Αὐτὸς μὲν γάρ, ὡς τεθάρρηκα, τοῖς ἀσθενοῦσιν ἀσθενὴς γίνεται, ἵνα τοὺς ἀσθενεῖς κερδήσῃ. See, finally, *Ep.* 188, c. 1: Courtonne, 2: 123.

[174] Campenhausen, *Greek Fathers*, p. 98.

[175] The notions of πλῆθος (plurality, multitude) and ἀξιοπιστία (trustworthiness, respectability) have been studied by P. F. Monticelli, "Collegialità episcopale ed occidente nella visione di san Basilio Magno. Le nozioni di πλῆθος e ἀξιόπιστον," *Annali della Facoltà di Magistero di Bari*, 6 (1967) 1-38; see esp. pp. 11-14. According to this author, in his letters Basil uses both terms interchangeably—thirty-seven times πλῆθος, sixteen ἀξιόπιστον. The reasons for Basil's preoccupation with the πλῆθος is thus explained by M. Richard: "En

Orient, les Nicéens étaient, au moins en apparence, en minorité et étaient traités comme tels par le pouvoir. Les Ariens profitaient naturellement de cette situation, qui, en leur donnant figure d'orthodoxie officielle, leur permettait d'attirer à eux tous les indécis. Mais si, au lieu de considérer l'Orient seul, on prenait l'Eglise entière, la situation se trouvait inversée. La majorité orthodoxe apparaissait écrasante. S. Basile, avec un sens catholique très réaliste, se rendait parfaitement compte de cette situation. Il pensait donc, peut-être avec raison, qu'une manifestation d'unité des évêques orientaux (nicéens) et occidentaux ouvrirait les yeux à bien des gens sur cette réalité œcuménique et les inciterait à renoncer à leur habitude de juger les affaires ecclésiastiques à l'échelle orientale" ("Saint Basile et la mission du diacre Sabinus," *AB* 67 [1949], p. 184). That "plurality" is not a criterion of the truth, see *De sp. s.* 79: Pruche, 528, and particularly the letter to the ascetics persecuted by the Arians, *Ep.* 257.2: Courtonne, 3: 99-100, "high priests, scribes, and elders devised the plot against the Lord, ... Remember that it is not the multitude (τὸ πλῆθος) who are being saved, but the elect of God." Are the ascetics to be considered among the elect? Nowhere more clearly than in this document from 376 Basil speaks of clergy (τῶν κληρικῶν) and people (τοῦ λαοῦ) as an indiscriminate multitude (πολυοχλία) that is "carried hither and thither by winds like the waters of the sea," and of the ascetics as the "little flock" of the holy ones (οἱ ὅσιοι).

3

The Charisma of the Leader of the Word

God creates the universe through his Logos; the Holy Spirit congregates the nations of the world into the one church of God through his kergyma.[1] The agents of the Holy Spirit in the establishment and furthering of the Kingdom of Christ on earth are not only the prophets and apostles in the technical sense but also all those whom the Spirit chooses for the purpose of communicating to others the riches of his grace.[2] In the context of the church as the charismatic community, the charisma of apostleship and of prophecy, it is true, occupies a preeminent place. The proclaimers of the gospel are, according to Basil, the lips and eyes of the body of Christ.[3] As lips they lend their voices to the Holy Spirit in order that he may write "the words of eternal life in the hearts of the faithful";[4] as eyes their function is to "discern between good and evil, and guide the members of Christ towards what befits each."[5]

The reasons behind the name leader of the word ($\pi\rho o\epsilon\sigma\tau\dot{\omega}\varsigma$ $\tau o\tilde{\upsilon}$ $\lambda\acute{o}\gamma o\upsilon$) are perhaps best explained in a passage from the homily *On Psalm 28*.[6] Drawing to a considerable degree on the allegorical method, Basil contends,

> [Like the rams], such are the leaders of the disciples of Christ [$o\dot{\iota}$ $\tau\tilde{\eta}\varsigma$ $\pi o\iota\mu\nu\tilde{\eta}\varsigma$ $\tau o\tilde{\upsilon}$ $X\rho\iota\sigma\tau o\tilde{\upsilon}$ $\pi\rho o\epsilon\sigma\tau\tilde{\omega}\tau\epsilon\varsigma$]. They lead them forth to the blooming and fragrant nourishment of spiritual doctrine, water them with living water with the concurrent assistance of the Spirit, raise them up and nourish them until they produce fruit; then they guide them to rest and safety from those who lay snares for them.[7]

---

[1] See *Hex.* 3.2: Giet, 192; *De sp. s.* 38: Pruche, 376-378; *In ps.* 48.1: 433A.

[2] See *In ps.* 48.1: 433A; *Reg. mor.* 80.13: 864C; cf. above, pp. 32-33.

[3] *In ps.* 44.4: 397A; *Reg. mor.* 80.15: 865A.

[4] *In ps.* 44.3: 396A.

[5] *Reg. mor.* 80.15: 865A; Clarke, p. 128.

[6] This homily is placed by J. Bernardi, *La prédication des Pères cappadociens: le prédicateur et son auditoire* (Paris, 1968), p. 25, "before 375."

[7] *In ps.* 28.2: 284A-B; Way, p. 195 (rev.).

Several points are made in this passage. Alongside the divine rule of universal providence[8] and the energizing activity of the Spirit in the church, Basil
recognizes the need that human souls won over to Christ be guided by
human leaders.[9] These leaders are not only to instruct in and lead their
disciples towards what befits each but their function is also to provide constant assistance to every member of the Christian community entrusted to
their care.[10] The father-child relationship also involves the function of
caring for (spiritually and materially) and of protecting the community from
all possible dangers to which it may be exposed.[11]

The other point which Basil is trying to make is that every leader of the
word is invested with a certain degree of authority at the moment he is
delivering the message.[12] This authority is not unqualified and seems to be
derived from the fact that a genuine leader is acting in response not only to
a divine but also to an *ecclesiastical* calling.[13] As we have seen, an act of
"recognition" (ἔγκρισις) had to precede the exercise of leadership in the
ascetic community. The same is now postulated for the exercise of the
charisma of the word ‘in the *Moralia*. This, of course, does not mean that
the charisma of the word (or any other charisma for that matter) is thus
created by the church but only that its meaningful and purposeful exercise is
only possible *in* and *through* the church.[14]

After these preliminary remarks let us now see in more detail some of the
main requirements and duties which Basil postulates in those in the community who are endowed with the leadership of the word.[15]

[8] See e.g. *Hex.* 9.5: Giet, 504; other passages ibid., 314, n. 1.

[9] Besides pp. 45 ff., above, see *Ep.* 223.2: Courtonne, 3: 10.

[10] See briefly *Reg. mor.* 70.16-21: 829B ff.; *Proem. in reg. br.*: 1080A; and the other
evidences given by M. M. Van Molle, "Vie commune et obéissance d'après les institutions
premières de Pachôme et Basile," *VSSt* 23 (1970) 214 f.

[11] See *In ps.* 33.8: 369B; *Reg. mor.* 70.21: 833B; *Ep.* 28.2: Courtonne, 1: 68.

[12] See the important *Reg. br.* 114: 1160A ff., which also illustrates Basil's recognition of
the charismatic principle of organization derived from Paul (see E. Schweizer, *Church Order
in the NT* [London, 1961], pp. 100 ff., and 221).

[13] A "calling," that is, that is subject to and authenticated by the "test" (ἔγκρισις) of
others; see *Reg. mor.* 72.3-5: 848B ff.; *Reg. br.* 148: 1180c. There is nothing in Basil to
support an indiscriminate claim to an authority directly derived from God or the Holy Spirit;
see in this context *Reg. mor.* 70.3: 820B. For some of the reasons see p. 46 and n. 41,
above.

[14] See above, p. 47, n. 48.

[15] Several other scholars have studied Basil's concept of proclamation, but none from the
ecclesial viewpoint. The difference of their approach from mine also lies in the use of the
sources. The point of departure of J. Bernardi's excellent study, *La prédication des Pères
cappadociens: le prédicateur et son auditoire* (Paris, 1968), is deliberately confined to the
textual analysis of the homilies of the three Cappadocians. S. Giet in *Les idées et l'action
sociales de s. Basil* (Paris, 1941) has mainly focused on the preacher as educator and social

A. THE "CALLING" OF THE LEADER OF THE WORD

Christian preaching (κήρυγμα) is not a self-chosen or self-imposed enterprise. It is a charisma (gift) of the Holy Spirit, a sacred ministry (λειτουργία) to be executed in the Christian community for the benefit of others.[16]

In the case of the bishop-proclaimer,[17] Basil clearly implies that God, through the agency of another member of the church, calls and chooses an individual for the ministry of his saints:[18]

> Blessed be God Who from age to age chooses [ἐκλεγόμενος] them that please Him, distinguishes [γνωρίζων] vessels of election, and uses them for the ministry [λειτουργία] of the saints. Although you were trying to flee, as you confess, not from me, but from the calling you expected through me [τὴν δι' ἡμῶν προσδοκωμένην κλῆσιν], He has netted you in the sure meshes of grace, and has brought you into the midst of Pisidia to catch men for the Lord, and draw the devil's prey from the deep into the light. You, too, may say as the blessed David said, 'Whither shall I flee from thy Spirit? or whither shall I flee from thy presence?'[19]

The biblical extraction of this passage is undisputed. It should perhaps be added that in all probability Basil here paraphrases the formula of clerical ordination in use in his church.[20] The term λειτουργία occurs in *Epistle 225*

---

reformer without making any significant use of the *Moralia* (see pp. 246-265). T. Špidlik's "sophiological" approach to Basil's writings led him to consider mainly the ascetic side of ecclesiastical preaching; see his *La sophiologie de s. Basile* (Rome, 1961), esp. pp. 246-259. Through the present investigation of the preacher as the leader of the word based chiefly on Basil's *Moralia* I intend to complement the valuable contributions of my predecessors. For the sake of brevity, the *Moralia* hereafter will simply be quoted by the number of the rule followed by that of the chapter, e.g. *Reg. mor.* 70.5 as 70.5, etc. Complementary to the present chapter are Appendices D and E below, pp. 169 ff.

[16] See *Proem. in reg. br.*: 1080A-B; *Proem. in reg. fus.*, 4: 900c; *De fide*, 1: 677A. For a definition of charisma in general see *Hom.* 11.5: 384A; *Reg. fus.* 7.2: 932A, and pp. 24 ff., above. See also *Reg. br.* 45: 1112B, for the description of proclamation as οἰκονομία τοῦ λόγου.

[17] There is no doubt that in *Reg. mor.* 70.1: 816D the expression "those to whom the proclamation of the gospel is entrusted" is referred to the bishops in the first place. See also Gregory of Nazianzus, *Oratio apologetica*: PG 35, 441. That this responsibility is shared with others see *Reg. mor.* 70.1 ff.

[18] The bishops, however, are not the only ones to have their vocation from the Lord. Calling in Basil implies (a) the general calling to be a Christian, and (b) the particular assignment of an individual within the community; see *Reg. br.* 225: 1232B ff.; 136: 1172c f.

[19] *Ep.* 161.1: Courtonne, 2: 92-93; Jackson, p. 214.

[20] Many of the theological axioms of Basil in one way or another derive from the liturgical practice of his church (see the arguments of the books *Contra Eunomium 3* and *De*

in the sense of ecclesiastical ministry conferred through the laying on of hands.[21] Elsewhere it is taken in the broader sense of service and ministration.[22] Τῶν ἁγίων in all probability should be rendered by "of the saints" rather than "of the holy things."[23] Within these boundaries is contained the "calling" of every Christian and more so, the "calling" of those entrusted with the charisma of the word and teaching in the church. They are called to be the servants and ministers (διάκονοι) of the word, God's fellow-workers, apostles and ministers of Christ. For the benefit of others they should lend their voices to the Holy Spirit so that he may write words of eternal life in the hearts of the faithful.[24] Because through the proclamation of the gospel they generate new members for the church, the leaders of the word are also referred to as fathers and nurses.[25]

In *Epistle 161* Basil also employs the biblical image of the "vessel" (cf. Acts 9.15). Every person whom God through his Spirit calls is a chosen instrument for the service of others. This image is complemented in *Homily 3* with that of the various crafts (τέχναι) and activities (πράξεις) which the members of the body of Christ exchange among themselves under the inspiration and guidance of the Spirit.[26] The term "calling" like "charisma" includes the (inborn?) suitability to perform a given task in the community, not, however, without the previous consent (recognition) on the part of the

---

Spiritu Sancto). From the explicit references to the function of ecclesiastical ministries it is very difficult even to surmise which of the extant formulae of clerical ordination was in use in Caesarea. To my knowledge, there are no parallels in his writings to the prayer "Divine Grace," despite the fact that Gregory of Nazianzus alludes to it in his works. In my opinion, a more in-depth study will with certainty reveal the direct dependence of Basil (or rather of the church of Caesarea) on the liturgical practices of the Syrian church. The formula "Divine Grace" is also unknown to the *Apostolic Constitutions*, a Syrian document of the fourth century, which together with its prototypes, the *Didache* and the *Didascalia*, provide several parallels to Basil's views, for instance, his conception of the itinerant ministry, charisma, the designation of the church as brotherhood, etc. On the whole question of clerical ordination formulae see briefly P. Jounel, "Les ordinations" in A. G. Martimort, ed., *L'Eglise en prière. Introduction à la liturgie* (Paris, 1961), pp. 480 ff. Also B. Botte, "La formule d'ordination 'La grâce divine...' dans les rites orientaux," *OS* 2 (1957) 285-296. Judging from Basil's writings, it seems also very unlikely that he knew the formula of ordination from the *Apostolic Tradition* of Hippolytus on which see J. M. Hanssens, *La liturgie d'Hippolyte. Ses documents, son titulaire, ses origines et son caractère* (Rome, 1959).

[21] 841A. However, this is not the most common meaning of λειτουργία. In the above sense the term ὑπηρεσία is rather to be expected; see *Ep.* 54: Courtonne, 1: 139-140.

[22] See *Epp.* 269.1: Courtonne, 3: 139; 301: ibid., 177.

[23] It is a Pauline term for all the baptized. For Basil see *In ps.* 44.12: 413c. Courtonne, 2: 92, translates "of the holy things."

[24] See p. 77, above, and pp. 99 ff., below.

[25] See p. 78, n. 11, above.

[26] For a brief analysis of this homily see pp. 7-8, above.

other members.[27] "Catch men for the Lord, and draw the devil's prey from
the deep into the light," describes the *apostolic* task of Amphilochius.[28]

The statement of these general principles concerning the calling of a
minister of the word is very important. But these principles could not by
themselves solve the complex problem when it came to decide in practice
who did and who did not possess the requirements for the discharge of the
ministry of the word. Despite Basil's early appeal to prayers and other good
works in the course of which the Lord was to make manifest his choice,
probably as a result of disappointing experiences, he strongly insisted that
some other prerequisites be met.[29] The screening of candidates for the
various ministries of the church was to be carried out with vigour.[30] Only
those were to be received who in their previous lives had no record of
criminal offences and who in addition had given positive proof of honesty
and moral integrity.[31] More than teaching by word of mouth the leaders of
the word were to teach by the example of their conduct.[32] Through the observance and practice of all divine commandments they were to give proof
of the authenticity of their calling (charisma) and the legitimacy of their
message.[33]

---

[27] Cf. p. 47, n. 48, above; also pp. 24 ff.

[28] For its sources see Mk 1.17 and Lk 1.79.

[29] See *Ep.* 28.2: Courtonne, 1: 69. The choice of Atarbius for the leadership of the
church of Neocaesarea proved disastrous for the relations of that see with Caesarea; see *Epp.*
65, 126, 175, 204, and 207.

[30] Cf. 70.1-2 with *Epp.* 53-54, and the following note.

[31] For the terms ἀνέγκλητος and δόκιμος see 70.1: 816D. In *Epistle 54* to the
chorepiscopi, from the beginning of his episcopate, Basil writes, "I am much distressed that
the canons of the Fathers have fallen through, and that the exact discipline of the church has
been banished from among you. ... According to the ancient custom observed in the churches of God, ministers in the church (ὑπηρετοῦντας τῇ Ἐκκλησίᾳ) were received after careful
examination (μετὰ πάσης ἀκριβείας δοκιμάζουσα); the whole of their life was investigated; an
enquiry was made as to their being neither railers nor drunkards, not quick to quarrel,
keeping their youth in subjection, so as to be able to maintain 'the holiness without which
no man shall see the Lord'" (Courtonne, 1: 139; Jackson, p. 157). This same letter specifies
further that "this examination was made by presbyters and deacons living with them. Then
they brought them to the chorepiscopi, after receiving the suffrages of the witnesses as to the
truth and giving information to the bishop, so admitted the minister to the sacerdotal order" (Courtonne and Jackson, ibid.). According to the Benedictines, among those in the
sacerdotal order Basil intended to include also the readers, singers and subdeacons (PG 32,
795D and 399D f.). It is highly probable that Basil himself, while still a reader, preached
and interpreted the Scriptures to the people (see Gregory of Nazianzus, *Or.* 43.27 and
Maran, *Vita*, 9.11). The subdeacons, readers and singers are, however, omitted in 70.1 and
71.

[32] See in this context *Ep.* 150.4: Rudberg, 200; *Ep.* 190.1: Courtonne, 2: 141-142; *Reg.
fus.* 43.1: 1028B-C; *Reg. mor.* 80.14: 864D.

[33] Cf. *Reg. mor.* 7.1: 712B with 72.1-2: 845D f.

When speaking of the establishment of the various church ministries Basil employs various terms: "recognition," "reception," "calling," "commissioning," "appointment," "ordination," "laying on of hands."[34] None of these terms seems to have consistency except perhaps for the idea that it is the "authority" (ἐξουσία) of the church (or of the community) "to discern" (κρίνειν) the suitability of a member-candidate to perform a given function.[35] But instead of a "democratic" vote we find in Basil the accumulation of the competence to make ecclesiastical appointments in the hands of the local leaders—the bishops and Basil himself.[36] In this way also the ordination of the leaders of the word is reserved for those to whom the proclamation of the gospel was primarily entrusted.[37]

B. The "Mission" of the Leader of the Word[38]

> That he who is chosen [ἐκλεγέντα] must not undertake the proclamation on his own initiative, but must wait for the time of God's good pleasure and begin proclaiming when he is commanded and proclaim to those to whom he is sent [ἀπεστάλη]. That he who is called [κληθέντα] to proclaim the gospel must obey at once and not procrastinate.[39]

These two statements clearly indicate the necessity of a mandate as a preliminary condition to exercise the charisma of proclamation in the church.

Although he is a mobile minister—an itinerant—the leader of the word is assigned to a precisely circumscribed territory.[40] At the beginning of his episcopate Basil requested from his chorepiscopi an exact list of the names and records of all the ministers working in his province.[41] One copy of the

---

[34] See in that order *Reg. fus.* 43.2: 1029A; *Epp.* 54: Courtonne, 1: 139; 161.1: ibid., 2: 92-93; *Reg. mor.* 70.3-4: 820B f.; 70.1: 816D; 70.2: 820A; *Epp.* 120: Courtonne, 2: 26; 122: ibid., 27; 225: ibid., 3: 22. Cf. also *Reg. mor.* 7.1: 712B.

[35] See e.g. *In ps.* 44.9: 408C, esp. 12: 413C cited above, pp. 8-9 and 10-12.

[36] See in this regard the way the whole affair of Nicopolis in 375 was handled (*Epp.* 227-230, esp. *Ep.* 230: Courtonne, 3: 35) with a retrospective look at what was stated in *Epistles 28* and *29* from 370-371. See also n. 29, above, and *Ep.* 290: Courtonne, 3: 161-162.

[37] Cf. 70.1-2: 816D ff.

[38] The term "mission" is used here not necessarily in the sense of the later (juridical) "missio canonica." It stands only to indicate the act of being commissioned, sent (ἀπεσταλθῆναι).

[39] 70.3-4: 820B ff.; Clarke, p. 120 (rev.).

[40] See 70.12: 825C and the testimony of Rufinus about Basil's early preaching in Pontus quoted below, p. 168. See also *In ps.* 114.1: 484B.

[41] See *Ep.* 54: Courtonne, 1: 140.

register was to be kept in the place where they lived, another sent to Basil.[42] In this way, in a time when the church's stability and order were threatened by external and internal pressures—the government of Valens from without and the theological disputes from within—Basil strove for a return to the original discipline exemplified in the model community of Jerusalem,

> 'The multitude of them that believed were of one heart and one soul' (Acts 4.32); *no one*, that is, maintaining his own desire, but all in common seeking in the one Holy Spirit the will of the one Lord Jesus Christ, Who said, 'I am come down from heaven, not to do mine own will, but the will of the Father that sent me' (Jn 6.38).[43]

As there were some ascetics who on the grounds of alleged charismata challenged the authorities, Basil endeavoured to restore in the church the order which was enforced in his cenobia: all charismata were to be placed under the administration (responsibility) of the charisma of the leader of the community.[44] Consequently also the charisma of utterance of the leader of the word had to be placed under the jurisdiction of the one who commissioned him.[45]

The main task, however, to which the proclaimer of the gospel is bound is: "Whatever things his good master has entrusted to his charge, for the benefit of his fellow servants, to preserve these for their use without adulteration or tricks of the trade."[46] Thus the two subsequent chapters of the *Moral Rule 70* stipulate, negatively, "that one must not teach different doctrine," and positively, "that we must teach those entrusted to us all that is ordered by the Lord in the gospel and through His apostles."[47] Should the leader of the word depart from this standard and introduce into the message fabrications of his own, he would no longer have the Lord as his master.[48] Any leader who does not teach the will of God as revealed in the Scriptures is "a false witness of God" (ψευδομάρτυς τοῦ Θεοῦ) and is "sacrilegious"

---

[42] According to *Ep.* 54, loc. cit., the roll (ἀναγραφή) was to contain the names of the persons, by whom they were accepted (εἰσῆχται), and what their mode of life was.

[43] *De jud.*, 4: 660c-d; Clarke, p. 81.

[44] See *Reg. fus.* 32.2: 996c-d; *Reg. br.* 235: 1240c. Cf. *Ep.* 156.2: Courtonne, 2: 82-83 (rejection of an hypothetical case of charismatic intervention in the government of the church). On the regime in Basil's cenobia see Clarke, *Ascetic Works*, pp. 39-46; E. Amand de Mendieta, *L'ascèse monastique de saint Basile* (Maredsous, 1948), pp. 128-144.

[45] See 70.3: 820b.

[46] *De fide*, 1: 677a; Clarke, p. 90.

[47] 70.5-6: 821b-c; Clarke, p. 121.

[48] See 70.30: 841a.

(ἱερόσυλος).[49] Under such conditions his message, after being tested, should be rejected by the hearers.[50]

In his mission the proclaimer should try to efface himself behind his message, which is not only the written testimony of the Scriptures but also Christ, the heavenly Logos.[51] After all, he is a herald (κῆρυξ) only, a messenger (ἀπόστολος), the lips of Christ (χείλη τοῦ Χριστοῦ), who after the example of St. Paul should have Christ, the Logos, speaking within himself.[52] He should lend his voice to the Holy Spirit so that the Spirit of Christ, through whose kerygma the church is built, may write the words of eternal life in the hearts of the faithful.[53] In his assignment, the leader of the word should so totally identify himself with the message entrusted him, that with the prophet he should be able to state before his audience, "I bring back to you the tidings (ἀγγέλλω) the Spirit taught me, and I say nothing of my own, nothing human."[54]

C. The Prophetic Role of the Proclaimer of the Gospel as Leader of the Word

Accused of having in his ministry used non-scriptural terms, Basil justified his procedure by claiming that he had been called to serve the spirit, not the letter of the New Testament.[55] In other words, Basil claimed to possess as the minister (διάκονος) of the New Testament the capacity to discern what non-scriptural terms could be used in the proclamation of the Christian message without adulterating and betraying its original purpose.[56] In order to explain the prophetic role of the leaders of the word let us begin by making some distinctions.

Concerning divine testimony in the church, in his writings Basil of Caesarea is distinctly aware of three major facts: (1) that there is an *explicit* testimony of Scripture regarding certain things; (2) that with regard to some items the utterances of Scripture are *obscure* and *cloaked in mystery*; (3) that concerning some other things there is *no explicit*

---

[49] *Reg. br.* 98: 1149D.
[50] See 72.1-2: 845D f.
[51] See *In ps.* 33.6: 364D.
[52] See *In ps.* 44.5: 397C; also *Reg. mor.* 80.12-13: 864B-C; *De sp. s.*, 62: Pruche, 472.
[53] See *In ps.* 44.3: 396A.
[54] *In ps.* 48.2: 436B-C.
[55] See *De fide*, 1: 677A. For the context see ibid.: 677B ff.
[56] See the whole context of the *De fide*, 1-2: 676D ff.

testimony of Scripture at all, that is, many things are completely passed over in silence by Scripture.[57] Basil comments,

> As for those things that are written, no man whatever has any authority to do anything that is prohibited or to leave undone anything that is prescribed: since the Lord once for all proclaimed, 'Thou shalt keep the word which I command thee this day; thou shalt not add to it nor take away from it.' For there remains a fearful expectation of judgment and a fierceness of fire about to devour those who dare such a thing.[58]

Regarding the obscure utterances (τὰ ἀσαφῆ) which Scripture uses and the things passed over in silence (σεσιωπημένα), Basil wants the leader of the word to be the eye and the lips on behalf of the other members of the body of Christ.[59] Thus *Rule 70*, which describes the mission of the proclaimer in the church, after saying that he must teach what is ordered by the Lord in the gospel and through his apostles, adds, "And whatever is consistent with this" (καὶ ὅσα τούτοις ἀκόλουθα).[60] Similarly *Rule 26* first says, "that every word or thing should be confirmed by the testimony of inspired Scripture," then proceeds, "that one should use illustrations drawn from nature and the familiar course of life for the confirmation of what is done or said."[61] In this perspective, the role of the obedient preacher is extended to include the functions of an enlightened leader. He is to be not only the servant of the word (διάκονος; ὑπηρέτης τοῦ λόγου) but also the leader of the word (προεστὼς τοῦ λόγου). This point is explained by Basil in somewhat more detail.

Rule 80.15 implies that the proclaimer of the gospel as an eye in the body of the church has the competence "to discern [διακρίνειν] between good and evil."[62] In things that are not prescribed in Scripture by way of command or prohibition he is urged to induce people "to do what is the better course."[63] No doubt this competence of discernment attributed to the leader of the word in the community implied the role of charismatic interpretation of the will of God and the responsibility of decision-making.[64] The leader fulfils in the community a prophetic task, and people, after testing him and his message against the scriptural witness, ought to receive

---

[57] See particularly *Reg. br.* 1: 1081A-C and *De sp. s.*, 66-67: Pruche, 478 ff.

[58] *Reg. br.* 1: 1081B; 303: 1297C-D; see also *Reg. mor.* 72.1: 845D f.

[59] See *De sp. s.*, 66: Pruche, 484; *Reg. br.* 1: 1081B; *Reg. mor.* 80.15: 865A.

[60] 70.6: 821C; Clarke, p. 121.

[61] 26.1-2: 744C f.; Clarke, p. 109.

[62] 865A.

[63] 70.8: 824B; Clarke, p. 121.

[64] See 70.7: 824A; *Reg. fus.* 24: 984A. See also Špidlik, *Sophiologie*, pp. 172 and 169 ff.

him as if he were the Lord himself.[65] It should be noted that in Basil's consciousness this function of the leader of the word is not marginal to the presence of the written testimony in the church. On the contrary, the charismatic role of reading and interpreting the will of the Master *donec veniat* stands in the same prophetic and charismatic line of interpretation as Scripture occupies vis-à-vis the will and judgment of God.[66] Of course, there must arise in the realization of this phenomenon and order of things an almost insoluble tension. We become aware of this in reading *Moral Rule 70.37*: the proclaimer who is the judging eye of the community has to be prepared to stand scrutiny and judgment "by the very people who are entrusted to him."[67] He is a leader who never ceases to be a servant as among Christians "the care of many entails the service of many" (ἡ τῶν πλειόνων ἐπιμέλεια πλειόνων ἐστὶ ὑπηρεσία).[68]

D. THE CREDENTIALS OF THE LEADER OF THE WORD

> Like the ram, an animal capable of leading, such are the leaders of the disciples of Christ [οἱ τῆς ποιμνῆς τοῦ Χριστοῦ προεστῶτες]. They lead them forth to the blooming and fragrant nourishment of spiritual doctrine, water them with living water with the concurrent assistance of the Spirit, raise them up and nourish them until they produce fruit; then they guide them to rest and safety from those who lay snares for them.[69]

The function of the leader of the word is to lead his disciples to the Word. Thus he could better be described as the leader *to* the Word than *of* the Word. This is what we may gather from Basil's discussion of the word and its ministers.

The first step to efficacious preaching is to become one with the message.

> As the nature of honey can be described to the inexperienced not so much by speech as by the perception of it through taste, so the goodness of the heavenly Logos cannot be clearly taught by doctrines, unless, examining to a

---

[65] See 72.3-4: 848B-C; 36.1: 756C.

[66] The reader can find a more extensive discussion of the role of the "superiors" with regard to the Bible and God's will in Špidlík, *Sophiologie*, pp. 186-188; also pp. 172 ff. This author rightly criticizes and supplements from other sources Gribomont's otherwise excellent study on "Obéissance et évangile," ibid., pp. 167 ff. See also Van Molle, "Vie commune," cited above n. 10.

[67] 845A.

[68] *Reg. fus.* 30: 993A; Clarke, p. 196. See also 70.24: 836C; *Reg. fus.* 43.2: 1028C.

[69] *In ps.* 28.2: 284A-B; Way, p. 195 (rev.).

greater extent the dogmas of truth, we are able to comprehend by our own experience the goodness of the Lord.[70]

Through assiduous works of justice, the leader of the word has to become a sharp arrow, one capable of penetrating gently and subtly into the souls of those who are being instructed. His mission is not to subdue souls to God by his words but to "prepare the people to fall under Christ."[71] He should not be the leader who forces the Word to take possession of the heart but one who prepares the soul to surrender to the commandments and the will of God in a voluntary fashion. He is indeed to be the leader *to* the Word more than the leader *of* the word.

However, one of the credentials by which his authenticity may be judged is the extent to which the contents of his message are exemplified in his personal life; that is, in order to lead effectively, the leader must himself possess what he brings to the souls of his people. The prohibition "that one must not teach different doctrine" thus becomes "that one must not put constraint upon others to do what he has not done himself," that is to say, "the leader of the word should make himself an example to others of every good thing, *practising first what he teaches.*"[72]

Basil makes no pretence that the preacher will not be judged by his listeners: "That the leader of the word must do and say everything with great circumspection and judgment, aiming at pleasing God, since he must be judged and borne witness to by the very people who are entrusted to him."[73] There are two ways of proving the authenticity of a minister of the word. First, "that such hearers as have been instructed in the Scriptures should test what their teachers say, and receive what agrees with the Scriptures but reject what disagrees; and sternly decline dealing with those who persist in such teachings." Second, "that those who have little knowledge of Scripture should recognize the stamp of sanctity in the fruits of the Spirit, and should receive those that show them, but reject those that do not."[74]

Scholars have wondered whether Basil made the sanctity of the preacher, that is, the testimony of his life the only test to prove the truth of his message.[75] Between efficacy of preaching and the personal holiness of the preacher Augustine of Hippo saw only a relationship of a psychological

---

[70] *In ps.* 33.6: 364D-365A; Way, p. 258.

[71] *In ps.* 44.6: 404A; Way, p. 287.

[72] 70.5: 821B; 70.9: 824C; 70.10: 824D; Clarke, p. 121.

[73] 70.37: 844D-848B; Clarke, p. 124.

[74] 72.1-2: 845D-848B; Clarke, pp. 124-125.

[75] See Špidlík, *Sophiologie*, p. 256; and in general see D. Grasso, *Proclaiming God's Message* (Notre Dame, 1965), pp. 158 ff.

nature. As with the sacraments, preaching can be effective without sanctity of life, although sanctity facilitates its action.[76] On the other hand, we know that in subsequent centuries the East was to establish an indissoluble link between sanctity of life and truth.[77] The Augustinian option seems to presuppose a notion of an abstract truth which need not necessarily be affected by practical conduct. It thus seems to overlook the intuitive side of a reality which is not only heard but also seen by the parties involved. And this, according to Basil, would be a monstrosity. If the Christian preacher could disassociate himself to such an extent from his message, he would be no longer a leader but an actor who is one "person" (πρόσωπον: persona) on the stage and another in real life; or he would resemble that hare chased by dogs who in order to escape from its pursuers feigns following one course while in reality it follows another.[78] It is not the veracity of an abstract truth that Basil is seeking to establish through the conduct of the preacher, but his credentials and very credibility, that is, the truth as experienced concretely by his audience. How can one ever trust a person who does not practise what he teaches? Or as Gregory of Nazianzus puts it, "How can we induce somebody to accept an opinion which is different from that which we have taught by our life?"[79] As Basil puts it, "The instruction how to lead a Christian life depends less on words than on daily example."[80] With Christian religion this is even more so, as the object of preaching is a truth known only in part and as it were in a mirror.[81] Thus the testimony of life is an essential part of the dialogue which is every homily (ὁμιλία).

Consequently, Basil wants the conduct of the leader of the word to be so irreprehensible that by his example alone the rectitude of those who follow the Lord can be established and the perversity of those who in any way whatsoever disobey him can be rebuked.[82] "Strive to give all a plain example by deed of whatever you teach by word," he writes to the presbyters of Nicopolis in a moment of general distress.[83]

---

[76] De doctrina christiana 4.59: CCSL 32, 4, 1, pp. 163-164; cf. ibid., 27, p. 135. These texts are not quoted in A. D. R. Polman, The Word of God according to St. Augustine (Grand Rapids, 1961), pp. 134-140. This author completely ignores the problem and is simply satisfied in justifying Augustine's position in the light of the Donatist controversy.

[77] See Špidlik, Sophiologie, p. 256.

[78] See De leg., 4: 573D ff.; Hom. 12.7: 401A.

[79] Carmen historicum 1.1: PG 37, 1204A-B (quoted in Grasso, Proclaiming, p. 165).

[80] Ep. 150.4: Rudberg, 200.

[81] See In ps. 33.6: 365A; De fide, 2: 681A.

[82] 80.14: 864D.

[83] Ep. 246: Courtonne, 3: 85.

For if this is the standard of Christianity, the imitation of Christ, according to the measure of His Incarnation as is appropriate to the calling of each, those who are entrusted with the guidance of the many ought by their mediation to lead on the weaker to the imitation of Christ, as the blessed Paul says, 'Be ye imitators of me, even as I also am of Christ.'[84]

E. Full Commitment to the Service of the Word

The function of the ministers of the gospel is to be "as God's fellow workers (συνεργοί), having given themselves wholly on behalf of the church to such works only as are worthy of God."[85] Negatively, this full involvement in the service implies the elimination of all obstacles that might impede the word of God from becoming a fountain of living water, springing up into life everlasting, in the hearts of the faithful. Many of the impediments are dealt with in *Moral Rule 70*:

(1) That we must not use the word of teaching in an ostentatious or huckstering way, flattering the hearers, and satisfying our own pleasures or needs; but we must be such men as speak for the glory of God in His presence.

(2) That the leader of the word must not abuse his authority (ἐξουσία) to insult those who are under him, nor even exalt himself over them, but must rather use his rank as an opportunity for practising humility towards them.

(3) That one must not proclaim the gospel by way of contention or envy or irritation against any.

(4) That one must not use human advantages in proclaiming the gospel, lest the grace of God be obscured thereby.

(5) That we must not imagine that the successful issue of preaching is secured by our own devices, but trust wholly in God.

(6) That he who is entrusted with the proclamation of the gospel should acquire nothing beyond his own necessities.

(7) That as regards care for worldly things a man must not put himself at the disposal of those who pay undue attention to them.

(8) That those who in order to please their hearers, neglect to declare God's will boldly, enslaving themselves to those they wish to please, no longer have the Lord for their master.[86]

From this lengthy presentation of the things that should be avoided in order that the message be not impaired and in order that the leader of the

---

[84] *Reg. fus.* 43.1: 1028B-C; Clarke, p. 216.
[85] 80.19: 865D; Clarke, p. 129.
[86] 70.23-30: 836A-841A; Clarke, p. 123 (rev.).

word maintain the distinctiveness and independence of his vocation, it is clear that he is a full-time minister of the church. Like some of the apostles, he should be able to earn his living from his job.[87] But he must not abuse his listeners by demanding from them more than is necessary for his physical well-being. It is noteworthy that Basil, following St. Paul, links together unworthy motives such as a desire to please or flatter the audience with motives of material self-interest.[88] The affirmation of the absolute necessity of the grace of God for successful preaching leads us to consider the positive side of the minister's commitment to the service of the word.

First should be the willingness and readiness to render to the listeners not only the gospel of God but even one's own soul.[89] This readiness entails $\pi\alpha\rho\rho\eta\sigma\iota\alpha$, boldness in proclaiming the word and bearing witness to the truth, even if some hinder and persecute us in one way or another, even unto death.[90] Complete devotion to the trade also involves perseverance unto death; continuous prayers of supplication for the advance of believers; periodic visitations aimed at strengthening those who receive the word of truth; material and not only spiritual assistance for all those who require it.[91] In short, "He who teaches should set before himself this aim: to bring all to a perfect man, to the measure of the stature of the fulness of Christ, yet each in his own order."[92]

F. The Aims of Preaching

(i) Edification of the Church and the Ecclesial Perspective

The church is the body of Christ, Christ its supreme head, and the Holy Spirit its indwelling soul.[93] As God creates the universe through his Logos, thus the Holy Spirit builds the church ($\dot{\varepsilon}\varkappa\varkappa\lambda\eta\sigma\iota\dot{\alpha}\zeta\omega\nu$) through his kerygma.[94] The heralds of the kingdom of Christ on earth are the prophets, apostles and the proclaimers of the gospel.[95] Through their proclamation they bring

---

[87] Nevertheless, some clergymen were engaged in other crafts; see *Ep.* 198.1: Courtonne, 2: 153, and also perhaps *Hom.* 3.4: Rudberg, 29.

[88] See 1 Thess 2.3-7 quoted in 70.23: 836c.

[89] See 80.18: 865c and 1 Thess 2.8, and *Reg. br.* 98: 1152a.

[90] See 70.13: 828a.

[91] See 70.19: 832b; 70.14: 828c; 70.18: 832a; 70.21: 833b. On the "Basiliada" see G. F. Reilly, *Imperium and Sacerdotium according to St. Basil* (Washington, D.C., 1945), pp. 125 ff.; Giet, *Idées,* pp. 419 ff.

[92] 70.31: 841a; Clarke, p. 123 (rev.).

[93] See *De jud.,* 3: 660a.

[94] See *Hex.* 3.2: Giet, 192; *De sp. s.* 38: Pruche, 376 f.; *In ps.* 48.1: 433a.

[95] See *In ps.* 48.1: 433a; 80.13: 864c.

all nations and people of all cultures into one church under the sovereign lordship of Christ.[96] Comparing the messengers of the gospel and their words to arrows sharpened through the power of the Spirit, Basil declares, "The arrows, falling in the hearts of those who were at some time enemies of the King, draw them to a love of truth, draw them to the Lord, so that they who were enemies to God are reconciled to Him through its teachings."[97] The power to edify the church is not dependent upon human resources. It is the result of divine grace operating through the charisma of the leaders of the word:

> Those outside the word of truth, despising the simplicity of expression in the Scriptures, call the proclamation of the gospel, folly; but we, who glory in the cross of Christ, 'to whom gifts bestowed on us by God were manifested through the Spirit, not in words taught by human wisdom', know that the grace poured out by God in the teachings concerning Christ is rich. Therefore, in a short time the teachings passed through almost the whole world, since grace, rich and plentiful, was poured out upon the proclaimers of the gospel, whom Scripture called even the lips of Christ. Moreover, the message of the gospel in its insignificant little words possesses great guidance and attraction toward salvation. And every soul is overcome by the unalterable doctrines, being strengthened by grace to an unshaken faith in Christ. Whence the apostle says, 'Through whom we have received grace and apostleship to bring about obedience to faith.'[98]

The necessity and relevance of preaching for the edification of the church is not diminished by the fact that people through the contemplation of nature (physical and human) can arrive at a knowledge of and faith in God.[99] In the present conditions only the church, bought and purified by the precious blood of Christ, has a mind trained ($\gamma\epsilon\gamma\upsilon\mu\nu\alpha\sigma\mu\acute{\epsilon}\nu\text{ov}$ $\nu\text{o}\tilde{\upsilon}\nu$) to recognize unmistakably the presence of God in the created world.[100] "Deceived by their inherent atheism it appeared to [the philosophers of

---

[96] See *In ps.* 48.1: 433A; *In ps.* 44.6: 404A.

[97] *In ps.* 44.6: 404A-B; Way, p. 288.

[98] *In ps.* 44.4: 396C-397A; Way, p. 283.

[99] Basil acknowledges that all people were created in the image and likeness of God in order that "the like may know the like" (*In ps.* 48.4: 449C). Thus, the universe as a whole including man as composed of body and soul, is a place where people can learn to know God (see *Hex.* 1.6: Giet, 110; *Hom.* 6.2: 221D ff.; *Hom.* 3.7-8: Rudberg, 34 ff.; *In ps.* 32.3: 329B; *Ep.* 235.1: Courtonne, 3: 44; *Hex.* 9.6: Giet, 512, 514; *Hex.* 10.1-2.6: Smets-Esbroeck, 166 ff.). Also led by nature, man can be good and honest (see *Reg. fus.* 2.1: 912A; *Hex.* 9.4: Giet, 496). However, because of sin the natural order has been upset and the "wounded" man is in need of grace (see *In ps.* 61.3: 473C; *In ps.* 44.8: 405B).

[100] See *In ps.* 44.10: 409A.

Greece] that nothing governed or ruled the universe, and that all was given up to chance."[101] Others worshipped the powers of nature and failed to recognize from their study of the universe the existence of a Creator. Thus, outside the influence of the "humble scriptural account" and the church redeemed by Christ, Basil hardly seems to recognize the validity of any θεωρία φυσική as an independent and alternate way of discovering the presence of God in the world.[102] Eyes alone without the light of faith are insufficient to infer the existence of God from the open book of the universe. It was in order to obviate this difficulty that Basil tried to give his people a "purified" presentation of the beginnings, relying not upon "the worldly wisdom" but upon the light given to God's servant Moses and the *logos* of the church.[103] Gregory of Nazianzus, who often turned to Basil's *Hexaemeron*, confessed, "Whenever I take his *Hexaemeron* in my hands and savor its words, I am put in the presence of the Creator, and understand the account of creation, and I admire my Creator more than before, using my eyes only as my teacher."[104]

But to edify the church, the treatment of any subject must be undertaken with the sole intention of expanding the faith of the listeners and not with the aim of satisfying their or one's own curiosity.[105] In his preaching the minister of the word should avoid dealing with idle questions (τὰ περίεργα), reject a too sophisticated method of scriptural exegesis, abstain from entering into disputed topics which could harm the simplicity of the Christian faith, for none of these approaches contributes to the edification (οἰκο-δόμησις) of the church or the salvation of its members.[106] Instead it should be his concern to provide through his homilies spiritual food for his listeners, encouragement and comfort in their struggle against the forces of evil, awareness of their duties and vocation.[107] Only such an approach to and understanding of the primary goal of preaching, which is to edify the church, is in keeping with the apostolic and evangelical kerygma, which in

---

[101] *Hex.* 1.2: Giet, 94; Jackson, p. 53.

[102] See *In ps.* 44.10: 409A and Špidlík, *Sophiologie*, pp. 225 ff.

[103] See *Hex.* 6.1: Giet, 324; 3.3: ibid., 202.

[104] *Or.* 43.67: PG 36, 585A; McCauley, p. 85.

[105] See *Hex.* 1.8: Giet, 120; 3.3: ibid., 202.

[106] See *De fide*, 5: 689A; *Ep.* 175: Courtonne, 2: 112; *Hex.* 9.1: Giet, 478 ff. (rejection of the allegorical method); *Ep.* 188, cc. 15-16: Courtonne, 2: 131 (rejection of an exegesis based on an excessive grammatical analysis); *Hex.* 7.6: Giet, 418 (εἴς μοι σκοπός, παντο-χόθεν οἰκοδομεῖσθαι τὴν Ἐκκλησίαν; cf. *Hex.* 11.8: Smets-Esbroeck, 248); *Hom.* 27.1: 1457c. Cf. K. Holl, *Amphilochius von Ikonium in seinem Verhältnis zu den grossen Kappadoziern* (Tübingen, 1904), pp. 130 ff.

[107] See *In ps.* 28.2: 284A-B; *Hex.* 6.11: Giet, 388; 8.8: ibid., 476; 3.10: ibid., 242; *In ps.* 59.1: 460A-B; *Hom.* 2.1: 183A-B; *In ps.* 48.8: 449B ff. Cf. *Ep.* 246: Courtonne, 3: 85.

its simple language about the crucified Lord conquered in a short time almost the whole world.[108]

In order to edify the church the leader of the word, in preparing and delivering his message, must also keep an eye on the ecclesial perspective. The church for Basil is not only a charismatic community, renewed constantly by the power (grace) of the life-giving Spirit, but also a people with a history, "with two hundred and more years of existence."[109] The church has a past of its own, a vocabulary, many traditions and customs that the preacher should reflect in his addresses to the people.[110] In this way an uninterrupted and unbroken continuity (ἀκολουθία) in the message can be preserved and ensured so that the church through the ages "as becomes her, may remain in a succession (διαδοχή) in no way degenerate from her past glory."[111] In this connection H. von Campenhausen writes:

> Both factors, the Bible and tradition, had already played an important part in the church in the second century. They were closely related in Origen. But whereas he saw the task as one of advancing ever further away from tradition, Basil turned back rather to Irenaeus. Basil stood for confinement rather than further expansion. ... Dogma and tradition again assume a decidedly defensive purpose, as a shield and safeguard.[112]

On this score, Basil pays the highest tribute of recognition to Musonius who in teaching his people "put forth nothing of his own, no novel invention; but as the blessing of Moses has it, he knew how to bring out of the secret and good stores of his heart, 'old store, and the old because of the new'."[113] Musonius deserves praise because he was "a guardian of the principles of the fathers; an enemy of innovation; exhibiting in himself the ancient fashion of the church, and making the state of the church put under him conform to the ancient constitution, as to a sacred model, so that all who lived with him seemed to live in the society of them that used to shine like lights in the world two hundred years ago and more."[114] To realize the

---

[108] See *In ps.* 44.4 quoted above, p. 92.

[109] *Ep.* 28.1: Courtonne, 1: 66. Actually the church is heir to all the Jewish Scriptures (see *In ps.* 59.2: 464B).

[110] See *De sp. s.* 16: Pruche, 298; 66: ibid., 478 f.; *Hex.* 3.3: Giet, 202; *In ps.* 28.3: 292B. Cf. Basil's frequent appeal to the ancient authorities (the canonical *Epistles 188, 199* and *217*; *Ep.* 160: Courtonne, 2: 88-92; *De sp. s.* 71-74: 500 ff.; *C. Eun.* 2.8: 585B-C).

[111] *Ep.* 229.1: Courtonne, 3: 34; see *De sp. s.* 79: Pruche, 530. Cf. also the definition of faithful minister in *De fide*, 1: 677A.

[112] *The Fathers of the Greek Church* (New York, 1959), p. 99.

[113] *Ep.* 28.1: Courtonne, 1: 66; Jackson, p. 132.

[114] Ibid.

benefits of such a policy of church-building it is enough, according to Basil, to look at the community of Neocaesarea, "For so far as I know, you alone or, at any event, you and but very few others, in the midst of such a storm and whirlwind of affairs, were able under his good guidance to live your lives unshaken by the waves."[115]

We should, however, avoid overemphasizing this yearning in Basil for the "good old order," as for him tradition is not so much a conglomerate of dead dogmas as a living organism.[116] In his attitude as a Christian leader Basil shows that within the ecclesial framework there is ample room for innovating. He not only had recourse to the ancient writers, the Scriptures and past records, but also emphasized the validity of contemporary religious experience as lived by simple countryfolk, the spiritual and charismatic people, the contemporary Christian community by and large.[117] Von Campenhausen writes that "indefatigably Basil advises all Christians to keep to the Nicene Creed and not be lured away from it by any subtle, captious questions."[118] Generally speaking this is correct, but we should not forget that Basil at the same time strongly advocated the distinction between the terms ὑπόστασις and οὐσία; he showed preferences for the ὅμοιος κατ᾽ οὐσίαν rather than the Nicene ὁμοούσιος; Basil, in other words, did admit within the ecclesial perspective an advance in the consciousness and teachings of the church induced by its apostolic spirit.[119]

The church continually grows and expands, thanks to the work of the Holy Spirit who operates in its midst through the instrumentality of men endowed with the charisma of utterance and teaching.[120] Perhaps the best description of a church growing thanks to the work of its charismatic members, especially parents and leaders of the word, is given in Basil's account of his own faith as a dynamic reality. From his parents, Basil tells us, he received the Christian faith in the form of a seed (σπέρμα) which was first tiny and then grew bigger, always however preserving its original identity (ταυτότης), never changing in kind (γένος) although gradually becoming perfected (κατ᾽ αὔξησιν τελειούμενον) through continually advancing stages.[121] This characteristic of steady growth without alteration of identity

---

[115] Ibid., 67.

[116] Cf. Špidlik, *Sophiologie*, p. 182: "La tradition n'est pas un ensemble de dogmes morts, mais un organisme vivant, bien vivant."

[117] See *De sp. s.* 16: Pruche, 298 f.; *Ep.* 229.1: Courtonne, 3: 33-34.

[118] *Greek Fathers*, p. 99.

[119] See *Epp.* 125.1: Courtonne, 2: 30 ff.; 9.3: ibid., 39. Cf. above, p. 72, for the apostolic spirit.

[120] See in this context the *Moral Rule 80.21*: 868B and *In ps.* 48.1: 433A.

[121] See *Ep.* 223.3: Courtonne, 3: 12-13.

was lacking in the faith and in the teachings of the heretics who, spurning the ecclesial perspective (λόγος), tried to fabricate new truths instead of nursing and further developing the ones existing in the church which has remained faithful to its apostolic principle.[122] Acting on the assumption that a change (μεταβολή) in the church was needed from "worse" (that is, the traditional faith) to something "better" (i.e. their own innovations: καινο-τομίαι), the heretics by inserting elements alien to the vine which is Christ did not contribute to the church's edification, growth and development but to its destruction.[123] Only progress understood in this way was unacceptable for Basil.

(ii) *Refutation of Errors*

Although Basil maintained friendly relations with some pagans, there are no traces of evangelization in his letters, nor in his preaching.[124] Nor is there extant any homily of any of the three Cappadocians intended for the conversion of the pagans. The opinions of pagan philosophers are occasionally refuted, but these are viewed more as weapons in the hands of the Christian Arians than as an antagonistic power or system opposed to Christianity.[125] The internal religious divisions and the presence of an unproportionately large number of catechumens in many churches seem to have constituted the major pastoral concern and problem at the time Basil became leader of the church of Caesarea.[126]

---

[122] That is, the church to which Basil believed he belonged; see above, p. 52, n. 78.

[123] See *Ep.* 223.5: Courtonne, 3: 14-15; *Reg. mor.* 80.20: 868A, and Špidlik, *Sophiologie*, pp. 211-214.

[124] At least some of the letters to Libanius are authentic (see J. Gribomont, "In tomum 32 PG adnotationes" [Turnhout, 1961], pp. 10-11).

[125] The futile attempt of Julian to revive the old Roman religion in the early 360s did not constitute a serious threat to the continuing expansion of Christianity. The *Invectives* of Gregory of Nazianzus—the only Cappadocian documents dealing directly with the revival of paganism—confront their opponent more on an abstract than existential level. Besides they were written after Julian's departure and were perhaps never pronounced in public (see J. Quasten, *Patrología* [Madrid, 1962], 2: 255). According to G. Dagron, during the fourth century the main opposition was not so much between Christianity and paganism as between orthodoxy and heresy within each group (see his "L'Empire romain d'Orient au ive siècle et les traditions politiques de l'hellénisme: Le témoignage de Thémistios," *Travaux et mémoires* [Paris, 1968], 3: 1-242).

[126] Actually not the catechumens per se but the attitude of some Christians, that is, of people born to Christian families, of indefinitely procrastinating the reception of baptism constituted the point of major concern. While the pagans in Cappadocia and Pontus were probably an insignificant minority, the number of catechumens must have been very sizable (see Bernardi, *Prédication*, pp. 352 ff. and 395 ff.). See *Ep.* 113 for the priority of the task of reuniting the divided Christendom, and *Ep.* 257.1 for the statement that a new type of persecution was under way; for the first time ever "Christians were persecuting Christians."

Both groups of people—the heretics and lukewarm Christians—are addressed in Basil's homilies.[127] The errors that Basil tries most of all to combat are two—a shallow understanding of the Christian calling and a spirit of selfishness among some of the disciples of Christ. In response to a merely nominal affiliation with Christianity, Basil tries to deepen the concept of Christian life, proposing to his followers not only the acceptance of baptism but of the ascetic life as well. To eradicate the spirit of self-love (φιλαυτία in the negative sense), Basil castigates those who have received from God more benefits, either spiritual or material, and refused to share them with the needy.[128]

The main error of the heretics in Basil's view is not so much their different understanding or refusal of a faith that is after all based on a partial knowledge of God, as their spirit of haughtiness, presumption (αὐθάδεια), that is to say, their claim and pretence of knowing everything which they exhibit thereby.[129] In his struggle against heresies, Basil distinguishes between the people and their ideas, or as he puts it, reading his own Christian bias into the words of Ps 45.10, "He shall destroy the bow, and break the weapons," between the adversaries and their tools (devices).[130] Only after all forms of care (ἐπιμέλεια) have been exhausted in the ministry to the disobedient (ἀπειθούντων) should the leader of the word retreat.[131] Also in the letters to the Westerners Basil demanded, as we shall see, not the condemnation as yet but a joint public denunciation of such prominent heretics as Marcellus of Ancyra, Apollinarius of Laodicaea, Eustathius of Sebaste and others.[132] The reason was that before reaching a final condemnation, one must first instruct his opponents with forebearance and meekness, waiting patiently for their repentance (μετάνοια) as the present time is not yet a time of judgment, but of divine mercy.[133]

---

[127] See *Hom.* 9, 23 and 24 on heretics. The rest of Basil's homilies could well be termed *Moral Homilies* (see S. Rudberg, *Etudes sur la tradition manuscrite de s. Basile* [Lund, 1953], p. 53 for this title in some MSS).

[128] See *Hom.* 6, 7; *In ps.* 7 and *In ps.* 14.1 and 2, all dealing with the rich. According to Bernardi, *Prédication*, pp. 335 ff. and 400 ff., the rich in Cappadocia were in great numbers. See also the study of Giet, *Idées*, pp. 110-142. This author sometimes appears intimidated by the "rigorisme" of Basil and unsuccessfully tries to disclaim Basil's "communism"; see ibid., pp. 96-110.

[129] See *Ep.* 52.1: Courtonne, 1: 134; *In ps.* 48.7: 449A.

[130] See the beautiful but very personal interpretation of Psalm 45 in the homonymous homily (428B-C).

[131] See 70.35: 814B and *Ep.* 128.3 quoted above, p. 74, n. 170.

[132] See *Ep.* 263.2-5 quoted and discussed below, pp. 111 ff.

[133] See 70.32: 841C; *Ep.* 223.6: Courtonne, 3: 15-16; *In ps.* 32.3: 332A; *Reg. mor.* 1.2: 700C.

The most powerful weapon in combating any errors and aberrant views is to set the example of a truly Christian life. This applies first to the leader of the word, but also to the community as a whole. According to Basil, all Christian believers ought to be in their environment "as light in the world, so that both they themselves be not receptive of evil and enlighten those who approach them to a knowledge of the truth, and that these either become what they should be or reveal what they are." Also they should be "as salt in the world, so that they who associate [κοινωνοῦντας] with them are renewed in the spirit unto incorruptibility."[134]

(iii) *Formation in Piety or the Building of the Church as the Community of Complete Christians*

In chapter one we discussed Basil's consciousness of the church and his ideal of sanctity.[135] The element that came most clearly into focus from the analysis of his ascetic writings was the corporate aspect of his conception of the church as the community of complete Christians. Only through communion (κοινωνία) with God and his neighbours can man achieve perfection, and the more intimate that communion is, the more perfect man is. In view of such an ecclesiology and anthropology it was almost natural for Basil to invite and even urge Christians to accept the ascetic life in its communal version. Accordingly, Basil's ascetic brotherhoods may in a way be regarded as the logical outcome of his preaching, which in its turn appears strongly coloured by eschatological motives. It would be difficult, if not impossible, to extricate from Basil's homilies elements that would be applicable only to Christians living in his communities in contrast to elements applicable to Christians living outside them.

Since, as we believe, both groups of people are simultaneously considered and addressed by Basil in his homilies (at least in the edited form in which they have been preserved), it should come as no surprise that in many of them he appears to be deliberately ambiguous. It is true that nowhere in his sermons does Basil go so far as to deny for Christians the possibility of being saved or made perfect in the "common life" (κοινὸς βίος, that is married life), or to exclude temporal occupations from the charismatic realm.[136] If compared with other Fathers of the church, Basil appears rather moderate and restrained in suggesting or recommending virginity, absolute

---

[134] 80.9-10: 864A-B; Clarke, p. 128.
[135] See above, pp. 15 ff.
[136] See *Hom.* 3.4 quoted above, p. 8 and *Reg. mor.* 73-79.

disposal of material possessions and total abandonment of the world. But, whether consciously or unconsciously, Basil does tend to insinuate what he deems to be the better course for a Christian: life in a church where all things are shared and possessed in common, where no one seeks what is his own, in other words, a type of life strongly marked by an eschatological preoccupation. It should be noted that in doing so Basil is far from being a visionary who would see the *parousia* of the Lord as imminent. In approaching the whole matter he proceeds rather as a cool rationalist who, after brooding upon the nature of spatial and temporal reality, discovers that nothing in the world is worthy of man's exclusive care and attention, that the perishable things should be used not abused so as to help man to achieve another more definitive goal which lies beyond his present existence.[137]

The most representative work of Basil dealing with the Christian church and its members is the *Moralia*. In it Basil reviews all the different charismata that Christians might possess. The functions surveyed range from those of the leaders of the church, in which category are included bishops, presbyters and the rest of the clergy, to the ethos of married people: husbands, wives, children, widows, soldiers, rulers and the order of virgins. This collection should probably be dated from the time of Basil's ecclesiastical reform, which he undertook at the beginning of his episcopate. It constitutes a kind of scriptural vade mecum for the use of all but particularly the leaders of the word.[138] No doubt in his preaching Basil often must have resorted to this biblical florilegium, especially during the time of his episcopate, when work and poor health did not allow him to read with diligence the whole of the inspired Scriptures.[139]

I shall quote excerpts from the last *Moral Rule 80*, which in Basil's own words constitutes a kind of summary of his views on the constitution of the church and the moral perfection of its members.[140] The paraphrased title of this section in the preface to the *Hypotyposis* reads, "The Logos of Christian Character [and the Leaders' of the Word of God's Teachings], in Brief and Concise Rule Form, Extracted from the Holy Scriptures."[141] Its

---

[137] See *Hex.* 1.3: Giet, 100; 6.10: ibid., 378; *Reg. fus.* 20.3: 976A. Cf. J. Gribomont, "Le renoncement au monde dans l'idéal ascétique de s. Basile," *Irénikon* 31 (1958) 300-301.

[138] Cf. the relatively lengthy description of their duties in *Moral Rule 70* with the rather summary account of the other functions.

[139] See *Ep.* 244.3: Courtonne, 3: 77.

[140] Cf. *Proem. ad hyp.*: 1512D.

[141] *Proem. ad hyp.*, ibid.

purpose should be interpreted in the light of *Moral Rule 70.31* which states
that the aim which the leader of the word should set before himself is, "To
bring all to a perfect man, to the measure of the stature of the fulness [πλήρ-
ωμα] of Christ, yet each in his own order."[142]

> What is the ethos [τὸ ἴδιον] of a Christian? Faith working through love.
> What is the mark of faith? Unhesitating conviction of the truth of the inspired
> words, unshaken by any argument. ... What is the mark of love towards God?
> Keeping His commandments with a view to His glory. What is the mark of
> love towards one's neighbour? Not to seek one's own good, but the good of
> the loved one for the benefit of his soul and body. What is the mark of a
> Christian? To be born anew in baptism of water end Spirit. ... What is the
> mark of those who eat the bread and drink the cup of the Lord? To keep in
> perpetual memory Him Who died for us and rose again. What is the mark of
> those that keep such a memory? To live unto themselves no longer, but unto
> Him Who died for them and rose again.[143]

This description of the individual Christian ethos corresponds to Basil's
ideal of the church as the community of perfect Christians. As was mentioned earlier, what matters is not so much the form of Christian life as the
quality and intensity of the desire to become conformed to the pattern of
what Christians see in Christ and hear from him.[144] In other words, the aim
of all Christians, but particularly of the leaders of the word, should be to
build a church differentiated not so much by its external appearance as by
its quality as the perfect body of Christ, "holy, pure, formed after the
likeness of God, and filled only with what pertains to the worship (λατρεία)
of God."[145]

We could not better conclude this short review of the qualities and functions of the leaders of the word than by quoting in full Basil's own words
from his *Moral Rule 80* which we have tried to interpret:

> What manner of men does Scripture wish those to be who are entrusted with
> the proclamation of the gospel? As apostles and ministers of Christ, and
> faithful stewards of God's mysteries, fulfilling only the things commanded by
> the Lord without falling short in deed or word; as heralds of the kingdom of
> heaven, for the destruction of him who holds the power of death in sin; as a

---

[142] 70.31: 841A; Clarke, p. 123. Cf. 80.1, 3, 8 and 15, 21: 860C-868B.

[143] 80.22: 868C-869C; Clarke, pp. 127-131 (rev.). Cf. *Hex.* 10.17: Smets-Esbroeck,
210.

[144] Cf. 80.1: 860C and above, pp. 15 ff.

[145] See 80.6, 8: 861C-D. This would be in contrast to the Eustathians' emphasis on the
externals, see below, pp. 160 f.

type or rule of piety, to establish the complete rectitude of those that follow the Lord, and to rebuke the perversity of those who in any way whatsoever disobey Him; as an eye in a body, since they discern between good and evil, and guide the members of Christ towards what befits each; as shepherds of the sheep of Christ, not even shrinking from laying down their lives for their sakes on occasion, that they may impart them the gospel of God; as doctors, with much compassion by their knowledge of the teaching of the Lord healing the diseases of souls, to win for them health in Christ and perseverance; as fathers and nurses of their own children, in the great affection of their love in Christ willing to render to them not only the gospel of God but even their own souls; as God's fellow workers, having given themselves wholly on behalf of the church to such works only as are worthy of God; as planters of God's branches, inserting nothing that is alien to the vine which is Christ, or that fails to bear fruit, but improving with all diligence such as belong to Him and are fruitful; as builders of God's temple, shaping the soul of each one so that he fits harmoniously on to the foundation of the apostles and prophets.[146]

---

[146] 80.12-21: 864B-868C; Clarke, pp. 128-129. On the hearers of the Word, the preaching and letter-writing see Appendices D and E below, pp. 169 ff.

4

Pastoral Solicitude
for Communion of All the Churches

In Basil's overall activity as leader of the church of Caesarea (370-379) it is possible to distinguish two major undertakings: (1) the reestablishment of unity, peace and order in the church of Caesarea, and (2) the initiative of restoring unity, peace and communion among the Christian churches. His first project consisted not only in appeasing and healing the internal faction which had arisen within his province following his episcopal election, but also in restoring discipline among his clergy, by promoting the ascetic life throughout the provinces of Cappadocia and Pontus and by raising the quality of Christian life among all the members of his church.[1] The transition from the first stage concerned with internal renewal into the next phase upon which Basil was soon to embark is presented by Gregory of Nazianzus in a manner which emphasizes conspicuously Basil's qualities not only as a local but also as an ecumenical leader:

> When he had settled affairs at home to his satisfaction, ... he conceived a far greater and loftier design. While all other men had their eyes only on that which lay at their feet and considered how they might safeguard their own interests—if, indeed, this is to safeguard them—without going any further or being capable of conceiving or accomplishing any great or noble purpose, Basil, though he observed moderation in other respects, in this knew no measure. But lifting his head high and casting the eye of his soul in every direction, he obtained a mental vision of the whole world through which the word of salvation had been spread. He saw the great heritage of God, purchased by His own words and laws and sufferings, the holy nation, the royal priesthood, in a miserable plight and torn asunder into an infinity of doctrines

---

[1] See on each of these accomplishments: *Epp.* 48, 58-60: Courtonne, 1: 128-129, 145-151; Gregory of Nazianzus, *Or.* 43.40: PG 36, 549ʙ ff.; *Epp.* 53-56: Courtonne, 1: 137-143; *Reg. mor.* 70, 71 and 80: 816ᴅ-845ᴅ, 860ᴄ-869ᴄ; *Epp.* 22-23: Courtonne, 1: 52-59; the *Great Asceticon* and the *Moralia*.

and errors. ... He did not think it enough to lament misfortune in silence and merely lift up his hands to God to implore deliverance from the pressing evils, himself remaining asleep. Rather he thought he was bound to render aid and to make some personal contribution.[2]

In this chapter we shall study Basil's efforts towards the reunification of the churches, mainly within the framework of his attempts to restore unity to the church of Antioch and in the context of the various negotiations undertaken for that purpose with the Western churches. We shall first outline the general situation of the Eastern churches under Valens. Basil diagnoses the causes that determined the precarious state of affairs; these we characterize as a want of a common orthodox front. To that effect we present his own analysis of contemporary moral and doctrinal anarchy and of the lack of unity and cooperation among the Christian churches in general. Against this general historical background we present Basil's concrete measures to remedy the situation, which consisted in promoting the creation of a united orthodox front over and above the geographical barriers. We begin by analyzing his awareness of the intrinsic limitations of the local church, his emphasis on the primacy of love, the various levels of human and Christian communion (κοινωνία) and finally the forms of ecclesiastical communion. It is obvious that, to be treated properly, each of these topics would require lengthier discussion which would far exceed the limits of a chapter or even a book. We shall therefore restrict ourselves to the essentials, referring whenever possible to the relevant literature.

A. EXTERNAL AND INTERNAL SITUATION OF THE CHURCHES

i. *The External Situation of the Eastern Churches under Valens (364-378)*

While the successors of Jovian—Valentinian in the West and Valens, his brother, in the East—from the beginning maintained the same tolerant attitude towards paganism, they sharply differed as to the course to be pursued in face of the parties which divided the post-Nicene church. The contrasting attitudes with regard to the unification of the Christian churches adopted by the two emperors, with Valens' strong support of the Arians, is fittingly characterized by L. Duchesne:

The religious policy of the emperor Valens was a melancholy contrast to that of his brother Valentinian. Many people in the East might well say that they

---

[2] *Or.* 43.41: PG 36, 549D-552B; McCauley, pp. 62-63 (rev.). In support of Gregory's statements see *Epp.* 69.1: Courtonne, 1: 162; 113: ibid., 2: 16.

lived there under an evil star. Even in the now far-off times of the Great Persecution, the West had scarcely had two years of suffering; in some countries, persecution had hardly touched them at all; whilst the East, from Diocletian to Galerius, from Galerius to Maximin, had had ten years of misery. Licinius and Julian had only shown their severity in the East. The Western bishops had only had to endure Constantius in the last years of his reign. And from the time of Julian's accession no one any longer thought of molesting them.[3]

From the first year of his reign Valens made up his mind to seek reconciliation of the warring parties around the formulary of Rimini. But it was only after his complete victory over his political opponents and the Goths in 370 that the emperor began to apply his measures to the Christian churches.[4]

The procedure adopted by the emperor was very simple.[5] All the bishops were presented, if they had not already signed it, with the formulary of Rimini, and steps were taken to make sure that they accepted communion with the leaders of the Anomoean party headed by Eudoxius. From those who refused, their churches were taken and turned over to the Arians. Against the resistance or disturbances caused by the recalcitrant clergy, a decree was signed and the opposition was broken down by arresting and banishing them from their churches. In his letters Basil often describes the deplorable scenes: "Shepherds are banished, and in their places are introduced grievous wolves harrying the flock of Christ. Houses of prayer have none to assemble in them; desert places are full of lamenting crowds."[6] Among the bishops exiled by Valens were Meletius of Antioch, Eusebius of Samosata, Pelagius of Laodicaea, Barses of Edessa, Abraham of Batna and many others. To the ascetics harassed by the Arians Basil wrote:

> In my judgment the war that is waged against us by our fellow countrymen is the hardest to bear. ... Our fathers were persecuted, but by idolaters; their substance was plundered, their houses were overthrown, they themselves were driven into exile by our open enemies, for the sake of Christ's name. The persecutors who have lately appeared hate us no less than they, but, to the

---

[3] *The Early History of the Christian Church* (London, 1912), 2: 317.

[4] The formula which under Constantius was adopted in Rimini in 359 replaced the ὁμοούσιος and ὁμοιούσιος with the more ambiguous term ὅμοιος (κατὰ πάντα). On Valens' motives in favouring this formula see Duchesne, *History*, 2: 290.

[5] For this part see Duchesne, *History*, 2: 310, G. Bardy in J. R. Palanque, et al., edd., *The Church in the Christian Roman Empire* (New York, 1953), 1: 313-337 (on Valens); 337-356 (on Basil), and F. Guillén-Preckler, "Basilio di Cappadocia e l'occidente," *Communio* 6 (1973) 5-32.

[6] *Ep.* 90.2: Courtonne, 1: 196; Jackson, p. 176.

deceiving of many, they put forward the name of Christ, that the persecuted may be robbed of all comfort from its confession, because the majority of simpler folk, while admitting that we are being wronged, are unwilling to reckon our death for the truth's sake to be martyrdom.[7]

Basil was among the very few orthodox bishops not exiled by the emperor. Although making some concessions to his opponents, Basil was a firm defender of the consubstantiality of the Son and of the Holy Spirit.[8] The emperor, despite signing a decree banishing Basil from Caesarea, withheld his decision and, when visiting the capital of Cappadocia in the winter of 371-372, even granted demesne lands for the construction of Basil's hospital. In 372 Basil was officially commissioned to set in order the religious affairs of the kingdom of Armenia and to ordain bishops there.[9] On the subject of Basil's dealings with the political power, it is perhaps also noteworthy that Basil hardly ever blames the civil authorities for the churches' malaise, attributing instead the cause of the major upheavals to the members of the Christian communities.[10]

ii. *Internal Causes of the Problems Confronting the Churches*

Besides blaming himself and his sins for the many crises that beset the churches of his day, Basil unveils other causes which he believed lay at the root of many ecclesiastical evils.

---

[7] *Ep.* 257.1: Courtonne, 3: 98-99; Jackson, p. 294.

[8] The concession was in not calling the Holy Spirit God publicly; see Gregory of Nazianzus, *Or.* 43.68: PG 36, 588b-c.

[9] On the mission and the causes of its failure see *Ep.* 99.1-3: Courtonne, 1: 214 ff. As possible motives for Valen's rather friendly attitude towards the bishop of Caesarea may be mentioned: (1) Basil's political prowess (see his "prudent handling" [*oikonomia*] of the question of the Holy Spirit); (2) his highly sophisticated humanistic training (Valens was a military uncultivated man of peasant origin; see A. H. M. Jones, *The Decline of the Ancient World* [London, 1966], p. 64; also A. Piganiol, *L'empire chrétien* [Paris, 1972], p. 171; on Valens' wife Dominica and her influence on his religious policies see J. H. Smith, *The Death of Classical Paganism* [New York, 1976], p. 136); (3) his social background; senatorial origin, according to B. Treucker, *Politische und sozialgeschichtliche Studien zu den Basilius-Briefen* (Bonn, 1961), and J. Bernardi, *La prédication des Pères cappadociens* (Paris, 1968), p. 241. In my view this theory, however, does not withstand critical examination of the sources (see above, p. 38, n. 4, and J. Karayannopulos in *BZ* 65 [1963] 356-359) also because the above scholars do not make a proper distinction between the social background of Basil's father and that of Basil's mother. More on this in my forthcoming biography of Basil, now in preparation.

[10] For more on Basil's stance towards the civil authorities see above, pp. 38 ff.; S. Giet, *Les idées et l'action sociales de s. Basile* (Paris, 1941), pp. 356 ff.

(a) Moral and Dogmatic Anarchy

> The doctrines of the true religion are overthrown. The laws of the church are in confusion. The ambition of men who have no fear of God, rushes into commanding offices, and first office is now publicly known as the prize of impiety. ... Holy things are trodden under foot; *those of the people who are sound shun the churches as schools of impiety* [ὡς ἀσεβείας διδασκαλεῖα].[11]

In this excerpt from a letter to the Westerners, Basil gives a summary account of the contemporary situation in many churches east of the Illyricum. The state of internal disarray is exposed again in the *De judicio*, a writing addressed to the members of an ascetic community. In his first preface to the *Moralia*, Basil compares his domestic experience as well as his later experience in the world of business with the contemporary ecclesiastical situation. Whereas at home and in all of his previous engagements he had been aware of a great harmony (συμφωνία) on the part of all those who were serious about their responsibilities, Basil confesses,

> in the church of God alone, for which Christ died and on which He poured out the Holy Spirit richly, I was seeing a great and exceeding discord [διαφωνία] on the part of many men both in their relations with one another and their views about the divine Scripture. And, what was most horrible of all, I was seeing its very leaders [προεστῶτες] differing so much from one another in sentiment and opinion, and so hostile to the commandments of our Lord Jesus Christ, and so mercilessly rending the church of God, and unsparingly agitating His flock, that then, if ever, when the Anomoeans were pressing hard [ἐπιφυέντων], was fulfilled the saying, 'From among your own selves shall men arise, speaking perverse things, to draw away the disciples after them.'[12]

According to Basil, churches were victims of a two-fold impiety (ἀσέβεια): the well-known and easily recognizable one of the Arians who denied outright the divinity of Christ and the Holy Spirit, and the other one, more subtle and concealed but no less pernicious than the previous, of all those who by word of mouth professed their faith in Christ but by their works failed to recognize him as their only true God and King.[13] The latter no less than the former are branded by Basil as "impious" (practical atheists):

> Where no harmony [συμφωνία] is preserved, no bond of peace kept, no meekness in the spirit treasured, but division and strife and jealousy are found—it would be very presumptuous to call such men members of Christ or

---

[11] *Ep.* 92.2: Courtonne, 1: 200-201; Jackson, p. 178 (rev.).
[12] *De jud.*, 1: 653A-B; Clarke, p. 77 (rev.).
[13] See ibid., 2: 656C and 656B.

to say they are ruled by Him. But a frank mind would say boldly that the mind of the flesh is ruler and king there.[14]

(b) Lack of Unity and Solidarity Among the Orthodox Leaders

While in the *De judicio* the misery and ruin of many Eastern communities was to a large extent attributed to moral and dogmatic unruliness (theoretical or practical impiety), in other writings the root of the ecclesiastical predicament is more specifically identified as the absence of unity and of a common orthodox front among Christian leaders. Basil is far from underestimating the seriousness of the external situation. In his own church, seeing the impending peril, he adopted a policy of "diplomacy" ($\mathit{o\grave{i}\varkappa o\nu o\mu \acute{i}\alpha}$) by avoiding the term "God" with regard to the Holy Spirit. Nevertheless, Basil believed that the real cause of the ruin and decay of many churches was some of its leaders who, in particular by isolating themselves from the rest of their companions, became easy prey to Arian attacks.[15] Using several of his writings, we shall briefly portray the contemporary situation of lawlessness and disunity that, according to Basil, dominated the ecclesiastical scenario of his day. It was from his acute awareness of the seriousness of this situation that his project of promoting the creation of a united orthodox front between all the churches stemmed.

The image which Basil most often applies to the contemporary situation is that of a naval confrontation.[16] He envisions the protracted theological dispute among the orthodox as a fratricidal war which "had arisen out of time old quarrels and has been fought by people who cherish a deadly hate against one another."[17] Writing to Epiphanius about the conditions prevailing in Asia Minor, Basil complained:

> Nowhere is pity to be seen; nowhere sympathy. ... Not persecutions for the truth's sake, not churches with all their people in tears; not this great tale of troubles closing round us, are enough to stir us to anxiety for the welfare of one another. We jump on them that are fallen; we scratch and tear at wounded places; we who are supposed to agree with one another launch the curses that are uttered by the heretics; men who are in agreement on the most important matters are wholly severed from one another on some one single point.[18]

---

[14] *De jud.*, 3: 660A; Clarke, p. 80; also *Ep.* 191: Courtonne, 2: 145; *Reg. fus.* 3.1: 917A-B; *Ep.* 265.2: Courtonne, 3: 129.

[15] See *Epp.* 65 and 203 analyzed below, pp. 115 ff.

[16] See *De sp. s.* 76: Pruche, 520; *Epp.* 82 and 90.1: Courtonne, 1: 184, 195.

[17] *De sp. s.* 76: Pruche, 520; Jackson, p. 48.

[18] *Ep.* 258.1: Courtonne, 3: 100-101; Jackson, pp. 294-295. See *De sp. s.* 78: Pruche, 526.

Not infrequently this domestic war was conducted under pretext of the vindication of orthodoxy.[19] "Others, afraid of being convicted of disgraceful crimes, madden the people into fratricidal quarrels, that their own doings be unnoticed in the general distress. Hence the war admits of no truce."[20]

The state of strife and division appeared even more awkward when the present was compared with the past. In early days the main boast of Christians was not miracles, visions, charismatic ecstasies, but a conduct nurtured by love and mutual regard. "Brothers from each church, travelling from one end of the world to the other, were provided with little tokens [σύμβολα], and found all men fathers and brothers."[21] Of this characteristically Christian feature, Basil feels, "the enemy of Christ's churches has robbed us. We are confined each in his own city, and everyone looks at his neighbour with distrust. What more is to be said but that our love has grown cold? Yet it is through [love] alone that, according to our Lord, His disciples are distinguished."[22] Addressing himself to the bishops of Pontus upset by the Eustathian propaganda, Basil reminds them of the Pauline analogy of the church as a body, and also that even the Gentiles in order to survive and to cope with an uncertain future, enter into alliances among themselves:

> Yet we, the sons of fathers who have laid down the law that by brief notes the proofs of communion should be carried about from one end of the earth to the other, and that all should be citizens and familiars with all, now sever ourselves from the whole world, and are neither ashamed at our solitariness [μονώσει], nor shudder that on us is fallen the fearful prophecy of the Lord, 'Because of lawlessness abounding, the love of many shall grow cold.'[23]

iii. *The Four Negotiations with the West for the Purpose of Building a United Orthodox Front (371-377 A.D.)*

Generally, Basil's diagnoses of the afflictions troubling the churches were applicable mainly to the Eastern part of the Byzantine empire. The churches under Valentinian in the meantime enjoyed peace, freedom, and unity since

---

[19] *Ep.* 92.2: Courtonne, 1: 201.
[20] *Ep.* 92.2, ibid.; Jackson, p. 178.
[21] *Ep.* 191: Courtonne, 2: 145; Jackson, p. 233. See also below, p. 122, n. 96.
[22] *Ep.* 191, ibid., see also *Reg. fus.* 3.1: 917β.
[23] *Ep.* 203.3: Courtonne, 2: 170-171; Jackson, p. 242. Cf. *Reg. fus.* 3.1: 917α, for the statement that man is not a "solitary" (μοναστικόν) being but a sociable one with *Hex.* 9.3: Giet, 490.

the emperor favoured the Nicene party.²⁴ The general confusion (σύγχυσις) in the East was aggravated by the presence of two warring orthodox bishops in the church of Antioch. As Basil puts it, "There not only heresy is divided against orthodoxy, but orthodoxy is divided against itself." ²⁵ Antioch in the eyes of Basil was one of the most vital (ἐπικαιριώτερον) organs of the whole *oikoumene*, and no solution could be reached for the existing problems without its internal unity.²⁶ As both East and West were responsible for the disorder in the church of Antioch, Basil was convinced that only through a combined effort of both parties unity could be restored.²⁷

In the spring of 371 Basil confided his plans to Athanasius of Alexandria, whom he wanted to act as an intermediary in the negotiations with the West.²⁸ The first mission, however, did not go beyond Alexandria.²⁹

²⁴ The bishop of Milan, Auxentius, a native of Cappadocia, was one of the very few adherents of the formulary of Rimini in the whole West. On his vague condemnation by Damasus at the instigation of Athanasius, see Duchesne, *History*, 2: 368, and the document "Confidimus quidem," n..29 below. Milan at the time was the residence of the Western emperor and Auxentius its bishop seemed to have been on good terms with Valentinian.

²⁵ *Epp.* 258.3: Courtonne, 3: 102; 92.3: ibid., 1: 202. The roots of the Antiochene conflict go back to 330, when the Eusebians, the opponents of the *homoousion*-formula of the Council of Nicaea, succeeded in deposing Eustathius of Antioch, a staunch defender of that Council's decisions. Until about 361 there was only one bishop in Antioch. Meletius who succeeded Eudoxius in 361 was deposed a month later by the emperor, and Euzoius, an Arian, replaced him as bishop of Antioch. Meletius, although an orthodox, belonged to the group of moderates, known as Homoeousians. Along with Cyril of Jerusalem, Eusebius of Samosata, Eustathius of Sebaste, and others, he favoured the distinction between the terms *hypostasis* and *ousia*, and was for the substitution of the ὅμοιος κατ' οὐσίαν for the Nicene ὁμοούσιος. In the West such new theological developments were viewed with suspicion, and no complete trust will be bestowed on Meletius and his group (for his sympathies with this movement since the early 360s see his *Epistle 9*), until late 379. The Antiochene conflict took a turn for the worse when in 362 a priest of the conservative Eustathian group by the name of Paulinus was consecrated bishop of Antioch. Because of his determined opposition to the aforementioned theological changes, Paulinus was soon favoured by the Westerners, gaining full recognition from Damasus in 375.

²⁶ See *Ep.* 66.2: Courtonne, 1: 158. Duchesne, *History*, 2: 318, n. 3, and Bardy, *The Church*, 1: 341, n. 1, understand under οἰκουμένη the East. However, Basil never uses that word in such a sense. In the same letter the East is called Ἀνατολή. It seems that the difficulty which is sensed also by Giet, *Idées*, p. 312, n. 4, has arisen from a mistranslation of the Greek which reads, τί δ' ἂν γένοιτο ταῖς κατὰ τὴν οἰκουμένην Ἐκκλησίαις τῆς Ἀντιοχείας ἐπικαιριώτερον: "What is more vital than Antioch for the churches of the world?" and not, as Bardy has it, "What is more important than Antioch among the churches of the world?"

²⁷ See *Epp.* 66.1, 90.1, and 92.2: Courtonne, 1: 157, 195, 200.

²⁸ With E. Amand de Mendieta, "Basile de Césarée et Damase de Rome. Les causes de l'échec de leurs négociations," *Biblical and Patristic Studies in Memory of R. P. Casey* (Freibourg, 1963), pp. 125 ff., I distinguish four separate missions and negotiations. See also Duchesne, *History*, 2: 318-329. The choosing of Athanasius as intermediary was probably dictated by his untarnished reputation as a defender of the Council of Nicaea and also his friendship with Damasus. As Basil continued to negotiate with the West long after

The second mission was undertaken almost immediately thereafter. Sabinus was returning to Rome in the spring of 372 and Basil took the opportunity of sending a packet of letters through him.[30] Instead of an answer to the pressing demands of the Easterners, Evagrius in the summer of the following year brought back with him from Rome *Epistles 90* and *92* which were judged unsatisfactory "to the more precise authorities there" (τοῖς ἀκριβεστέροις τῶν ἐκεῖ) and the formula "Confidimus quidem" which was to be signed by the Easterners without the change of a single word.[31] Basil was not only saddened by the meagre outcome of this second mission, but the death of Athanasius (2 May 373) and the breach of communion with Eustathius of Sebaste which occurred shortly after increased the pain in his already troubled soul. The tone of *Epistle 243*, which Basil sent to the Western episcopate through Sanctissimus and Dorotheus in 376, bears

---

Athanasius died I discard as unlikely the hypothesis of Amand de Mendieta according to whom Basil chose to act through Alexandria because that church could supply financial aid for the costly trips to the West. Athanasius most of the time was residing abroad, so was Peter. One of the reasons for Basil's move could have been that in the eyes of many Westerners he was relatively unknown; thus he needed someone with a more established reputation in order to make a stronger case for the strife-ridden Eastern churches.

[29] Dorotheus, the bearer of Basil's *Epistle 70*, on arriving at Alexandria, was dissuaded from embarking for Italy, as Sabinus arrived from Rome with a synodical letter, probably the "Confidimus quidem," in which Damasus at the head of ninety-two bishops notified Athanasius of the condemnation of Auxentius and of the Council of Rimini. For a critical edition of the letter "Confidimus quidem," see E. Schwartz, "Ueber die Sammlung des cod. Veronensis 60," *ZNW* 35 (1936), pp. 19-20. See also ibid., pp. 21-23, and M. Richard, "La lettre 'Confidimus quidem' du Pape Damase," *Annuaire de l'Institut de philologie et d'histoire orientales* 11 (1951) 323-340. On the likelihood that Athanasius procured an additional copy of the letter and addressed it to Basil, see M. Richard, "Saint Basile et la mission du diacre Sabinus," *AB* 67 (1949) 170-202. At any rate, the document "Confidimus quidem" could not have pleased Basil or any of the supporters of the "three *hypostaseis*, one *ousia*," as it spoke of the Father, the Son and the Holy Spirit as "unius deitatis, unius figurae, unius substantiae."

[30] *Epistle 90* was addressed "to the holy brethren, the bishops of the West"; *Epistle 91* to Valerian of Aquileia, and *Epistle 92*, written in the name of Meletius, Eusebius and thirty-two other bishops, "to the Italians and Gauls." It is possible that separate copies of *Epistles 90* and *92* were addressed and sent to each individual church and that the present global address comes from the scriptorium of Caesarea (see J. Gribomont, "Rome et l'Orient. Invitations et reproches de saint Basile," *Seminarium* 27 [1975] 340, n. 24).

[31] See *Ep.* 138.2: Courtonne, 2: 56. Duchesne writes: "These proceedings, we must admit, were scarcely friendly. They were not softened by a demand that the Eastern prelates should themselves repair to Rome, in order that there might be some reason for making them a return visit. Basil was offended; from that time forward he had only a poor opinion of the Westerners, and their chief, Pope Damasus, impressed him as a man of haughty and merciless temper" (*History*, 2: 321). See also Amand de Mendieta, "Basile et Damase," p. 128, and Richard, "Basile et la mission de Sabinus," pp. 197-198. See also following note on Basil's characterization of Damasus.

signs of a bitter disappointment and frustration with the way the Westerners and Damasus, their *coryphaeus*, were handling the situation:

> Do not think only of your being yourselves moored in a safe haven, where the grace of God gives you shelter from the tempest of the winds of wickedness. Reach out a helping hand to the churches that are being buffeted by the storm, lest, if they be abandoned, they suffer complete shipwreck of the faith. ... Polytheism has prevailed. ... Our opponents have the command of baptisms, ... they communicate the mysteries. All these things, as long as the performance of them is in their hands, are so many ties to bind the people to their views. ... You may now take as a proof of the sore straits in which we are placed the fact that we are not even free to travel abroad. For if any one leaves his church, even for a brief space, he will leave his people at the mercy of those who are plotting their ruin.[32]

Again, the results of the third mission were rather modest and in one respect altogether disappointing. No one came from the West. Dorotheus did, however, bring back a letter in which Basil's "zeal was acknowledged, and it was stated that a strong effort had been made to assist him."[33] The letter "Ea gratia" also denounced the errors of Marcellus and of Apollinaris, but without mentioning them by name. The term "substantia" was substituted for the transliteration of the Greek οὐσία and attention was called to a more strict observance of the canons in the ordination of bishops and clergy.[34] But a lethal blow to Basil's hope for dialogue and cooperation between Eastern and Western communities came when, after a long period of hesitation, probably under the influence of Peter of Alexandria, Rome recognized not Meletius but Paulinus as the only head of the orthodox church of Antioch. Through "his son" Vitalis, Damasus wrote officially to Paulinus, giving him authority to deal with questions of communion. But

> Damasus was badly informed; he did not know at this time that Vitalis was on the side of Apollinaris. ... While Paulinus was boasting at Antioch that he had been recognized by Rome, new messengers were on their way to him; one,

---

[32] *Ep.* 243.4-5: Courtonne, 3: 72-73; Jackson, pp. 284-285. See also *Ep.* 215: Courtonne, 2: 207. The following description is probably aimed at Damasus: "What good could accrue to the cause by communication with a man proud and exalted, and therefore quite unable to hear those who preach the truth to him from a lower standpoint." See also *Ep.* 239.2: Courtonne, 3: 60: "I am moved to say, as Diomed said, 'Would God, Atrides, thy request were yet to undertake; ... he's proud enough.' Really lofty souls, when they are courted, get haughtier than ever" (Jackson, pp. 255, and 280).

[33] Duchesne, *History*, 2: 325. See the text of "Ea gratia" in Schwartz, "Sammlung," pp. 20, and 21.

[34] Duchesne, *History*, 2: 325, is of the opinion that the last remark was aimed at Meletius.

to warn him that difficulties had supervened; the other, to give him in relation to Vitalis more complete instructions. ... The affair of Vitalis brought matters to a crisis. The Meletians already considered Apollinaris and Vitalis as heretics; after the letter of Damasus it was impossible for Paulinus to receive them into his Church. They founded another Church, and Vitalis himself became its bishop.[35]

The fourth negotiation took place in the spring of 377. Dorotheus and Sanctissimus were setting out for Rome with *Epistle 263* addressed by Basil "to the Westerners" in the name of the Easterners collectively.[36] According to most scholars, in his letter, Basil asked the Westerners, in the name of his colleagues, "*to condemn in express terms* Eustathius, the chief of the Pneumatomachi; Apollinaris, who taught the millenial reign and disturbed everyone by his doctrine as to the Incarnation; and finally, Marcellus, whose disciples found too much support from Paulinus."[37] But the term "condemn" or rather "judge" ($\varkappa\rho\acute{\iota}\nu\omega$) is used in the letter only once in connection with Eustathius' previous excommunication by one of Basil's predecessors, the bishop Hermogenes of Caesarea.[38] When referring to the problems at hand and demanding immediate action, Basil employs the words $\delta\eta\mu o\sigma\iota\epsilon\acute{\upsilon}\omega$ and $\delta o\gamma\mu\alpha\tau\acute{\iota}\zeta\omega$.[39] After recognizing that the Arians of whom the Westerners spoke in every letter were no longer much of a threat to the orthodox in the East, Basil addresses the "men clad in sheep's clothing, and presenting a mild and amiable appearance, but within unsparingly ravaging Christ's flocks," who "find it easy to do harm to the simpler ones, because they came from us."[40]

> It is these who are grievous and hard to guard against. It is these that we implore your diligence *to make known publicly* [$\delta\eta\mu o\sigma\iota\epsilon\upsilon\theta\tilde{\eta}\nu\alpha\iota$] to all the churches of the East; to the end that they may either turn to the right way and join with us in genuine alliance, or, if they abide in their perversity, may keep their

[35] Duchesne, *History*, 2: 326-328. Cf. Basil's harsh comments on Damasus' letters to Paulinus in *Ep.* 214.2: Courtonne, 2: 203-204.

[36] Cf. also *Ep.* 129.1-3: Courtonne, 2: 39 ff., in which Basil explains to Meletius the format of this new project.

[37] Duchesne, *History*, 2: 328-329 (italics not in the original). See also in the same vein Giet, *Idées*, pp. 346-351; E. Schwartz, "Zur Kirchengeschichte des vierten Jahrhunderts," *ZNW* 34 (1935) 171-177, esp. pp. 186-188; Amand de Mendieta, "Basile de Césarée et Damase de Rome," p. 131; P. Galtier, "Le Tome de Damase," *RSR* 26 (1936) 404-410; H. Lietzmann, *History of the Early Church* (Cleveland, 1961), 4: 29-31.

[38] *Ep.* 263.3: Courtonne, 3: 123.

[39] *Ep.* 263.2: Courtonne, 3: 122. For the use of the terms $\varkappa\acute{\eta}\rho\upsilon\gamma\mu\alpha$ and $\delta\acute{o}\gamma\mu\alpha$ in the sense of a "public decree," "ordinance," see *Epp.* 270 and 263.2: Courtonne, 3: 142, 123.

[40] *Ep.* 263.2: Courtonne, 3: 122; Jackson, p. 302.

mischief to themselves alone, and be unable to communicate their own plague to their neighbours by unguarded communion.[41]

From these words it is obvious that Basil is not asking for an outright condemnation—at least not yet. The only thing he is urgently demanding is a public and official statement (δόγμα: decree) of the errors attributed to Eustathius, Apollinaris, and Marcellus. The Westerners although partly responsible for the chaotic situation (as were they who indiscriminately gave letters of communion and recommendation to Eustathius and other chance-comers from the East) should not, however, for the time being interrupt their relations with the innovators but only make a statement concerning their future policy. With those who have perverted the doctrines of the church they will be in communion but only if they amend; however if the innovators determine to abide by their innovations (καινοτομίαι), the Westerners will separate from them.[42]

From the reply of the Westerners there is no doubt that both parties understood this procedure in the same way: there should be no condemnation or excommunication before a public warning was issued.[43] At first Basil wanted such an official policy-statement to be prepared with both the Eastern and Western leaders "sitting in synod" (ἐν κοινῇ σκέψει).[44] But after six years of unsuccessful attempts at having such an "ecumenical" synod assembled and fearing that the time factor was in favour of the innovators, Basil asked the Westerners to draft such a document on their own.[45] As they obviously lacked direct knowledge of many details, Basil further suggested that they make their mind up on the basis of his letter and the information that his messengers will be able to supply.[46]

We do not possess written records of the conversations which were held between Dorotheus, the chief negotiator of Basil, and the Westerners. But judging from the heated discussion which ensued between Basil's envoy and Peter of Alexandria, the chief adviser of Damasus, with charges and coun-

---

[41] Ibid.

[42] Ep. 263.5: Courtonne, 3: 125; Jackson, p. 303. Cf. above, p. 74, n. 170.

[43] In all probability the answer to Epistle 263 is contained in the fragments "Non nobis quidquam" and "Illud sane miramur." For a critical edition of these documents see Schwartz, "Sammlung," pp. 21-23. Our opinion regarding an agreement of views between the Westerners and Basil differs from the one proposed by the authors quoted above, n. 37. We reject as ill-founded any insinuation of Basil's having asked an explicit condemnation of the people mentioned in his Epistle 263. For some of the possible reasons see above, p. 74, n. 170.

[44] Ep. 263.5: Courtonne, 3: 125. Cf. Ep. 66.1: ibid., 1: 157.

[45] Ep. 263.5, ibid.

[46] See Ep. 263.5: Courtonne, 3: 126.

tercharges regarding among other things the orthodoxy of Meletius and Eusebius, the protégés of Basil, it is safe to say that neither party had at hand particularly competent people for conducting such delicate negotiations.[47] In his customary manner, Basil attributed to his own bad judgment and to his sins the failure of his undertakings.[48] But there certainly was more involved in the situation than could be dealt with by one person. "On the men of this time who were well intentioned there weighed the consequences of the long war in which Eusebius of Nicomedia had embroiled the Easterners, first against Alexandria, and then against the Roman Church."[49] If we add the immense geographical distances, the difficulties and slowness of communication, the linguistic barriers, the factors of a political and cultural order, the inaccuracy of reports (this in particular applies to the letters of Jerome to Damasus), the differences of theological emphases, we can perhaps begin to understand the causes for Basil's failure to create during his lifetime between East and West a united orthodox front.[50] It was only after Basil's death that most of his "ecumenical" efforts were crowned with success. By 381 the Antiochene dispute was resolved, and peace and unity were restored to the Eastern churches. Also in the same year the Council of Constantinople condemned the heresy of the Pneumatomachians, along with other offshoots of Arianism, and solemnly proclaimed the catholic teaching of the consubstantiality of the Holy Spirit.[51]

---

[47] The incident is related in *Epistle* 266.2: ibid., 135, written by Basil to Peter of Alexandria who most of the time resided in Rome. According to this letter, Meletius and Eusebius were reckoned among the Ariomaniacs by Peter. This provoked the anger of Dorotheus who in turn attacked Peter with some vehemence. Basil apologized, but at the same time drew Peter's attention to the fact that Meletius and Eusebius who had suffered so much from the Arians, deserved better treatment.

[48] See *Ep.* 266.2: Courtonne, 3: 135.

[49] Duchesne, *History*, 2: 329. See also Bardy, *The Church*, 1: 352: "Between East and West an *entente* had never been easy; it was now more difficult than ever. The two halves of the Church did not speak the same language; they did not employ the same expressions; they had not the same aims" (follows a quotation from Jerome's *Ep.* 15).

[50] Some of these causes have been studied in a more general context by Y. M. J. Congar, *After Nine Hundred Years; the Background of the Schism between the Eastern and Western Churches* (New York, 1959). See also the assessment of Basil's character—a natural temperament at once too sensitive and too pugnacious; his health always poor, etc.—in Duchesne, *History*, 2: 334-335, and Bardy, *The Church*, 1: 356. For a different interpretation of the "parting of the ways" between East and West see P. Brown, "Eastern and Western Christendom in Late Antiquity: A Parting of the Ways," in D. Baker, ed., *The Orthodox Churches and the West* (Oxford, 1976), pp. 1-24. See also the remarks of W. de Vries in his review of the above work, *OCP* 43 (1977) 211-212.

[51] A fine assessment of Basil's work and accomplishments as a church politician can be found in Gribomont, "Rome et l'Orient," p. 345.

B. Theological Presuppositions of Communion and of Pastoral Care for All Churches

Following this historical survey of some of the major events that took place between 371 and 377, I now propose to outline some of the theological antecedents that might have warranted and guided Basil's efforts to constitute a united orthodox front among all Christians despite their cultural and national differences.[52]

i. *Intrinsic Limitations of the Local Church*

One of the conclusions which Basil soon arrived at was that not only is one man in need of others, but no single community of people can survive without the cooperation of others. It was for this reason that the pagans also, although living in a self-sufficient (αὐτάρκης) country, entered into (defensive and offensive) alliances (συμμαχίαι) with each other, and sought mutual cooperation in order to be able to cope more efficiently with an uncertain future.[53]

But Christians have many other more compelling reasons to think of themselves as in need of the friendship and cooperation of their fellow members, and this not only on an individual level but also on a corporate basis. Speaking on behalf of his community, which, following the administrative division of Cappadocia into two provinces, was severed from one of its parts, Basil confessed:

> Others may be great and powerful and self-confident, but I am nothing and worth nothing, and so I could never take upon myself so much as to think myself able to manage matters without support. ... Truly, from our own bodily constitution the Lord has taught us the necessity of fellowship [κοινωνία]. When I look to these my limbs and see that no one of them is self-sufficient [αὐτάρκης], how can I reckon myself competent to discharge the duties of life? One foot could not walk securely without the support of the other; ... the grasp is made firmer by the fellowship of the fingers. In a word, of all that is

---

[52] Unlike Amand de Mendieta (see his "Basile et Damase," cited above, n. 28) I am not interested here in seeking the causes of Basil's apparently unsuccessful attempts at winning the cooperation of the Western churches for his project of universal Christian solidarity. My main concern is to discover some of the theological presuppositions which led Basil in the first place to seek such universal cooperation (or rather σύμπνοια: "spiritual, mutual, dynamic accord") among all Christian leaders, and this not only for the settlement of impending problems but also for the creation of a strong, self-respecting community of Christians, capable of surviving any future contingencies and of adequately fulfilling its responsibilities independently of the state. See in this respect M. Richard's quotation above, p. 76, n. 175 and Gribomont, "Rome et l'Orient," p. 345.

[53] See *Ep.* 203.3: Courtonne, 2: 170.

done by nature and by the will, I see nothing done without the concord [σύμ-πνοια] of fellow forces. Even prayer, when it is not united, loses its natural strength.[54]

We spoke earlier of a noticeable lack of imperial sentiment in Basil.[55] This is not only because Basil considered that for a Christian all the earth is his home, but also because, as an heir of the first disciples of the Lord, he strongly objected to any individualism based on geographical distribution.[56] After asserting that contemporary Christians were deprived by the enemy of Christ's churches of the spirit of love and brotherhood which, according to Basil, prevailed among the first Christians when "brothers from each church, travelling from one end of the world to the other, were provided with little tokens and found all men fathers and brothers," Basil sadly adds this comment, "we are confined now each in his own city, and everyone looks at his neighbour with distrust. What more is to be said but that our love has grown cold? Yet it is through [love] alone that, according to our Lord, His disciples are distinguished."[57]

Let us examine two of Basil's letters written to the bishops in which he condemns as unchristian and also as a move fraught with danger any tendency to isolate one church from the other on grounds that it is competent and self-sufficient in dealing with its problems.

(a) *Epistle 65* from 372 A.D.

Basil did not take part in the election of the new bishop of Neocaesarea.[58] He hoped, however, that the Christians of that church would elect a man

---

[54] *Ep.* 97: Courtonne, 1: 210-211; Jackson, p. 181. There can perhaps be detected some political undertones in this letter addressed to the senate of Tyana, the new capital of Cappadocia II. The letter was written in 372 following the partition of Cappadocia into two provinces and the elevation (or self-proclamation) of Tyana as the metropolis of Cappadocia II. (See *Epistles 74-76*, and for the best interpretation of the events, A. H. M. Jones, *The Cities of the Eastern Provinces*, 2nd ed. [Oxford, 1971], pp. 182-185, and R. Teja, *Organización económica y social de Capadocia en el siglo IV, según los Padres Capadocios* [Salamanca, 1974], pp. 196-201.) Despite Basil's vigorous protests and opposition Anthimus became metropolitan of Cappadocia II. Nonetheless, the principles enunciated in *Epistle 97* fully agree with Basil's teaching expounded elsewhere (see e.g. *Reg. fus.* 7: 928B ff.; 3: 916c ff.).

[55] See above, pp. 38 f., and F. Morison, *St. Basil and His Rule* (Oxford, 1912), pp. 6-7.

[56] In *Epistle 191* quoted next Basil voices his strongest opposition to the tendency found among certain bishops to adopt in their churches a *polis*-like constitution involving Hellenic style self-sufficiency (αὐτάρκεια) and independence (αὐτονομία). This he considers contrary to the spirit of Christian *koinōnia*.

[57] *Ep.* 191: Courtonne, 2: 145.

[58] See *Ep.* 28.1: Courtonne, 1: 65-66 and ibid., 3: 70.

with whom he could be in good relations, better anyway than those he had had with Musonius. The people with the clergy chose a cousin of Basil, probably an ascetic, by the name of Atarbius. For a very long time Atarbius refused to send Basil his "enthronistic" letter.[59] Basil, in spite of his rank and seniority, had to be the first to extend his hand to Atarbius. Important for us are the concepts expressed on the occasion. Basil observes that the enemies of the church, in order to destroy the orthodox faith, go to all kinds of pains and troubles. "If we were not to make as strenuous efforts on behalf of the churches as the opponents of sound doctrine make to subvert and utterly destroy them, you may be quite sure that there is nothing to prevent the truth from being swept away."[60] Basil exhorts Atarbius to expel from his mind the idea that he needs communion with no one else.

> To cut one's self off from connexion with the brethren is not the mark of one who is walking by love. ... I do wish you, with all your good intentions, to take into account that the calamities of the war which are now all around us may one day be at our own doors, and if we too, like the rest, have our share of outrage, we shall not find any even to sympathize with us, because in the hour of our prosperity we refused to give our share of sympathy to the wronged.[61]

(b) *Epistle 203* from 375 A.D.

Basil wrote a long expostulatory letter to the bishops of Pontus who lived on the Black Sea. This region of Asia Minor was not hit so hard by the persecutions as the other provinces from the hinterland. The bishops considered themselves safe and without obligations towards their less fortunate colleagues. At first Basil expected to pay them a visit, but the poor condition of his health and the many cares caused by the struggles against the Arians did not allow this. His desire to meet them was not motivated by any canonical ordinance, but because in a moment when Eustathius of Sebaste was campaigning against him they "were wanting to him."[62] Basil more than anybody else was exposed to the attacks of the enemies of the orthodox. After having reminded them that love is the distinguishing mark of all the true disciples of the Lord and that peace is the greatest gift that

---

[59] That is, a letter officially informing his colleagues of his election and ordination whereby his name would be entered in the list of the bishops belonging to the same communion.

   [60] *Ep.* 65: Courtonne, 1: 155; Jackson, p. 163. See also *Ep.* 136.2.

   [61] *Ep.* 65: Courtonne, 1: 156; Jackson, p. 163.

   [62] *Ep.* 203.1: Courtonne, 2: 167; and ibid., 170.

Christ has bequeathed us, Basil invites them to show him regard in one of the following manners: by visiting him; if this is not possible, by sending somebody who would be able to examine the situation and report back to them; or by sending friendly letters.[63] The third paragraph of *Epistle 203* contains a brilliant and at the same time strongly motivated presentation of the mutual need and expectation of help felt by every human. What a neighbour is for an ordinary person, one church is for another church. As in the *De judicio*, Basil reminds the maritime bishops that it is not necessary to be Christian to see and understand all this.[64] It is enough to realize how the pagans proceed: whenever they want to achieve a goal they enter into alliances ($\sigma\upsilon\mu\mu\alpha\chi\iota\alpha\iota$). In this way they also protect themselves against the uncertainties of the future.[65]

> Let not this consideration influence you. 'We dwell on the sea, we are exempt from the sufferings of the generality, we need no succour from others; so what is the good to us of foreign communion?' For the same Lord Who divided the islands from the continent by the sea, bound the island Christians to those of the continent by love. Nothing, brethren, separates us from each other, but deliberate estrangement. We have one Lord, one faith, the same hope.[66]

Both documents strongly emphasize the corporate and communal dimensions of Christian calling. The reality that no man is an island becomes the basis for the conviction that no Christian is an island. This particular line of reasoning Basil pursues even further: not only is an individual member of the community incapable of taking adequate care of his needs but neither is a church (as a local brotherhood) competent to provide for all its needs or to withstand the attacks of those threatening its existence.[67] Solidarity and mutual cooperation among the churches are the essential requirements for the survival of Christianity in a world threatened by centrifugal forces—the evil of hatred and self-love. The need, individually and collectively speaking, to seek complementarity ($\pi\lambda\acute{\eta}\rho\omega\mu\alpha$) for one's personal shortcomings through fellowship ($\kappa o\iota\nu\omega\nu\iota\alpha$) with others is also argued by Basil on the basis of the varied and uneven distribution of the charismata: no church, as no individual, can boast to have all the charismata. But these are given with the explicit purpose that we may minister through them not to

---

[63] Ibid., 4: 171-172.
[64] Cf. *De jud.*, 2: 656B; *Ep.* 203.3: 170.
[65] See the text quoted above, p. 107.
[66] *Ep.* 203.3: Courtonne, 2: 170; Jackson, p. 242.
[67] Cf. *Reg. fus.* 7.1: 928c f.; *Ep.* 65: Courtonne, 2: 156.

ourselves, but that we serve the needs of others.[68] Dealing specifically with the church of Neocaesarea Basil recalls this to have been precisely the order that once regulated its relations with Caesarea:

> Ask your fathers and they will tell you that though our districts were divided in position, yet in mind they were one, and were governed by one sentiment [μιᾷ γνώμῃ ἐκυβερνῶντο]. Intercourse [ἐπιμιξίαι] of the people was frequent; frequent the visits of the clergy; the pastors, too, had such mutual affection [ἀγάπη], that each used the other as teacher and guide in things pertaining to the Lord.[69]

ii. *The Supremacy of Love and the Charismatic Order*

Besides the above arguments derived from immediate experience, Basil adduces another in favour of a more strict collaboration between the single ecclesiastical communities: it is the law of *Agape*, grounded and inferred from the sociable nature of man, "a tame and sociable, not a wild and solitary being."[70] Love is not a law that imposes itself from outside; more than a law based on convention, it is a *logos spermatikos* based on man's intimate structure. Like every man, the Christian leader possesses its seeds from his first constitution (σύστασις). Thus under no circumstances can he escape the imperative demands of this natural drive towards fellowship. If he tried, he would cease to be not only a Christian, but a man.[71]

Love is the principle of cohesion among the various parts of the church, the body of Christ, effecting that unity and order without which the church would cease to be a brotherhood:

> As the charismata of the Spirit are different, and neither is one able to receive all nor all the same charismata, ... all should be harmonious with one another in the love of Christ, as members in a body.[72]
> For we all are 'members one of another, having different charismata according to the grace of God that is given us.' Wherefore 'the eye cannot say to the hand, I have no need of thee; nor again the head to the feet, I have no need of you,' but all together complete [συμπληροῖ] the body of Christ in the unity of the Spirit, and render to one another the needful aid that comes of the charismata. ... 'The members have the same care for one another,' according

---

[68] See *Reg. mor.* 60 quoted above, p. 42; also pp. 7 f., 21 f., and 24 ff.

[69] *Ep.* 204.7: Courtonne, 2: 180; Jackson, p. 245; see also *Reg. fus.* 35.3 quoted above, pp. 34 ff. Cf. *Ep.* 156.1: Courtonne, 2: 82.

[70] *Reg. fus.* 3.1: 917A; see *Reg. fus.* 2.1: 908B ff.

[71] Besides *Reg. fus.* 2.1 cited in the preceding note, see *De sp. s.* 78: Pruche, 528; Jackson, p. 50, "We have become more brutish than the brutes," etc.

[72] *Reg. mor.* 60.1: 793A-B; Clarke, p. 117 (rev.).

to the spiritual communion of their inborn sympathy. ... And as parts in the whole so are we individually in the Spirit, because we all 'were baptized in one body into one spirit.'[73]

All these and similar passages indicate that in Basil, as in Paul, the charismatic order is far from being purely pneumatic. On the contrary, the charismata constitute the elements of liaison and cohesion among the various members of the brotherhood. "Like all social relations, those established in the church, are based on the necessary exchange of services."[74] Throughout his works Basil insists that everything is to take place in the church and the ascetic community "decently and in order."[75] Basically this order is the order of selfsubordination effected by the Spirit who inspires every member not to seek what is his own but what is the common good.[76] The leaders of the church witness to this order of the Spirit when they are "subject to one another," that is, when they rule the church "through mutual accommodation ... by the ancient kind [εἶδος] of love."[77]

iii. *The Various Levels of Communion*

Man communicates in God's life because he was created in his image and because after his downfall he was redeemed and reinstated to his original dignity through the dispensation of Christ.[78] As sin alienates (ἀλλοτριόω; χωρίζω) man from God, so love unites (συνάπτω; οἰκειόω) him with his Creator and Redeemer.[79] "Love cannot be taught. ... Its learning does not come from outside," but from his first constitution man has been endowed with the *dynamis* and *logos* of love.[80] Between love for God and for one's neighbours there is such close connection that God "transfers to Himself benefits conferred on one's neighbours."[81]

---

[73] *De sp. s.*, 61: Pruche, 470. See ibid., 39 quoted above, p. 45.

[74] Giet, *Idées*, p. 173. The meaning of charisma in Basil is "function," "service," involving both natural and "supernatural" aptitudes required in the performance of the various assignments: see above, pp. 28 ff.

[75] The quotation from 1 Cor 14.40, "Let all things be done decently and in order" occurs very often in Basil in key passages (see *Reg. fus.* 24: 981D; *Reg. br.* 72: 1133A; 108: 1156C; 138: 1241C; 276: 1276C). See the brief but incisive comments on this passage in L. Goppelt, *Apostolic and Post-Apostolic Times* (London, 1970), p. 187.

[76] See *De jud.*, 4: 660C; *Epp.* 28.3 and 65: Courtonne, 1: 65, 155.

[77] *Ep.* 191: Courtonne, 2: 144; *Reg. fus.* 35.3: 1005C. See *Ep.* 70: Courtonne, 1: 164.

[78] See *In ps.* 48.8: 449B ff.; *De sp. s.*, 35: Pruche, 364. On baptism as sacrament of Christian regeneration see *Reg. mor.* 20.1-2: 736C ff.; 80.22: 868D ff.; *De sp. s.*, 26: Pruche, 336 f.

[79] See briefly *Hom.* 9.6: 344A-C.

[80] *Reg. fus.* 2.1-2: 908B ff.

[81] *Reg. fus.* 3.1: 917B; Clarke, p. 157.

From man's instinctual drive to love God and his neighbours there follows the need to associate and communicate (κοινωνέω).[82] Man communicates with God by adhering to his saving commandments, through a life of openness and service to his neighbours.[83] As was mentioned earlier, of all the charismata bestowed by the Spirit, the charisma of love is the highest; it is the summary of all man's obligations towards God and his neighbours.[84] To love is mutually to care for and to share with another in all goods whether material or spiritual.

The church, as the body of Christ animated by the Spirit, is a place of sharing and communicating κατ' ἐξοχήν. One of its distinguishing features is love translated into participation, action, hospitality, willingness to serve, and even to give one's own life for the sake of others.[85]

iv. *Ecclesial Communion*

The church is the assembly of all those whom the Holy Spirit calls with his kerygma to salvation through the agency particularly of prophets, apostles, and those who in succeeding generations are ackowledged to be endowed with the charisma of the word and teaching.[86] The church is not only internally variegated and manifold according to the various charismata and degrees of participation in knowledge of God, but it is also a multinational, multicultural, and ecumenical community.[87] The church is a brotherhood, whose members are scattered all over the *oikoumene*.[88] But although coming from different cultural and national backgrounds "all believers in Christ are one people; all Christ's people, although He is hailed from many regions, are one church."[89]

(a) Signs of Personal Communion

The ontological unity of the church is warranted by the life-giving (ζωοποιόν) presence and activity of the Holy Spirit. I propose now to review briefly some of the signs of its unity which, according to Basil, witness to this fellowship of the Spirit at the empirically observable level. The term

[82] Ibid.: 917A.
[83] See *Reg. mor.* 3-5: 705c ff.; 18.1-6: 729A ff.
[84] See above, p. 33, n. 167.
[85] See *Hom.* 11.5: 384A ff.; *Reg. br.* 85: 1144A.
[86] See above, p. 77.
[87] See *Reg. mor.* 60.1: 793A-B; *In ps.* 44.11: 412A ff.; *Hom.* 3.4: Rudberg, 28-29; *In ps.* 48.1: 433B.
[88] *Ep.* 133: Courtonne, 2.47; *In ps.* 44.4: 396c-397A.
[89] *Ep.* 161.1: Courtonne, 2: 93; Jackson, p. 214.

communion (κοινωνία) appears very often in this connection in Basil's letters. Its equivalents are "peace" (εἰρήνη), "agreement" (ὁμόνοια), "unity" (ἕνωσις), and above all "love" (ἀγάπη).

Communion at the ecclesial level denotes first the unity effected by God's salvific economy, embodied in the fellowship of all those who were regenerated in baptism performed in the name of the three divine hypostases, by which people who were until then separated and divided by their ethos became united in the church through reciprocal love.[90] In the church, people communicated with God and each other by partaking at the same altar of the body and blood of Christ, and by sharing their possessions.[91] Although regarding the Eucharist as a symbol of ecclesial unity, Basil speaks much more frequently about prayer (εὐχή) as the organ of fellowship.[92] When many churches were turned over to the Arians, people in disapproval preferred to pray to God in the open, "in the wilderness, in heavy rain, in the snow, the gales and the frost of winter as well as in summer under the blazing heat of the sun." All this they suffered because they refused to communicate in "the wicked leaven of Arius."[93] Although on friendly terms with Apollinaris of Laodicea, Basil never admitted the clerics of his church to the communion of prayers.[94] Again, when Theodotus disagreed with Basil because of the latter's communion with Eustathius of Sebaste, he excluded Basil from the morning and evening prayers held in his church at Nicopolis.[95]

Personal communion was also expressed by provision of hospitality to travelling Christians. "Brothers from each church, travelling from one end of the world to the other, were provided with little tokens [σύμβολα: "tesserae"], and found all men fathers and brothers."[96]

---

[90] See *In ps.* 48.1: 433c-d.

[91] See *Epp.* 93: Courtonne, 1: 204; 53.1: ibid., 138. On the importance of the altar as a sign of fellowship and unity see *Ep.* 251.3: Courtonne, 3: 91, where Eustathius is said to have overthrown the altars of those who were no longer of his communion. On the sharing (*koinōnia*) of properties see *Reg. br.* 85: 1144a; 92: 1145c ff.; 187: 1208b f.; *Reg. mor.* 48.1-2: 768c-d.

[92] About prayer in this sense see the fundamental statement in *Ep.* 150.2: Rudberg, 197. About prayer in general see F. Morison, *St. Basil and His Rule* (Oxford, 1912), pp. 58-78. That for Basil Eucharist and prayer were the instruments of personal communion see P. Maran, PG 32, 561d, n. 2.

[93] *Ep.* 242.2: Courtonne, 3: 67; Jackson, p. 283.

[94] See *Ep.* 224.2: Courtonne, 3: 19.

[95] See *Ep.* 99.1: Courtonne, 1: 214.

[96] *Ep.* 191: Courtonne, 2: 145; Jackson, p. 233; see also *Ep.* 203.3: ibid., 170-171. The tokens served to identify the orthodoxy of the church to which the traveller belonged: see G. D'Ercole, *Communio-Collegialità-Primato e sollicitudo omnium Ecclesiarum dai Vangeli a*

(b) Exchange of Letters

Exchange of letters was the natural substitute for lack of and in the absence of visits. For Basil letters in general possessed the same force as face-to-face meetings. As we are speaking about his letter-writing in general elsewhere, we shall consider here only those letters which had a bearing upon ecclesial communion, namely, "enthronistic" and synodal letters.[97]

No sooner was a bishop installed than either he or those who installed him sent an official document witnessing to his orthodoxy and expressing the desire of being in communion with all those who shared the same faith.[98] The letters of enthronement usually contained a formula, sometimes in abbreviated form, of the symbol of faith in usage in the given church. As the situation grew complicated, Basil was not satisfied with the Nicene creed; from those who sought his communion he required in addition a mention of the non-creaturehood of the Holy Spirit.[99] It is for this reason also that he established himself as an authority with regard to whom other bishops should or should not send letters of communion.[100]

Not all the letters exchanged by bishops were necessarily letters of communion in the technical sense but only those drawn up according to the rule ($τύπος$) of the church, probably the ones in which a bishop was given his title.[101] It should also be noted that letters of communion as a means of pastoral solicitude were not always sent to the bishops of a see, but in cases of heresy they were addressed to the presbyters or even private individuals.[102]

(c) Synods

Pastoral solicitude could not always be exercised by means of letters alone, as there were many problems requiring a more accurate examination

---

Costantino (Rome, 1964), and L. Hertling, *Communio: Church and Papacy in Early Christianity* (Chicago: Loyola, 1972). If the traveller was a bishop in the churches of his communion he was not only admitted to prayers and given shelter but also invited at times to preach in the church. Probably *Reg. mor.* 36.1, 38.1, and 72.1-2 are to be referred to such situations.

[97] See below, pp. 166 ff. and above, p. 116, n. 59.

[98] *Ep.* 197.1 is probably a reply to Ambrosius' "enthronistic"; see also *Epp.* 65 and 203.

[99] See *Epp.* 113-114, and 140. As we have seen Basil even viewed with suspicion the Westerners' "Confidimus quidem" in which no distinction was made between $ὑπόστασις$ and $οὐσία$ (see above, p. 109, n. 29).

[100] See *Epp.* 82: Courtonne, 1: 185; 129.3: ibid., 2: 41; 265.3: ibid., 3: 131 ff.

[101] *Ep.* 129.3: Courtonne, 2: 41; see PG 32, 561, n. 2.

[102] Basil even encouraged people to disassociate themselves from their leaders who fell into heresy; see *Ep.* 151: Courtonne, 2: 76 f. See in this light the statement in *Ep.* 257.2: ibid., 3: 99-100.

and discussion. Besides, letters could often be intercepted. For this reason Basil invites his colleagues to pay him visits. In the majority of cases, Basil invites the bishops of his communion and closer friends to visit him in Caesarea on the occasion of the πανηγύρεις—festivities ("festal assemblies") in honour of the local martyrs.[103] Precisely for the reason that such conferences were held on the occasion of liturgical festivities, the latter are frequently referred to by the name of synods.[104] The term most often employed by Basil to designate such episcopal meetings is συντυχία.[105]

The objectives of such "high-level" encounters were varied. Let us review some cases.

Epistle 92, addressed "to the Italians and Gauls," requests the convocation of an "ecumenical" synod. Its purpose would be to restore the creed of Nicaea, "proscribe the heresy, and, by bringing into agreement all who are of one mind, speak peace to the churches."[106]

Epistle 95: Meletius and Theodotus invited Basil to a meeting (συντυχία) to be held at Phargamus in the middle of June 372, in order to discuss and clarify Basil's relations with Eustathius of Sebaste. The conference was to be held both "in proof of love and for remedying the troubles."[107] From *Epistle 98* we learn that Basil did not participate in the meeting because Theodotus did not ratify the invitation, nor send anyone to escort Basil.[108]

Epistle 100: The episcopal conferences at Caesarea were usually held each year on the occasion of the festivity of the local martyr St. Eupsychius.[109] With Eusebius of Samosata who regularly attended such πανηγύρεις, Basil hopes to discuss the following points: the appointments of new bishops in the kingdom of Armenia, and the measures to be taken in face of the synods held against him by his brother Gregory of Nyssa.[110]

---

[103] See *Ep.* 176: Courtonne, 2: 112. *Homily 29* gives the most detailed explanation of the πανήγυρις, calling it "that remnant of the ancient love of the Fathers," and a means of spiritual renewal and reconciliation (ibid., 2: 1489B-C). See also *PGL*, s.v.

[104] See *Epp.* 100: Courtonne, 1: 219; 98.1: ibid., 212; 126: ibid., 2: 35. Synods, besides the festal gatherings, were designated also the congregations of the bishops and the people assembled for purposes of liturgical prayers and worship; see *Epp.* 138.2: Courtonne, 2: 56; 141.1: ibid., 63. The meaning of synod in *Ep.* 286: Courtonne, 3: 156, is church; see also *Ep.* 278: ibid., 151.

[105] See *Epp.* 95: Courtonne, 1: 207; 98.2: ibid., 212; 201: ibid., 2: 166; and Gregory of Nazianzus, *Ep.* 197: Gallay, 143.

[106] *Ep.* 92.3: Courtonne, 1: 202; see also *Epp.* 66.1: ibid., 157; 70: ibid., 164-166; 69.1: ibid., 162; cf. also 263.5: ibid., 3: 125.

[107] *Ep.* 95: Courtonne, 1: 207.

[108] *Ep.* 98.1: Courtonne, 1: 212.

[109] See *Epp.* 100: Courtonne, 1: 219; 176: ibid., 2: 112; 252: ibid., 3: 93.

[110] See *Ep.* 100: Courtonne, 1: 219.

Epistle 176 shows that synods were also occasions to interchange spiritual gifts, meaning probably the rendering of services on the part of the bishop-guest to the visited church.[111]

Epistle 201 indicates, as does *Epistle 98*, that synods were held especially to secure advice "on the matters in hand" and to discuss in general current church affairs.[112]

In *Epistle 202* Basil speaks of a synod of bishops which he was not able to attend. "If the matter can be postponed for a few days, I will, by God's grace, join you and share your anxieties. If the business presses, do with God's help what has to be done; but reckon me as present with you and as participating in your worthy deeds."[113]

From this review of some of Basil's letters it would appear that episcopal synods were aimed above all at clarifying matters of faith.[114] In face of the many accusations regarding his orthodoxy, Basil was constrained to organize several meetings in order to explain his position vis-à-vis heresy and some of its promoters.[115] In all these meetings participated all who were officially invited; they could, however, if they wanted, extend the invitation to others.[116] It is difficult to determine who presided over such meetings. For instance, Poemenius the bishop of Satala, a small town, played a decisive role in the synod held to discuss the succession of Theodotus.[117] Also in the latter case, at least in Basil's version, great weight seemed to have been attached to the spiritual charismata, whereas the canonical prohibition against transferring a bishop from one church to another was completely disregarded. From *Epistle 28* it would follow that Musonius, although a junior, in virtue of many charismatic gifts, frequently presided over many episcopal assemblies.[118]

There are two things that seem to emerge quite clearly from the examination of Basil's letters dealing with the synods. (1) No decisions could be taken regarding a church whose bishop was not present; (2) no major initiative could be undertaken by a bishop without the express consent of the bishops of his communion.[119]

---

[111] See *Epp.* 176: Courtonne, 2: 113; cf. also above, p. 122, n. 96.

[112] See *Epp.* 201: Courtonne, 2: 166; 98.1: ibid., 1: 212.

[113] *Ep.* 202: Courtonne, 2: 166-167.

[114] See *Epp.* 92.3: Courtonne, 1: 202-203; 205: ibid., 2: 181-182; 126: ibid., 36.

[115] See *Epp.* 95: Courtonne, 1: 207-208; 203.1-4: ibid., 2: 167 ff.

[116] See *Ep.* 98.1: Courtonne, 1: 212.

[117] See *Epp.* 227-230: Courtonne, 3: 29 ff.

[118] See *Ep.* 28.1: Courtonne, 1: 67. Cf. *Ep.* 65: ibid., 155.

[119] See *Ep.* 265.3: Courtonne, 3: 132. Basil, who undertook the negotiations with the West, could do little in view of the persistent indifference and opposition of some of his colleagues; see *Ep.* 141.2: Courtonne, 2: 63-64, and the Ben. n. 89 in PG 32, 589.

Like the letters of communion and the visits, the synods were a form of collective government.[120] More than a legislative or executive body, they appear in Basil as a means of sharing anxieties with one's colleagues, of soliciting advice on urgent matters and as an expression of love and brotherhood. On the other hand, as events, synods served to emphasize even more the insufficiency of every local community if left to itself. Such a conviction in Basil, more than a result of abstract thinking, was the outcome of historical circumstances. It was perhaps Basil's greater experience, a more intimate acquaintance with his office, and the disturbing confusion of the moment that compelled him to seek continuously the advice of his colleagues and to arrange periodic meetings with them. Basil was reluctant to trust his own insights for fear of making irretrievable mistakes; he preferred rather to be dependent upon others.[121]

Basil's desire to communicate with others was sometimes interpreted as an intrusion, as a political manœuvre to acquire influence over the churches of the neighbouring provinces. Some people have even wished "to see in him the founder of a kind of Patriarchate, with a jurisdiction corresponding to the 'diocese' of Pontus." But from the examination of all of his writings it is evident that Basil had no authority in the western provinces of Asia Minor, those of Bithynia, Galatia, and Paphlagonia; nor did he exercise any real authority in the churches of the seaboard and interior of Pontus.[122]

v. *The Elements of Church Unity*

(a) Common Confession of the Trinitarian Faith

Faith in the trinity of divine hypostases, nurtured by the Scriptures and the ecclesiastical traditions, is for Basil the ultimate norm of action. The church's unity consists of and depends on the common confession of faith in the three divine hypostases, the acknowledgment of their ὁμοτιμία, and a life patterned on the infinite number and great variety of its demands that follow. In virtue of the multiformity of functions (charismata), each member of the body is capable of preserving and developing his own particular abilities without losing his identity in making his charisma available to others.

[120] See G. D'Ercole, *Communio*, pp. 325 ff.

[121] See in general his letters to Eusebius of Samosata; also Meletius of Antioch, PG 32, *ad ind.*

[122] I summarize here the opinion of Duchesne, *History*, 2: 335, which my own research had proved independently.

From all the letters of Basil to the Westerners it is apparent that faith in the trinity of divine hypostases was endangered not only by the original Arian heresy but by its many derivatives: the Anomoeans, Pneumatomachi, the innovations of Apollinaris and Marcellus. It is also evident from the same sources that Basil was reluctant to coin or sign new formulas of faith. The Nicene symbol, he thought, was sufficient to unite Christians with the only exception that it should be supplemented by the mention of the non-creaturehood of the Holy Spirit.

Unity of faith and Christian communion cannot be achieved either by adhering to the Scriptures alone or to the traditions alone. According to Basil the source of faith is the baptismal formula derived from the Bible and interpreted by the church. The Christian ethos should be derived from this single source: membership in a church abiding by the words of God, guided by his life-giving Spirit, and ministering to him and to all people in a self-subordinated love; that is, "faith working through love" (πίστις δι' ἀγάπης ἐνεργουμένη) is the Basilian definition of Christian being and acting.[123]

The Holy Spirit is the architect of the church's ethos. He operates in a lordly fashion as a sovereign; thus, in his activities he is not bound by space or formulas.[124] However, his presence is infallibly with the church built by his charismata, in the written testimony of the inspired Scriptures, in the sacraments of baptism and confirmation, in ecclesiastical proclamations, instructions and prayers.

This trinitarian faith rooted in and stemming from the baptismal formula, this ministering love, Basil saw threatened by the Arian heresy, by the innovations of the *technologoi* such as Eunomius, the Anomoeans, the Pneumatomachi, and by a mere nominal orthodoxy.

(b) Tokens of Love, or Love Grown Cold

While σύμβολα τῆς ἀγάπης, "tokens of love" represented what Basil had believed was the order and original ethos of the Christian church, ἐψύξαμεν τὴν ἀγάπην, "we have let our love grow cold" was a statement about the present conditions.[125]

In *Epistle 70* to Damasus bishop of Rome, Basil speaks of a two-fold love: of material and spiritual assistance. When *ca.* 264 Cappadocia was invaded by the Goths and its churches were plundered and Christians taken

---

[123] See *Reg. mor.* 80.22: 868c; *Ep.* 295: Courtonne, 3: 170. In general see *Reg. mor.* 3.1-2; 9.1-5; 18.3; *De jud.*, 4.

[124] *De sp. s.* 61-62: Pruche, 466 ff.; cf. *Ep.* 229.1: Courtonne, 3: 33-34.

[125] See *Epp.* 191: Courtonne, 2: 145; 172: ibid., 107; 203.3: ibid., 171; *De sp. s.* 78: Pruche, 528.

into captivity, Dionysius, the bishop of the Roman church, "visited" (ἐπισκεπτόμενον) the church of Caesarea by letters and sent contributions to pay for the ransom of the prisoners.[126] His gesture was so momentous that its memory was kept to Basil's day. Now, in 371, in a yet more painful and gloomy situation Basil turns to Damasus. This time not bodies and material buildings are destroyed but souls are carried away into captivity by the champions of heresy. From Damasus Basil asks not legal intervention but spiritual comfort:

> To renew laws of ancient love, and once again to restore to vigorous life that heavenly and saving gift of Christ which in course of time has withered away, the peace, I mean, of the Fathers. ... I have been constrained to beseech you by letter to be moved to help us, and to send some of those who are like-minded with us, either to conciliate those at variance and bring back the churches of God into friendly union, or at any event to make you see more plainly who are responsible for the unsettled state in which we are, that it may be obvious to you for the future with whom it befits you to be in communion. In this I am by no means making any novel request, but am only asking what has been customary in the case of men who, before our own day, were blessed and dear to God, and conspicuously in your own case.[127]

Material assistance, however, is also a constitutive element of church unity and Christian brotherhood. In his letters and writings Basil often speaks of this second aspect of Christian solicitude, solidarity, care, and affection. He pleads for material support for the poor and needy, for widows and orphans, for foreigners and travellers, for Christians and non-Christians. Most commonly this expression of love assumes in Basil an organized form.[128]

These two aspects of Christian *agape* should never be disassociated. Spiritual and material assistance are the two correlative expressions of Christian love. We shall see now their combined manifestation as the most infallible sign of church unity.

About 374, by a decree of the emperor, many bishops were sent into exile; among those were Eusebius of Samosata and Barses of Edessa. No sooner had Basil learned of the exile of Eusebius than he wrote to the presbyters and the senate of Samosata to exhort them to perseverance and loyalty towards their leader.[129] To the bishop Barses, deported first to the

---

[126] *Ep.* 70: Courtonne, 1: 165-166.
[127] Ibid., 164 ff.; Jackson, p. 166.
[128] About Basil's hospital see *Ep.* 94: Courtonne, 1: 205, and above, p. 38; also pp. 52 f.
[129] See *Epistles 182, 183, 219* and *268.*

island of Arada and then confined to the fortress of Philo in Egypt, Basil wrote twice promising to assist him with his prayers.[130] In *Epistle 267* he announces the dispatch of some gifts for the venerable confessor.[131] Another missive was forwarded by Basil to the Egyptian bishops, Eulogius, Alexander and Harpocration, banished by the emperor to Palestine. The letter sent to these bishops is full of Christian hope: unsearchable are the judgments of divine righteousness; now the Lord avails himself of the involuntary and forced presence of these champions to communicate and spread the light of the gospel in the regions of Palestine. Basil assures them of his communion although he is somewhat puzzled by the way they granted their communion to the Marcellians without first verifying their orthodoxy.[132]

Not infrequently in his letters Basil asks others to assist him in the management of his affairs by their prayers, visits, letters of good advice and sympathy.

Nothing could better illustrate Basil's concern and solicitude for others than the following excerpt from his letter to the Alexandrians. Basil certainly did not intend to claim any jurisdictional authority over the Alexandrian community, at this time without its leader since Peter, the successor of Athanasius, resided in Rome. However, he feels compelled to write to those Christians, severely tested by the cruel persecution roused by Valens shortly after the death of Athanasius, in order to comfort them and to ask them to pray for him.

> Had it but been possible for me to travel to you I should have liked nothing better than to meet you, that I might see and embrace Christ's athletes, and share your prayers and spiritual charismata. But now my body is wasted by long sickness, so that I can scarcely even leave my bed, and there are many who are lying in wait for me, like ravening wolves, watching the moment when they may be able to rend Christ's sheep. I have therefore been compelled to visit you by letter; and I exhort you first of all most earnestly to pray for me, that for the rest of my remaining days or hours I may be enabled to serve the Lord, in accordance with the gospel of His kingdom.[133]

[130] See *Epp.* 264: Courtonne, 3: 126-127 and 267 cited next.
[131] *Ep.* 267: Courtonne, 3: 137.
[132] See *Ep.* 265.1-3: Courtonne, 3: 127 ff.
[133] *Ep.* 139.3: Courtonne, 2: 59; Jackson, p. 203.

General Conclusion

Basil of Caesarea lived at a time when orthodox Christianity was engulfed in a severe crisis of doctrinal and institutional identity. The "honeymoon," if there was any at all, between state and church came to an end, at least in the eastern section of the Roman empire, when Valens made up his mind to endorse the supporters of the Council of Rimini. More than external, the crisis seemed to be internal, as Christians were entangled in a domestic war against Christians. The most critical level of tension was reached in Antioch where not only heresy was divided against orthodoxy, but orthodoxy was divided against itself.

The doctrinal crisis entailed an institutional crisis, as the emperor could no longer be regarded by many Christians as the supreme lawgiver and protector of orthodoxy since he had compromised himself by supporting heresy.

This book has studied the awareness of this critical period of uncertainty and darkness in the life of Basil of Caesarea whose public service in the church corresponded almost exactly with the reign of Valens—365 to the end of 378. Gregory of Nazianzus, who closely followed the events, could find no better illustration for his theoretical disquisition on clerical and Christian dignity than, in a supplement to his *Oration 42*, to portray the image of Basil as an ideal bishop, a local and ecumenical leader $\kappa\alpha\tau$' $\dot{\epsilon}\xi\sigma\chi\dot{\eta}\nu$.[1]

As we have pointed out several times, it was from his realization of the gulf between the precarious contemporary situation and the original spirit of Christianity that Basil decided to become an ascetic and reformer of the church. Basil embraced a type of asceticism which was to be developed not outside of or on the margins of the church but which would be capable of influencing it from within. His ascetic brotherhood was intended to recreate the life of the early Christian community, "in which all things were common, whose members were united by the same faith and brotherly love, 'all

---

[1] See *Oration 43* and Bernardi, *La prédication des Pères cappadociens. Le prédicateur et son auditoire* (Paris, 1968), p. 238.

in common seeking in the one Holy Spirit the will of the one Lord Jesus Christ'."[2] In this fashion also the two distinctive features of the church as a holy and charismatic community were to flourish once again. Even if Basil insisted to a great extent on the importance of the charisma of love and other gifts of the Holy Spirit, it seems that he avoided falling into either sheer pneumatism or authoritative legalism. His charismatism appears rather to be tempered by insistence on the self-subordination of love and order of services in the community.[3]

Basil not only yearned for the return of the pre-Constantine model of the church, but he also used a terminology and strove for a type of church government which so resembled the one prevailing in the church of the first three centuries that at times the reader of his letters is tempted to consider them as documents belonging to that period rather than the one in which Basil lived. We have seen several expressions of this archaic mentality such as "brotherhood," "brotherhood of churches," "fellowship of the Spirit," "church administration ($o\grave{\iota}\varkappa o\nu o\mu\acute{\iota}\alpha$) based on the ancient type of love," "leader," "leader of the word."

As the leader of the church of Caesarea, Basil endeavoured to exemplify in his conduct many of the principles related to the revival of the primal spirit of love, brotherly interrelations, mutual sharing ($\varkappa o\iota\nu\omega\nu\acute{\iota}\alpha$) in material and spiritual goods and exchange of services (charismata), that were enforced in his ascetic brotherhoods. In his role as defender of the orthodox faith Basil, it is true, stood for confinement rather than further expansion, but it is also undeniable that most of the time the bishop of Caesarea was on the offensive rather than the defensive in protecting church interests against a compromised government. His concept of Christian love involved material as well as spiritual assistance to the needy, broadmindedness in matters of belief, and friendly although uncompromising relations with the outsiders.

Referring to the Holy Spirit as the ambiance ($\chi\acute{\omega}\rho\alpha$) of Christian sanctification and divine worship, Basil attributed to the Paraclete the function of building the church of Christ. Human instrumentality in the edification of the church is most conspicuous in Basil's emphasis on the relevance and necessity of ecclesiastical proclamation ($\varkappa\acute{\eta}\rho\upsilon\gamma\mu\alpha$) for the purposes of edifying the church, fighting errors, and forming souls in piety ($\varepsilon\grave{\upsilon}\sigma\acute{\varepsilon}\beta\varepsilon\iota\alpha$). Between the proclamation and the hearers' part in testing its soundness there is such a close association in Basil that anything resembling passive or

---

[2] See above, p. 24.
[3] See above, pp. 32 ff., 45 ff., and 118 ff.

blind reception of the message was far from his mind and intention. The hearers, in order to ensure the building of the church through proclamation, are called to collaborate actively with those who announce the Christian gospel first by testing its soundness and consistency with the faith of the church, and second, by assimilating ("digesting"), becoming one with the message, in a purified mind and in quietude of heart. The contact between the leaders and their followers, as is pointed out in Appendix E, was to be made not only through live addresses, homilies, and meetings but also through literary activity, especially through letter-writing as one of the most efficacious means for becoming acquainted with the "brothers" living in remote regions and for realizing the ideal of "one soul and one heart."

Chapter four endeavoured to apply most of the principles laid down in the foregoing chapters concerning the defense and proclamation of the faith to a broader audience, the ecumenical church. The present study confirms the observations made by H. von Campenhausen:

> Basil realized from the outset that the Church's dogmatic problems could not be solved on a particularistic basis. It is true that it would have been comparatively easy for him to keep to his own Cappadocian circle. ... But he would have regarded that as a betrayal of the common cause of all Christians. Basil required an 'ecumenical' outlook of all bishops.[4]

Not only did dogmatic issues require solution on an ecumenical and universal level, but the whole trend of Christian life was to be conducted and developed in a spirit of universal love and regard for others' needs and concerns. In order to fulfil its mission the church needs to be a brotherhood trusting the diversity of people, solid but not inflexible in its commitments, caring most of all for not being a hindrance to those who are being saved.

In assessing Basil's character and indicating that which prevented the bishop of Caesarea from reaching more lasting results from his "ecumenical" endeavours, L. Duchesne has pointed among other things to Basil's fragile health, the ill-will of the government, the often stupid but nonetheless persistent opposition from some ecclesiastics, and to the fact that "Basil brought to the service of a programme of reconciliation, a natural temperament at once too sensitive and too pugnacious."[5] One could perhaps add that Basil also not infrequently showed a certain lack of practical judgment (this in spite of some authors making him the most practical-minded of the three Cappadocians). Indications of this can be seen in his

---

[4] *The Fathers of the Greek Church* (New York, 1959), p. 95.
[5] *The Early History of the Christian Church* (London, 1912), 2: 334.

choice of friends, in the appointment of Gregory of Nazianzus and Gregory, his brother, to the bishoprics of Sasima and Nyssa respectively, in his enthusiastic friendship and then determined animosity towards Eustathius of Sebaste; also, as was pointed out in chapter four, his choice of the deacon Dorotheus to act as his authorized representative in Rome proved rather unfortunate as the extremely delicate and high level negotiations required a more dispassionate mind than the deacon of Meletius could provide.

These shortcomings in no way should diminish Basil's greatness which remains indisputable, and they should be considered only as accounting for part of the aborted efforts at forming a Christian "commonwealth." Nor should Basil be the only one to bear responsibility for the failure of the programme of reconciliation. Undoubtedly others like Athanasius and Damasus who had the power and opportunity to do more should be held partially responsible for having failed to contribute their share to the grand cause of Christian reunion. In the light of the events that followed Basil's death—notably the Council of Constantinople which not only proclaimed the *homoousion* of the Spirit but also initiated the squabble for jurisdictional supremacy and the title "New Rome" for the imperial city—we may say that, after Basil, some of the church leaders continued to pursue a policy of estrangement rather than *rapprochement*. Basil's rather idealistic portrayal and vision of a Christian community, "one soul and one heart," found only an imperfect realization in the religious-monastic establishments promoted by other great idealists such as Augustine of Hippo, Benedict of Nursia, Theodore of Studios, and the medieval founders. Throughout history, however, although there has never existed a fully unified church, *in actu* many valuable services have been rendered to the needy on the part of those endowed with charismatic love, thus bearing witness to the life-giving and energizing presence of the Spirit of Christ in the world.

It may not be inappropriate to conclude this inquiry into the ecclesial consciousness and functions of church leaders in the life and thought of Basil of Caesarea by quoting the final words from the treatise *On the Holy Spirit*:

> If you find what I have said satisfactory, let this make an end to our discussion of these matters. If you think any point requires further elucidation do not hesitate to pursue the investigation with all diligence, and to add to your information by putting any uncontroversial question. Either through me or through others the Lord will grant full explanation on matters which have yet to be made clear, according to the knowledge supplied to the worthy by the Holy Spirit.[6]

---

[6] *De sp. s.*, 79: Pruche, 530; Jackson, p. 50.

Appendix A

A Revised Provisional Chronology of the
Life and Works of Basil of Caesarea (330-379)

In this table we follow essentially the chronology of Basil's life and works as established by P. Maran in his *Vita Basilii* (PG 29, v-clxxvii); all references to Maran are to chapter and paragraph. This chronology has no claim to finality. It constitutes only a modest attempt to up-date provisionally, "salvo meliore iudicio," in the light of the most recent scholarship and some of my own endeavours, the course of events in the life and literary activity of Basil of Caesarea.

For maps and synopses of other events not mentioned in this chronological table see J. Stevenson, *A New Eusebius* (London, 1968), pp. 409-416, and idem, *Creeds, Councils, and Controversies* (London, 1973), pp. 371-377.

i Chronological Table of the Life and Works of
Basil of Caesarea

330 (or 329)

Basil born at Caesarea in Cappadocia. His father, Basil of Neocaesarea, by profession a sophist-rhetorician, was descended from a family of rich landowners in Pontus. Emmelia, his mother, was from a noble family from Cappadocia. Basil's grandparents on both sides demonstrated heroic loyalty to Christianity during various persecutions. Basil of Neoceasarea and Emmelia had ten children of which we know the names of five: Macrina the Younger, Basil, Naucratius, Gregory, and Peter.

330

Inauguration of Constantinople as capital of the Roman-Byzantine empire.

337

The Emperor Constantine dies and is succeeded by Constantius in the East and Constans in the West.

341/342

The council of Gangra condemns some of the extreme ascetic propositions and practices of the followers of Eustathius of Sebaste.

See below, Appendix B.

345/347

Sometime during this period, after the death of his father, Basil continues his secondary education at Caesarea. Meets Gregory of Nazianzus.

Gallay, *La vie*, 31-32.[1] Basil's father was a sophist, a teacher of rhetoric of students aged 15-18. If Basil did indeed study with him the ἐγκύκλιος παιδεία (see Gregory of Nazianzus, *Or.* 43.12), he must have died no sooner than 345.

346

Pachomius the Egyptian dies.

349/350

Basil pursues his studies at Constantinople.

Maran, *Vita*, 2.1.[2]

350

Constans is killed. (Constantius sole emperor from 353.)

350/351

Basil travels to Athens for further education; joins Gregory of Nazianzus.

Marrou, *History of Education*, 204, n. 33;[3] Gallay, *La vie*, 55 f.

352

Basil's brother Naucratius forsakes his rhetorical career and becomes an ascetic near Annesi.

Maraval, *Grég. de Nysse*, 165 ff.;[4] Aubineau, *Grég. de Nysse*, 52-53.[5]

353/354

Probable exchange of letters (not extant) between Basil and Apollinaris of Laodicea.

---

[1] P. Gallay, *La vie de s. Grégoire de Nazianze* (Lyon, 1943).

[2] P. Maran, *Vita s. Basilii Magni*, PG 29, v-clxxvii.

[3] H. I. Marrou, *A History of Education in Antiquity* (New York, 1956).

[4] P. Maraval, ed. and trans., *Grégoire de Nysse, Vie de sainte Macrine*, SCh 178 (Paris, 1971).

[5] M. Aubineau, ed. and trans., *Grégoire de Nysse, Traité de la virginité*, SCh 119 (Paris, 1966).

See *Ep.* 361: Courtonne, 3: 220, and Maran, *Vita*, 2.5, where some of the other sources are indicated. *Contra* Prestige, *St. Basil*, 31-32,[6] who, however, takes as too certain Apollinaris' ordination to the priesthood in 346 and overlooks the evidence from the above cited sources.

355

Basil returns home.

> Aubineau, *Grég. de Nysse*, 54, with n. 3; Maraval, *Grég. de Nysse*, 161, n. 7. The assumption here is that Basil never met Julian and that the latter's arrival in Athens in the summer of the same year should be considered a *terminus ante quem* to Basil's departure. Maran, *Vita*, 2.5, on the contrary, refers to Julian's sojourn as *terminus post quem* and delays Basil's return until 356. He also accepts the authenticity of Basil's correspondence with Julian.

355/356

Basil spends a short time teaching rhetoric at Caesarea.

> Gallay, *La vie*, 67, n. 4; *contra* Gribomont, "Voyages," 121;[7] see, however, Aubineau, *Grég. de Nysse*, 54, n. 7, who successfully disputes Gribomont's interpretation of Gregory of Nazianzus' passage from *Or.* 43.25 and, in confirmation of the traditional view, adduces the often neglected testimony from Gregory of Nyssa's *Epistle* 13.4; see likewise G. Lazatti, "Basilio," 284-292.[8]

Among Basil's students was probably his brother Gregory.

> Aubineau, *Grég. de Nysse*, 54-55.

356

17 January: Antony the Egyptian dies.
February: Athanasius of Alexandria is exiled.

> For both dates see Chitty, *The Desert a City*, 36, with n. 178.[9] I do not know on what evidence this author gives the date of 7 February for Athanasius' exile. The attempt on Athanasius' life took place on the night of 8 February. See Szymusiak, *Athanase*, 116;[10] see also ibid., 35, where only the month of February is given; for other references, see ibid., n. 1.

---

[6] G. L. Prestige, *St. Basil the Great and Apollinaris of Laodicea* (London, 1956).

[7] J. Gribomont, "Eustathe le Philosophe et les voyages du jeune Basile de Césarée," *RHE* 54 (1959) 115-124.

[8] G. Lazatti, "Basilio di Cesarea insegnò retorica?" *SMSR* 38 (1973) 284-292.

[9] D. J. Chitty, *The Desert a City, an Introduction to the Study of Egyptian and Palestinian Monasticism* (Oxford, 1966).

[10] J. M. Szymusiak, *Athanase d'Alexandrie, Apologie à l'empereur Constance, Apologie pour sa fuite*, SCh 56 (Paris, 1958).

At Caesarea Basil is baptized and ordained reader (admitted into the clergy) by Dianius.

> Maran, *Vita*, 3.2; Aubineau, *Grég. de Nysse*, 55, n. 5; compare *De sp. s.* 29: Pruche, 502, with Greg. Naz., *Or.* 43.27: PG 36, 533ʙ.

Converted to asceticism, Basil follows Eustathius (of Sebaste?) on a tour of the monastic settlements in Syria, Mesopotamia, Palestine, and Egypt; owing to an illness (or just poor health and exhaustion), he is detained at Alexandria.

> Spring-summer of 356; summer-fall of 357. Maran, *Vita*, 3.5, followed by Gribomont, "Voyages," and others, places Basil's trip in 357. The reason seems to be that, while in Alexandria, Basil did not see Athanasius: *Ep.* 80: Courtonne, 1: 181-182. However, as we now know (see above), Athanasius was exiled in February 356, and Basil could not have set out on his tour until around Easter, late spring or early summer of 356; see *Epistles 48*; *121*, and Gorce, *Les voyages*, 12.[11] But if Eustathius also, whom Basil seems to have been following (see *Ep.* 1), could not travel until that time of the year, Basil more likely left home later rather than earlier in the year. The itinerary he followed was (a) Mesopotamia, (b) Coele Syria, (c) Palestine, (d) Egypt: *Epp.* 1; 223.2, and Maran, *Vita*, 3.5. The trip by land was very difficult and expensive, and if Basil had wanted to return by the same route it would have taken him almost a full year to complete it: ibid.; Gorce, *Les voyages*, 12. However, I would be inclined to think that Basil returned by sea in the summer or fall of 357 before the Mediterranean closed for the winter season (November-March of each year); see *Ep.* 1 for his determination to return home as soon as possible in order to see Eustathius; see also Maran, *Vita*, 3.5. That travelling by sea was faster and also much less expensive see Brown, *Late Antiquity*, 12-13;[12] Jones, *Ancient World*, 310 ff.[13] There are also some other equally important reasons to anticipate rather than delay Basil's trip to the south. The interval between his return from Athens and his conversion to asceticism could not be less than one full academic year (that is, if we assume as we ought to that he taught rhetoric for a while, although Gribomont would deny this: see above, 368). If Basil, as is almost certain, did not see Julian during the latter's visit to Athens in the summer of 355, he then must have returned home at the end of the academic year 354/355; Marrou, *History of Education*, 204. Also Basil's first period at Annesi, before 359, should be lengthened rather than shortened (for an opposite

---

[11] D. Gorce, *Les voyages, l'hospitalité et le port des lettres dans le monde chrétien des ivᵉ et vᵉ siècles* (Paris, 1925).

[12] P. Brown, *The World of Late Antiquity* (London, 1971).

[13] A. H. M. Jones, *The Decline of the Ancient World* (London, 1966).

view see Gribomont, "Voyages," 120) for when he was joined by Gregory of Nazianzus in 360 the results of his personal ascetic endeavours were quite conspicuous, which in order to have happened must have required some time: Maran, *Vita*, 6.3; not all obviously should be attributed to a ready-made inheritance from Eustathius; see Gregory's *Epistles 1-2, 4-6*, and *Oration 43*.

357

Basil returns from his trip to the south. From Caesarea, Cappadocia, writes *Epistle 1* (before the winter; to Eustathius the Philosopher, probably Eustathius of Sebaste).

　　Gribomont, "Voyages."

Council of Sirmium (summer). Second formula of Sirmium: the Father is greater than the Son; prohibition of the use of the term *ousia, homoousios*, and *homoiousios*. Hosius of Cordova and Liberius of Rome sign the formula.

357/358

In Pontus, on a family estate at Annesi, Basil joins in a rather secluded ("semi-eremitical") type of asceticism practiced by his mother Emmelia, sister Macrina, and their entire household.

　　Gregory of Nyssa, *Vita Macrinae*, 5-8; Maraval, *Grég. de Nysse*, 155-169. In his writings Basil refers to his place at Annesi as ἐρημία; ἐσχατία: *Epp.* 2.1: Rudberg, 156-157; 210.1: Courtonne, 2: 190.

Sometime during this period or earlier Basil's brother Naucratius dies in an accident.

　　Vita Macrinae: Maraval, *Grég. de Nysse*, 169 ff.; see Gribomont, "Eustathe," 1721.[14]

Epistles 3 (to Candidianus), *4* (to Olympius).

358

Council of Ancyra (before Easter). Condemnation of Anomoeanism; substitution of the *homoiousios* for the *homoousios*. (Beginning of Homoiousianism: Basil of Ancyra, Eustathius of Sebaste, Meletius of Antioch, and others.)

358/359

Gregory of Nazianzus returns from Athens to Nazianzus. For a while he teaches rhetoric in his hometown.

　　Gallay, *La vie*, 65; *Briefe*, xiv.[15]

---

[14] J. Gribomont, "Eustathe de Sebaste," *DHGE* (Paris, 1967), 16: 26-33.
[15] P. Gallay, *Gregor von Nazianz, Briefe*, GCS (Berlin, 1969).

Basil invites Gregory to join him at Annesi; Gregory hesitates.

> Letters not preserved: Gallay, *La vie*, 68. Gregory's *Epistle 2* is wrongly quoted here as a reply to Basil's lost letter; see the same author's *Briefe*, xiv, and Maran, *Vita*, 6.3.

359

Fourth formula of Sirmium (the "Dated Creed": 22 May). "Expression of the vaguest and most inconsistent Homoianism."

Council of Rimini (July). Rejection of the "Dated Creed"; reiteration of the symbol of Nicea (by the orthodox majority).

Council of Seleucia (27 September). Basil attends it in the company of Basil of Ancyra, Eustathius of Sebaste, and Cyril of Jerusalem. The majority abides by the Dedication Creed of Antioch (341).

Epistle 361 (to Apollinaris of Laodicea; from Seleucia).

> Prestige, *St. Basil*, 7, 17-18.

Athanasius writes *De_ synodis* (October/November).

At Nicé delegates from the Councils of Rimini and Seleucia are made to assent to a version of the "Dated Creed."

360

Council of Constantinople (first days of January). Defeat of Anomoeanism, orthodoxy, and triumph of Homoianism. Basil publicly debates with the Anomoeans (Aetius, and Eunomius?).

When Dianius of Caesarea signs the formulary of Nicé-Constantinople, Basil breaks off communion with him and returns to Annesi. On his way to Pontus he writes

Epistle 14 (to Gregory of Nazianzus)

> Gallay, *La vie*, 69-70. For the placement of *Ep. 14* before *Ep. 2*, see Gallay, ibid., 70, n. 3; Giet, *Sasimes*, 38, n. 1;[16] *contra* Maran, *Vita*, 7.5.

Epistles 5 (to Nectarius, consolatory), *6* (to Nectarius' wife, consolatory; both letters written after Basil's trip to Seleucia).

361

In view of Gregory's indecision to join him (see Gregory's *Ep. 2*), Basil writes *Epistle 2* (to Gregory of Nazianzus). This letter signals Basil's conversion from rhetoric to philosophy.

---

[16] S. Giet, *Sasime, Une méprise de s. Basile* (Paris, 1941).

For an explanation of these terms see Ruether, *Gregory of Nazianzus*, 10.[17]

Gregory joins Basil at Annesi. Both friends work on the *Philocalia*, an anthology from Origen's works. Also they begin collecting Scriptural passages bearing upon the Christian ascetic life from which later on will develop Basil's *Moralia*.

> See below, pp. 152 ff. Gribomont, "Les succès," 32, n. 33,[18] refers to this early compilation as the first edition of Basil's *Moralia*. However, if we have in *Epistle 22* an intermediary form of this work, the early collection of Scriptural passages seems to be a first draft rather than first edition of the later *Moralia*.

On the Spirit ("De Spiritu," a cento from Plotinus' works; "sometime between 359-364").

> Dehnhard, *Das Problem*, 67.[19]

Bishop Meletius is transferred from the church of Sebaste to the church of Antioch. After a month he is sent into exile.

Death of Constantius. Julian becomes sole emperor (3 November).

362

Epistles 9 (to Maximus the Philosopher), *363* (to Apollinaris of Laodicea; early part of the year).

> Prestige, *St. Basil*, 12.

Synod of Alexandria (March/April). Adoption of the formula μία οὐσία, τρεῖς ὑποστάσεις. Athanasius' *Tomus ad Antiochenos*.

Basil attends the deathbed of Dianius at Caesarea. Dianius dies reconciled with the church. Basil returns to Annesi.

Election, baptism, and ordination of the decurion Eusebius as bishop of Caesarea.

On his way to Antioch, Julian pays a brief visit to Caesarea (early July).

> Prestige, *St. Basil*, 12.

Martyrdom of Eupsychius (7 September).

362/363

Epistles 11 (without address, for friendship's sake), *12* and *13* (to Olympius), *17* (to Origen), *18* (to Macarius and John).

---

[17] R. R. Ruether, *Gregory of Nazianzus, Rhetor and Philosopher* (Oxford, 1969).

[18] J. Gribomont, "Les succès littéraires des Pères grecs et les problèmes d'histoire des textes," *SE* 22 (1974/1975) 23-49.

[19] H. Dehnhard, *Das Problem der Abhängigkeit des Basilius von Plotin* (Berlin, 1964).

Death of Julian (27 June 363). Accession of Jovian.

364

Death of Jovian (17 February). Valentinian, emperor in the West (26 February); Valens, his brother, in the East (28 March).

Basil ordained presbyter by Eusebius at Caesarea.

> Around September: Maran, *Vita*, 9.2; or perhaps, more likely, earlier in the year as the following homilies seem to have been preached during Lent at Caesarea.

Homily 12 ("In Prov 1.1-5").

> Maran, *Vita*, 9.3; see Bernardi, *Prédication*, 56.[20]

Homily 11 ("De invidia").

> Bernardi, *Prédication*, 59.

Homily 20 ("De humilitate").

> Bernardi, *Prédication*, 67.

Homily 3 ("Attende tibi ipsi").

> Bernardi, *Prédication*, 67.

Alienation between Basil and Eusebius. In order to avoid an internal schism in the church of Caesarea Basil retires to the Pontus.

At Eusinae, Basil holds talks with Eustathius of Sebaste who in the company of other bishops is about to leave for the Council of Lampsacus. Eustathius' stenographers take dictation of Basil's confutation of the *Apology* of Eunomius, his books

Contra Eunomium 1-3.

> See *Ep.* 223.5: Courtonne, 3: 14; also *C. Eun.* 1.1: 497A ff. That this work was written when Basil was presbyter, cf. *C. Eun.* 1.5: 517B with *Proem. in reg. fus.* 4: 900C.

Council of Lampsacus. Annulment of all the decisions of the Council of Constantinople; legitimation of the *homoiousios*.

> Autumn: Maran, *Vita*, 10.5-6; or 365: Gribomont, "Les succès," 31.

For the Young on How They Might Derive Profit from Hellenic Literature ("De legendis libris gentilium").

> In 364 : Schucan, *Das Nachleben*, 38;[21] during the academic year

---

[20] J. Bernardi, *La prédication des Pères cappadociens. Le prédicateur et son auditoire* (Paris, 1968).

[21] L. Schucan, *Das Nachleben von Basilius Magnus "Ad adolescentes." Ein Beitrag zur Geschichte des christlichen Humanismus* (Geneva, 1973).

362/363: Moffatt, "The Occasion," 83-86,[22] believing that Basil was ordained presbyter in 362.

365

Epistles 20 and *21* (to Leontius the Sophist).

On the impending visit of Valens to Caesarea (October), Eusebius decides to recall Basil.

> Re October: Piganiol, *L'empire chrétien,* 172.[23] Maran, *Vita,* 9.7; Gallay, *La vie,* 85; see ibid., 85-87 for Gregory's part in bringing Basil over.

From now on, until Eusebius' death in 370, Basil will remain closely associated with him, becoming the actual leader of the church of Caesarea.

A work from Basil's presbyterate composed over a long period is his *Small Asceticon.*

> See *Scholion* 2 in Gribomont, *Histoire,* 152;[24] for some of the other early references see Aubineau, *Grég. de Nysse,* 79, n. 6.

Placed between 365 and 370 should also be, according to Bessières, the following letters from Basil's correspondence with Libanius: *Epistles 335-342, 344* and *346.*

> Bessières, *La tradition,* 168-173.[25]

Sometime during this period fall also *Epistles 7* and *19* (to Gregory of Nazianzus), *35* (without address), *46* (to a fallen virgin), *15* (to Arcadius, *comes rei privatae*; sometime between 364 and 373).

366

Pope Liberius dies (24 September). Damasus wins his succession.

368

Epistle 22 (without address; the title to be preferred is that of the codex Marcianus, 11th century: Κανὼν ἀκριβῆς τῆς κατὰ τὸ εὐαγγέλιον τοῦ Χριστοῦ ἀσκητικῆς πολιτείας).

Epistle 23 (to a solitary).

> These letters are placed by Gribomont, "In t. 32," 7,[26] "after 368."

---

[22] A. Moffatt, "The Occasion of St. Basil's *Address to Young Men,*" *Antichton* 4 (1972) 74-86.

[23] A. Piganiol, *L'empire chrétien (325-395),* 2nd ed. (Paris, 1972).

[24] J. Gribomont, *Histoire du texte des Ascétiques de s. Basile* (Louvain, 1953).

[25] M. Bessières, *La tradition manuscrite de la correspondance de saint Basile* (Oxford, 1923).

[26] J. Gribomont, "In tomos 29, 30, 31, 32 PG ad editionem operum S. Basilii Magni introductio," *S. Basilii Magni Opera omnia* (rpt. edition, Turnhout, 1959).

Epistles 24 (to Athanasius, father of Athanasius bishop of Ancyra), *25* (to Athanasius, bishop of Ancyra), *26* (to Caesarius, brother of Gregory of Nazianzus).

Epistle 27 (to Eusebius, bishop of Samosata).

> Autumn: Loofs, *Eustathius*, 50.[27]

Homily on Psalm 114.

> Bernardi, *Prédication*, 26.

Famine in Cappadocia. Basil organizes a programme of relief.

369

Epistle 31 (to Eusebius of Samosata).

> Spring: Loofs, *Eustathius*, 50.

Homily 9 ("Quod Deus non est auctor malorum").

> Spring: Bernardi, *Prédication*, 60.

Homily 6 ("In destruam").

> End of spring or beginning of summer: Bernardi, *Prédication*, 61.

Homilies 7 ("In divites"), and *8* ("In famem").

> Both in summer: Bernardi, *Prédication*, 61; see also Teja, *Organización*, 151.[28]

Epistle 34 (to Eusebius of Samosata).

> Autumn: Loofs, *Eustathius*, 50.

Epistles 32 (to Sophronius the Master), *33* (to Aburgius).

370

Death of Eusebius, bishop of Caesarea (June); Basil elected his successor (September).

> Maran, *Vita*, 13.4.

Epistles 53 and *54* (to the chorepiscopi), *55* (to Gregory, the presbyter), *56* (to Pergamius), *52* (to the canonicae).

371

Homily 13 ("In baptisma").

> Probably 6 January: Bernardi, *Prédication*, 68.

Homily 1-2 ("De ieiunio").

> Lent: Bernardi, *Prédication*, 72.

---

[27] F. Loofs, *Eustathius von Sebaste und die Chronologie der Basiliusbriefe* (Halle, 1898).

[28] R. Teja, *Organización económica y social de Capadocia en el siglo IV según los Padres Capadocios* (Salamanca, 1974).

Epistles 28 (consolatory to the church of Neocaesarea), *29* (consolatory to the church of Ancyra).

> Both in the spring: Loofs, *Eustathius*, 50.

Epistles 48 (to Eusebius of Samosata), *49* (to Arcadius the bishop), *36* (without address), *37* (without address), *57* (to Meletius of Antioch), *58* (to Gregory his brother), *59* and *60* (to Gregory his uncle).

Epistle 79 (to Eustathius of Sebaste).

> Schwartz, "Zur Kirchengeschichte," 169.[29]

Death of Emmelia, mother of Basil.

Epistle 30 (to Eusebius of Samosata).

> June: Loofs, *Eustathius*, 50.

Epistles 61 (to Athanasius of Alexandria), *62* (consolatory to the church of Parnassus), *63* (to the governor of Neocaesarea), *64* (to Hesychius).

Epistle 66 (to Athanasius of Alexandria).

> "Before Epistle 65": Loofs, *Eustathius*, 42-46; Lietzmann, *Apollinaris*, 52.[30]

Epistle 68 (to Meletius of Antioch).

Epistles 69 and *67* (to Athanasius of Alexandria).

> In that order: Loofs, *Eustathius*, 42; Lietzmann, *Apollinaris*, 51; Richard, "S. Basile," 187.[31]

Epistles 70 (without address; to Damasus of Rome?), *71* (to Gregory of Nazianzus; after 7 September), *72* (to Hesychius), *73* (to Callisthenes).

Basil makes visitation tour of his churches (October/November).

> Maran, *Vita*, 19.3.

After receiving news of the planned division of Cappadocia, returns to Caesarea.

Epistles 74 (to Martinianus), *75* (to Aburgius), *76* (to Sophronius the Master), *77* (about Therasius), *78* (on behalf of Elpidius).

Basil threatened by Arian bishops. Meets Modestus.

Epistle 80 (to Athanasius of Alexandria).

---

[29] E. Schwartz, "Zur Kirchengeschichte des vierten Jahrhunderts," *ZNW* 34 (1935) 129-213.

[30] H. Lietzmann, *Apollinaris von Laodicea und seine Schule* (Tübingen, 1904; reprinted Hildesheim-New York, 1970).

[31] M. Richard, "S. Basile et la mission du diacre Sabinus," *AB* 67 (1949) 170-202.

Homilies on Psalm 14, 1 and *2.*

> "Before 372": Bernardi, *Prédication,* 25.

Failure of the first negotiation with the West.

> See above, p. 108.

372

The Emperor Valens attends at Caesarea the liturgy on the Epiphany of the Lord, 6 January.

> Hauser-Meury, *Prosopographie,* 41, n. 47.[32]

Interviews between Basil and Valens. The emperor grants demesne lands for Basil's hospital (*Ptochotrophium*). Despite Basil's protests, during the same year he proceeds with the division of the province into Cappadocia Prima and Secunda.

> On this see Jones, *Cities,* 182-185,[33] and Teja, *Organización,* 196-201.

Epistle 65 (to Atarbius of Neocaesarea).

> Perhaps later in the year; "before 373": Maran, *Vita,* 16.5.

Epistle 82 (to Athanasius of Alexandria).

During the spring Basil visits Eusebius of Samosata.

Feud with Anthimus who claims the metropolitan dignity at Tyana, the new capital of Cappadocia Secunda. Basil forces Gregory of Nazianzus to accept ordination as bishop of Sasima; Gregory, Basil's brother, is created bishop of Nyssa. Gregory of Nazianzus flees; breach of friendship with Basil.

Lent: Second negotiation with the West (see above, p. 109 f.).

Draft of *Epistle 92.*

> Actually *Epistle 242*: Loofs, *Eustathius,* 41, 43; Lietzmann, *Apollinaris,* 52; Schwartz, "Zur Kirchengeschichte," 129.

Sabinus bearer of the letters to the Westerners (spring): *Epistles 90* (to the bishops of the West), *91* (to Valerianus of Illyricum), *92* (to the Italians and Gauls), *89* (to Meletius of Antioch).

> In that order: Loofs, *Eustathius,* 42-46; Lietzmann, *Apollinaris,* 52; Richard, "S. Basile," 189-197. Schwartz, "Zur Kirchengeschichte," 180-181, however, places all these letters in 373.

Homily 10 ("De ira").

> Bernardi, *Prédication,* 72-73.

---

[32] M. M. Hauser-Meury, *Prosopographie zu den Schriften Gregors von Nazianz* (Bonn, 1960).

[33] A. H. M. Jones, *The Cities of the Eastern Roman Provinces,* 2nd ed. (Oxford, 1971).

Homily 14 ("In ebriosos").

    Easter?: Bernardi, *Prédication*, 74-76.

Epistles 83 (to a magistrate), *84* (to the president), *85* (against taking oaths), *86* (to the governor), *87* (without address), *88* (about exaction of taxes).

Homily 21 ("Quod rebus mundanis").

    July: Bernardi, *Prédication*, 76; Gribomont, "Intr. 31," 6.

Homilies 4 ("De gratiarum actione") and *5* ("In Julittam").

    Both "*ca.* 372": Bernardi, *Prédication*, 80.

Homily 16 ("In verbum").

    "Before *Hom.* 15": Bernardi, *Prédication*, 87.

Homily 15 ("De fide").

    7 September?: Bernardi, *Prédication*, 86.

Epistles 93 (to Caesaria, concerning communion), *94* (to Elias, governor of Cappadocia), *95* (to Eusebius of Samosata), *96* (to Sophronius the master), *97* (to the senate of Tyana), *104* (to the prefect Modestus), *106* (to a soldier), *107* (to the widow Julitta), *108* (to the guardians of the heirs of Julitta), *109* (to the Count Helladius), *110* (to the prefect Modestus), *111* (to the same), *112* (to Andronicus, a general), *113* (to the presbyters of Tarsus), *114* (to Cyriacus at Tarsus), *115* (to the heretic Simplicia), *116* (to Firminius), *118* (to Jovinus, bishop of Perrha), *119* (to Eustathius of Sebaste).

Epistle 105 (to the deaconesses, the daughters of Count Terentius).

    Autumn: Loofs, *Eustathius*, 33; or 373: Hauschild, *Briefe*, 158.[34]

Epistle 99 (to Count Terentius).

    End of the year: all authors except Hauschild, *Briefe*, 156: August 373.

Epistle 150 (to Amphilochius).

    Hauschild, *Briefe*, 167; or 373: ibid.

373

Homily on Psalm 33.

    "After 372": Bernardi, *Prédication*, 27.

Homily 18 ("In Gordium").

    Either 3 January, or in the spring: Bernardi, *Prédication*, 80.

Homily 19 (In xl. martyres").

    Bernardi, *Prédication*, 85.

---

[34] W. D. Hauschild, *Basilius von Caesarea, Briefe*, 2 (Stuttgart, 1973).

Homily 23 ("In Mamantem").

> Bernardi, *Prédication*, 85.

Failure of the second negotiation (see above, p. 109 f.). Death of Athanasius of Alexandria (2 May).

June: Basil by imperial commission travels to the kingdom of Armenia to appoint new bishops there. At Sebaste meets for two days with Eustathius of Sebaste who consents to the signing of the Nicene formula. Difficulties with Theodotus of Nicopolis because of Basil's friendship with Eustathius.

> For the dating of these events see Hauschild, *Briefe*, 13; Dörries, *De Spiritu Sancto, passim*,[35] and Gribomont, "Intr. 32," 2, place them in 372.

Epistles 102 and *103* (to the people of Satala).

> June: Loofs, *Eustathius*, 29-30, 46; autumn of 373 or spring of 374: Hauschild, *Briefe*, 158.

Epistle 98 (to Eusebius of Samosata).

> End of June: Hauschild, *Briefe*, 155.

Epistle 128 (to Eusebius of Samosata).

> Summer: Hauschild, *Briefe*, 163.

Epistle 133 (to Peter of Alexandria).

> Summer: Hauschild, *Briefe*, 165.

Epistle 101 (consolatory).

> Late summer: Hauschild, *Briefe*, 157.

Epistles 100 and *127* (to Eusebius of Samosata).

> August: Hauschild, *Briefe*, 157.

Epistle 125 (transcript of the formula signed by Eustathius).

> August: Hauschild, *Briefe*, 162.

Epistles 123 (to the monk Urbicius), *124* (to Theodorus), *134* (to the presbyter Paeonius), *135* (to Diodorus of Tarsus), *137* (to Antipater appointed governor of Cappadocia), *138* (to Eusebius of Samosata), *139* (to the Alexandrians suffering persecution), *140* (to the church of Antioch).

> All these letters, autumn: Hauschild, *Briefe*, 165.

Epistles 141 (to Eusebius of Samosata), *142* (to the prefect's accountant on tax exemptions for hospitals), *143* (to an accoutant), *144* (to the prefect's officer), *145* (to Eusebius of Samosata).

---

[35] H. Dörries, *De Spiritu Sancto, Der Beitrag des Basilius zum Abschluss des Trinitarischen Dogmas* (Göttingen, 1956).

These letters, September/October: Hauschild, *Briefe*, 167.

Epistles 146 (to Antiochus), *147* (to Aburgius), *148* and *149* (to Trajan), *151* (to Eustathius, the physician), *152* (to Victor, the commander), *153* (to Victor, the ex-consul), *154* (to Ascholius of Salonika), *155* (in the case of a trainer).

Epistle 161 (on the ordination of Amphilochius as bishop of Iconium).
Winter 373/374: Hauschild, *Briefe*, 169.

374

Epistles 156 (to the presbyter Evagrius), *157* and *158* (to Antiochus).
All three from the beginning of the year: Hauschild, *Briefe*, 168-169.

Epistle 159 (to Eupaterius and his daughter).
Beginning of the year: Hauschild, *Briefe*, 169; or from 375: ibid.

Epistle 136 (to Eusebius of Samosata).
Spring: Hauschild, *Briefe*, 165.

Epistles 162 (to Eusebius of Samosata), *163* (to Count Jovinus), *164* (to Ascholius), *165* (to Soranus, duke of Scythia), *168* (to Antiochus), *172* (to Sophronius, the bishop), *173* (to Theodora the canoness), *174* (to a widow), *175* (to Count Magnenianus), *176* (to Amphilochius of Iconium), *177* (to Sophronius the master), *178* (to Aburgius), *179* (to Arintheius), *180* (to the master Sophronius, on behalf of Eumathius), *181* (to Otreius, bishop of Melitene), *182* (to the presbyters of Samosata), *183* (to the senate of Samosata), *184* (to Eustathius of Himmeria), *185* (to Theodotus of Beroea), *186* (to the governor Antipater), *188* (to Amphilochius of Iconium concerning the canons), *190* (to Amphilochius of Iconium), *191* (to a bishop), *192* (to Sophronius the master).

Homily on Psalm 28.
"Before 375": Bernardi, *Prédication*, 25.

Eusebius of Samosata is sent into exile; also Barses of Edessa, and others.
Summer: Hauschild, *Briefe*, 171.

Death of Gregory Nazianzenus, father of Gregory of Nazianzus. Death of Auxentius and consecration of Ambrosius as bishop of Milan (7 December).
Duchesne, *History*, 2: 369.[36] In a letter of 1 November 1976 Hauschild has agreed that *Epistle 197* should be placed in 375 and not in 374 as in his *Briefe*, 177.

---

[36] L. Duchesne, *The Early History of the Christian Church* (London, 1909-1924).

375

Death of Valentinian. Gratian and Valentinian II, emperors of the West. Synod of Illyria, and *Letter to the Orientals.* Semi-Arian Council of Cyzicus. Demosthenes, vicar of Pontus, harasses the orthodox. Gregory of Nyssa deposed.

Homily on Psalm 32.

> "*Ca.* 375": Bernardi, *Prédication*, 27-28.

Homilies on Psalms 33 and *45.*

Epistles 120 (to Meletius of Antioch), *121* (to Theodotus of Nicopolis), *122* (to Poemenius of Satala), *129* (to Meletius of Antioch), *130* (to Theodotus of Nicopolis), *131* (to Olympius), *132* (to Abramius of Batnae).

> All these letters at the beginning of the year: Hauschild, *Briefe*, 161; spring: Loofs, *Eustathius*, 29-30; Lietzmann, *Apollinaris*, 50; Schwartz, "Zur Kirchengeschichte," 177; Dörries, *De Spiritu Sancto*, 107.

Epistle 198 (to Eusebius of Samosata).

> Beginning of the year: Schwartz, "Zur Kirchengeschichte," 184, and others.

Epistle 126 (to Atarbius of Neocaesarea).

> Summer: Hauschild, *Briefe*, 163 and 16 ff.

Epistle 160 (to Diodorus of Tarsus).

> Hauschild, *Briefe*, 169.

Epistles 193 (to Meletius the physician), *194* (to Zoilus), *195* (to Euphronius of Colonia), *196* (to Aburgius), *197* (to Ambrosius of Milan), *199* (to Amphilochius of Iconium concerning the canons), *200, 201* and *202* (to Amphilochius of Iconium), *203* (to the bishops of the sea coast), *204* (to the Neocaesareans), *205* and *206* (to Elpidius the bishop), *207* (to the clergy of Neocaesarea), *208* (to Eulancius), *209* (without address), *210* (to the notables of Neocaesarea), *211* (to Olympius), *213* (without address), *214* (to Count Terentius), *215* (to the presbyter Dorotheus), *216* (to Meletius of Antioch), *217* (to Amphilochius of Iconium on the canons), *218* (to Amphilochius of Iconium), *219* (to the clergy of Samosata), *220* and *221* (to the Beroeans), *222* (to the people of Chalcis), *223* (against Eustathius of Sebaste), *224* (to the presbyter Genethlius), *225* (to Demosthenes, the vicar of Pontus, as from the synod of bishops), *226* (to the ascetics under him), *227* (consolatory to the clergy of Nicopolis), *228* (to the magistrates of Colonia), *229* (to the clergy of Nicopolis), *230* (to the magistrates of Nicopolis), *231* (to Amphilochius of

Iconium), *253* (to the presbyters of Antioch), *254* (to Pelagius of Laodicea), *255* (to Vitus of Carrae), *256* (to the persecuted presbyters, deacons and ascetics).

De Spiritu Sancto. The first draft of ch. 10-27 comes probably from the minutes of the two-day talk held at Sebaste with Eustathius of Sebaste in June 372 or 373. Ch. 1-9 and 28-30 were added after 9 September 374. The then completed treatise was sent to Amphilochius of Iconium by the end of 375.

> See Dörries, *De Spiritu Sancto, passim*. See *Ep.* 231: Courtonne, 3: 37.

376

Epistle 212 (to Hilarius).

> Hauschild, *Briefe*, 182.

Epistles 232-236 (to Amphilochius of Iconium), *237* (to Eusebius of Samosata), *238* and *240* (to the presbyters of Nicopolis).

Epistle 239 (to Eusebius of Samosata).

> Middle of the year: Lietzmann, *Apollinaris*, 48; 377: Schwartz, "Zur Kirchengeschichte," 185-186.

Epistle 241 (to Eusebius of Samosata).

Third mission to the West through Sanctissimus and Dorotheus carriers of *Epistle 243* (see above, 109 ff.).

Epistles 244 (to Patrophilus of Aegea), *245* (to Theophilus the bishop), *246* and *247* (to the Nicopolitans), *248* (to Amphilochius of Iconium), *249* (without address: commendatory), *250* (to Patrophilus of Aegea), *251* (to the people of Evaesae), *252* (to the bishops of the Pontic diocese), *257* (to the monks harassed by the Arians).

Epistle 258 (to Epiphanius the bishop).

> Lietzmann, *Apollinaris*, 56; Dörries, *De Spiritu Sancto*, 116.

Epistle 51 (to Bishop Bosporius).

> Dörries, *De Spiritu Sancto*, 115.

Synod of Iconium. Against the Pneumatomachi under the presidency of Amphilochius whose "Synodic" heavily draws upon Basil's treatise, *On the Holy Spirit*.

Hypotyposis ("outline," "sketch") *of the Ascetic Life*. A collection of ascetic treatises prepared by Basil himself for a Pontic community of ascetics.

> Gribomont, "In tomum 31," 9. This edition of collected works included the *Moralia* with its two prefaces, the *De judicio* and the *De fide*, and the *Great Asceticon* (the *Longer* and *Shorter Interrogations* with their prefaces): see *Proem. ad hyp.*: 1512B-D; Gribomont, *Histoire*, 280-

282. There are strong internal and external indications that each of these works has been written over a period of some ten to fifteen years, sometime between 361 and 376, or perhaps even longer, 360 to 377. This is true of the *Great Asceticon* which constitutes a substantial revision of the *Small Asceticon* (above, 143; for the additions see Gribomont, *Histoire*, 151 ff., and 252 ff.). I believe that also the *Moralia* with its present two prefaces and eighty *Moral Rules* is a work of accretion. The first draft was made by Basil, with the aid of Gregory of Nazianzus, in the early 360s (see above, 141). No copy of this first draft or edition has survived (Gribomont, "Les succès," 32, n. 33). The second revision was included in *Epistle 22*, written in 368/369 to a Pontic community. In it Basil stated: "Many things are set forth by inspired Scripture as binding upon all who are anxious to please God. But, for the present, I feel I need only send you a brief memorandum concerning the questions which have recently been raised among you, so far as I have learned from inspired Scripture itself. I shall leave behind me instructions on each point, easily understood, for the information of those with leisure to study them; who in their turn will be able to inform others" (Courtonne, 1: 52). After becoming bishop of Caesarea in 370, Basil could not find time to honour his promise. He was pressured to do so apparently after his breach with Eustathius of Sebaste, 372-375. Through their leaders, some of the ascetics living in Pontus and neighbouring Armenia requested from Basil a statement of his faith as a condition for remaining in communion with him after he broke off with their common teacher Eustathius. It was not enough for Basil to write *Epistle 226* and to send a representative, the presbyter Meletius. The ascetics demanded a more tangible proof of his orthodoxy and attachment to the Scriptural teaching. Through his *Hypotyposis*, and notably the *Moralia*, Basil (1) fulfills a longstanding promise: "Let us now strive to fulfil ... our promise concerning the *Moralia*. ... My first wish was to append to the *Rules* the passages of the Old Testament. ... But since the need was so urgent, and the brethren in Christ now more eagerly demanded from us our longstanding promise," etc. (ἀπαιτησάντων ἡμᾶς τὰ πάλαι ἐπηγγελμένα: *De fide*, 6: 692A-B). Basil (2), although reluctant to produce new symbols of faith (see *Epistles 140.2* and *175*), accedes to the wishes of his ascetics and submits to them a statement of his faith—a kind of "private creed" (*De fide*, 4: 685A ff.). It should be noted that in this confession Basil avoids technical terms and distinctions, doubtlessly to please his conservative audience. He also defines the Christian ethos almost exclusively in excerpts from Scripture, although without excluding arguments and traditions consistent with Scripture (*Reg. mor.* 70.6: 821C; 26.2: 745A). Some authors while admitting that the second preface to the *Moralia* could have been written either entirely or most of it in the 370s, had thought that the *De judicio* was a work of Basil's

early manhood, that is, early 360 (Maran against Tillemont; Clarke, Gribomont, and others). The evidence for this chronology was taken mainly from the words νῦν ... τῶν Ἀνομοίων ἐπιφυέντων (De jud., 1: 653ʙ), which Maran translates "exortis Anomoeis, nunc," and Gribomont "maintenant que se répandent les Anoméens" ("Les succès," 32, n. 33). However, ἐπιφυέντων is not a present participle (Gribomont, ibid.), but a second aorist passive. As such it only indicates the harshness without specifying the time of the Anomoean attack. Because the leading verb of the sentence is ἐθεώρουν, an imperfect, νῦν means "then" (time of the Anomoean onslaught) not "now" (time of composition of the De judicio; see our translation above, p. 105). It should further be noted that the main theme of Basil's discourse was the bitter antagonism developed among church leaders, not the upstart Anomoeans; the latter he adduced only as an aggravating circumstance: the church leaders were fighting each other at a time when the Anomoeans were pressing hard on the orthodox. (As a parallel see the last two chapters of the De Spiritu Sancto.) The time of Anomoean offensive referred to in the text could well have been 357-361. However, from the context it cannot be inferred that Basil was writing when that event was taking place, that is, between the years 357 and 361. He was probably writing sometime later and, as I believe, during his episcopate, close to 375-376. (1) It is readily assumed that in the De judicio 1-3 Basil speaks as a novice, "as yet without an established position" (Clarke, Ascetic Works, 15)[37] who feels the need to apologize in front of an unknown audience (Gribomont, Histoire, 287). However, a very similar style is used by Basil in Ep. 223.2-5: Courtonne, 3: 10 ff., where he also speaks of his childhood and travels. Epistle 223 is certainly from 375. (2) Far from showing timidity and being apologetic, through the use of such a literary device Basil intends to dispel any misunderstanding concerning his orthodoxy (see in this regard Epistles 204 and 210 to the Neocaesareans). The only conclusion that can be drawn is that he is writing his De judicio to a community of ascetics somewhat baffled by his falling out with Eustathius of Sebaste (see also Ep. 244.1: Courtonne, 3: 74). (3) In none of his extant writings that can be placed before 370 does Basil speak so openly of the evils of the church and the inability of its leaders to come to an agreement, "both in their relations with one another and their views about the divine Scripture," as he does in the De judicio (above quotation from De jud., 1: 653ʙ; see as parallels Hom. 23.4: 596ᴄ; Epp. 66, 69, 80, 82, 90, 92, etc.). If we now turn from the prefaces to the work Moralia itself, in many of its Rules we find such a tremendous theological insight and maturity of thought that they can be

[37] W. K. L. Clarke, trans., The Ascetic Works of Saint Basil (London, 1925).

considered as coming from the same time as the *De Spiritu Sancto*, and not just the third book *Against Eunomius* (cf. e.g. *Reg. mor.* 80 with *De sp. s.*, chapter 15). Also we may add that it is at the end of his life that Basil more than ever turned Scriptureward (see, for instance, the homilies on the *Hexaemeron* placed now in 378, and which embody Basil's attempt similar to that in the *Moralia* to subsume under the Scriptural *logos* all human activities, not only practical behaviour but also theoretical knowledge). If the authenticity of the *De baptismo* is to be accepted, this work should also be dated from Basil's episcopate. It would, however, have to be posterior to the *Moralia*, 376-378. (On the authenticity of the *De baptismo*, see Gribomont, *Histoire*, 306-308; idem, "In tomum 31," 12; and now, U. Neri, *Basilio de Cesarea*.[38] For the opinion of Hauschild, *Die Pneumatomachen*, 217 ff., that this would be a work of Eustathius of Sebaste, see A. M. Ritter in *ZK* 80 [1969] 397-406. See also A. J. M. Davids, "On Ps.-Basil, *De baptismo*," *SP* 16 [Berlin, 1976] 302-306.)

377

(Between 368 and 377): *Homilies on Psalm 7, 29, 44, 59, 61*, and *115*.

Epistles 259 (to the monks Palladius and Innocent), *260* (to Optimus the bishop), *261* (to the Sozopolitans), *262* (to the monk Urbicius).

Fourth mission to the West (see above, p. 111 ff.).

Epistles 263 (to the Westerners), *264* (to Barses of Edessa, in exile), *265* (to the Egyptian bishops in exile).

> All at the beginning of the year: Lietzmann, *Apollinaris*, 62; summer: Loofs, *Eustathius*, 39. The fourth negotiation, however, took place in the spring: Duchesne, *History*, 2: 328).

Epistles 267 (to Barses of Edessa, in exile), *268* (to Eusebius of Samosata, in exile), *269* (to the wife of Arintheus, the general, consolatory), *270* (without address, concerning raptus).

Epistle 266 (to Peter of Alexandria).

> End of the year: Lietzmann, *Apollinaris*, 62; beginning of 378: Loofs, *Eustathius*, 48.

378

Homilies on the Hexaemeron 1-11

> *1-9* between Monday 12 March and Friday 16 March: Bernardi, *Prédication*, 47; *Homilies 10-11* were probably only delivered, or just sketched out. After Basil's death, his notes would have been edited by a "modest" secretary: see Hörner, *Auctorum*, vii-viii,[39] and Gribomont,

---

[38] U. Neri, *Basilio di Cesarea, Il battesimo* (Brescia, 1976).

[39] H. Hörner, ed., *Auctorum incertorum, vulgo Basilii vel Gregorii Nysseni, sermones de creatione hominis, sermo de paradiso* (Leiden, 1972).

"Les succès," 38-39. See also for their authenticity the edition of A. Smets and M. van Esbroeck. I consider unwarranted the scepticism of both E. Amand de Mendieta in *JThS* 22 (1971) 240-242; *BZ* 66 (1973) 91-95, now also in *Zetesis. Festschrift E. de Strycker* (Antwerp, 1974), pp. 695-716; and E. Gallicet in *Atti della Accademia delle Scienze di Torino* 109 (1975) 319-342.

Homily 24 ("Adversus Sabellianos, et Arium et Anomoeos").
> After the death of Valens, 9 August: Bernardi, *Prédication*, 88; after 372: Dörries, *De Spiritu Sancto*, 94-97.

Eusebius of Samosata and Meletius of Antioch return from exile.

Epistles written in the last years of Basil's life, or of uncertain date: *271-320, 322-334.*

Homilies 26 ("In Lacizis"), *27* ("In Christi generationem"), *29* ("Adversus eos qui per calumniam dicunt dici a nobis tres deos").

379

1 January: death of Basil at Caesarea of Cappadocia.

Theodosius becomes Augustus.

381

Council of Constantinople: proclamation of the *homoousion* of the Holy Spirit, a crowning of Basil's lifelong efforts. Condemnation of the Anomoeans, Arians, Pneumatomachi, Sabellians, Marcellians, Photinians, and Apollinarians.
> See Dörries, *De Spiritu Sancto, passim*; Ritter, *Das Konzil*,[40] *passim.*

382

1 January: Gregory of Nazianzus delivers his eulogy of Basil *(Oration 43)* at Caesarea.
> Gallay, *La vie*, 215. On the subsequent cult, the relics and iconography of Basil, see Stiernon, "Basilio il Grande," 923-944.[41]

ii Spurious or Dubious Works of Basil of Caesarea

The following works have been set aside, at least as primary sources, in this study of Basil's ecclesial consciousness because of dubious authenticity, or because modern scholarship has proved them to be spurious. For the

[40] A. M. Ritter, *Das Konzil von Konstantinopel und sein Symbol* (Göttingen, 1965).
[41] D. Stiernon, "Basilio il Grande, Vita, opere, culto, reliquie, iconografia," *Bibliotheca Sanctorum* (Rome, 1962), 2: 910-944.

claims and counter-claims of scholars before 1959, see the introductions of
Gribomont to PG 29, 31, 32, and of the monks of Chevetogne to PG 30.
For the most recent scholarship up to 1974 (only the works that appeared
after that year will be cited below) and some of the other works ascribed to
Basil and not found in Migne, see M. Geerard, *Clavis Patrum graecorum*
(Turnhout, 1974), vol. 2, nos. 2835-3005. The dubious or spurious works
of Basil are reviewed below in the order they occupy in PG 29-32.

Volume 29

Contra Eunomium 4-5.
>   See Geerard, no. 2837, and now E. Cavalcanti, "'Excerpta'," in the
>   Bibliography.

Volume 30

Homilia in Psalmum 28, 37 and *132.*

Enarratio in prophetam Isaiam (Is 1-16).
>   This is certainly the work of a Cappadocian of the fourth century.

Liber de vera Virginitatis integritate ad Letoium, Melitensem episcopum.

Sermo de contubernalibus.

Rationes syllogisticae contra Arianos.
>   A compilation from Basil's authentic works prepared by Francisco
>   Torres (16th cent.).

*Expositio SS. PP. NN. Magni Basilii et Gregorii theologi De sancta et ortho-
doxa fide.*

Fragmentum homiliae de commemoratione Beatae Mariae Virginis. ...

Eunomii impii Apologetica.
>   Eunomius of Cyzicus.

Eustathii in Hexaemeron S. Basilii Metaphrasis Libri IX.
>   Latin translation of the first nine *Homilies of the Hexaemeron*; see the
>   critical edition of E. Amand de Mendieta and S. Y. Rudberg, *Eustathius,
>   ancienne version latine des neuf homélies sur l'Hexaéméron de Basile de
>   Césarée* (Berlin, 1958).

Volume 31

Homilies 17 ("In Barlaam"), *25* ("De Spiritu Sancto"), *28* ("De poeni-
tentia"), *30* ("De libero arbitrio"), *31* ("In Prov 4.4: Ne dederis som-
num"), *32* ("De ieiunio 3"), *33* ("De perfectione vitae monasticae"),
34 ("De misericordia et iudicio"), *35* ("Consolatoria ad aegrotum").

Sermones ascetici: "Praevia institutio"; "De renuntiatione saeculi"; "De
ascetica disciplina"; "Sermo asceticus"; "Prologus asceticus".

Constitutiones asceticae.

> Some of the *Epitimia* are probably authentic; see Gribomont, *Histoire*, 294-297, 320-321.

De consolatione in adversis.

De laude vitae solitariae.

Admonitio ad filium spiritualem.

Volume 32

Epistles 8, 10, 16.

Epistle 38.

> See in the Bibliography, P. J. Fedwick, R. Hübner, and Ch. von Schönborn.

Epistles 39-41.

Epistles 42-45.

> See Geerard, no. 2900.

Epistles 47, 50, 81, 166-167, 169-171, 189, 197.2, 321, 347-359, 360, 365-368.

Appendix B

The Pachomian and
the Eustathian Type of Asceticism

In the fourth century Pachomius was a typical representative of the more moderate version of the so-called desert-type of asceticism, which later became universally known under the name of monasticism.[1] Pachomius built his monasteries, it is true, within the boundaries of the local ecclesial communities. From the total isolationism enforced by Antony, he brought the anchorites closer to the Christian world. And yet Pachomius' foundations were to thrive for the most part, not *within* the confines but on *the margin and outskirts* of the local church organizations. Pachomian cenobia indeed constituted communions of their own outside the range and even independent of the episcopal authority, with the abbot as their foremost leader and spiritual father. There was little or no interest shown on the part of the monks in becoming involved in the undertakings of the church living in the world, or in taking part in the assemblies for public worship and instructions from the bishops. The few times the monks of

---

[1] A bibliography on Pachomius can be found in J. Quasten, *Patrología* (Madrid, 1962), 2: 161-166. See also P. Tamburrino, "Die Beziehung 'Monasterium' - 'Kirche' im frühen pachomianischen Mönchtum," *Erbe und Auftrage* 43 (1967) 5-21. Of great importance are the following studies of M. M. Van Molle, "Essai de classement chronologique des premières règles de vie commune connue en chrétienté," *VSSt* 21 (1968) 108-127; "Confrontation entre les règles et la littérature Pachômienne postérieure," *VSSt* 21 (1968) 394-424; "Aux origines de la vie communautaire chrétienne, quelques équivoques déterminantes pour l'avenir," *VSSt* 22 (1969) 101-121; "Vie commune et obéissance d'après les institutions premières de Pachôme et Basile," *VSSt* 23 (1970) 196-225 (the latter study renders obsolete some of the opinions expressed by E. Amand de Mendieta in "Le système cénobitique basilien comparé au système cénobitique pachômien," *RHR* 152 [1957] 31-80). See finally A. Veilleux, "La théologie de l'abbatiat cénobitique et ses implications liturgiques," *VSSt* 21 (1968) 351-393 (also in English, without some subdivisions, in *Monastic Studies* 6 [1968] 3-45). On Antony see the excellent study of J. Gribomont, "Antonio l'eremita, santo," in *DIP* (1974), 1: 700-703. On Egyptian and Palestinian monasticism in general see D. J. Chitty, *The Desert a City* (Oxford, 1966).

Nitria and Thebaida descended to Alexandria were for other than missionary purposes. Their journeys were undertaken not in order to meet the spiritual needs of their fellowmen struggling in the world—rather secular Christians would have to go to the monasteries in search of guidance—but solely for periodic business transactions.[2] The monastic rules moreover forbade their followers to accept and exercise pastoral responsibilities.[3] Whereas we are not quite sure if Antony in his twenty years of seclusion was ever able to receive the Eucharist, Pachomius advised communion twice a week, on Saturday and Sunday.[4] Also, common prayers and meetings were held periodically. Nonetheless, in its whole outlook on Christian righteousness and holiness, the monks made only insignificant use of the Bible. It is true they often memorized whole books but

> this learning by heart was nothing more than a superficial accomplishment, ascetic in character. ... This mechanical memorization did not penetrate the heart; it gave indeed only the faintest Biblical tinge to the world of ideas in which the monks lived. A study of the *Sayings of the Fathers* reveals an astonishing paucity of citations from the Bible, and even these are quoted for their value as admonitions to the practice of asceticism.[5]

When Father Amun was asked by a disciple whether they were to use sayings from the Bible, he replied, "It is preferable to use the *Sayings of the Fathers* and not passages from the Bible; it is very dangerous to quote the Bible."[6]

This characterization of the desert-type asceticism as promoted by Pachomius and adopted especially by the monks is limited to the ecclesial viewpoint. There were undoubtedly values inherent in such a philosophy of life and numerous saints came from the ranks of monks. However, throughout all the external changes—from a life in total seclusion to a life in the company of other like-minded men but aloof from society—monastic

[2] See H. Lietzmann, *History of the Early Church* (Cleveland, 1961), 3: 149: "The monasteries developed into factories producing woven goods of every kind, and carried on a steady trade with the capital in the Delta. If an abbot with well-developed business instincts was at the head of the monastery, vessels would be built on his wharves, and the profits would go to the purchase of additional farm-lands and forests. Granted that the more rigorous-minded brethren would voice their protests if commerce of this kind went beyond certain limits, nevertheless, in course of time, all the monasteries had adapted themselves in one way or another to the economic necessities of the situation." See also ibid., p. 144.

[3] Cf. John Cassian: "Omnimodis monachum fugere debere mulieres et episcopos" (*Instituta*, 11.18: CSEL [1888], 17.1: 203).

[4] On the first cf. L. Duchesne, *The Early History of the Christian Church* (London, 1912), 2: 390; W. K. L. Clarke, *St. Basil the Great. A Study in Monasticism* (Cambridge, 1913), p. 35, on the second.

[5] Lietzmann, *History*, 3: 153.

[6] Ibid., p. 154.

asceticism undeniably remained isolated, both in its outlook and in its form, from the concern and religious awareness of the vast majority of Christians.[7]

Somewhat different in its orientation was the ascetic movement initiated and presided over by Eustathius of Sebaste in the northern provinces of Asia Minor.[8] The Eustathians had kept perhaps too close to the churches— trying to influence the mass of Christians with their ideas and way of life. The little we know about this movement comes from a synod assembled about 342 at Gangra in which the bishops of the neighbouring churches vehemently criticized and condemned the Eustathians. There were mainly two scores: (1) their tendency to innovate in matters of discipline and customs; (2) their endeavour to impose some of their practices on all Christians.[9] The Eustathians, it is true, displayed a certain spirit of insubordination towards the local church authorities; they also tended to despise the married clergy, but they never tried to separate themselves from the church by retreating to total seclusion. On the contrary, they remained within its ranks trying to influence its course. Some of their extravagant practices are mentioned in the canons. The Eustathians are blamed for wearing extraordinary costumes, for refusing to attend the services held in the local churches, for disrupting many Christian homes by preaching the impossibility of salvation in the married state. Also their views on wealth and their contemptuous attitude towards traditional practices are met with severe criticism. However, all in all, the indelible impression conveyed by these conciliar measures is one of excessive rather than defective involvement in the life of the local church.

[7] In the judgment of Clarke "the Pachomian monasteries were cenobitic only in outward appearance; their inner essence was individualist" (*Monasticism*, p. 120; cf., ibid., p. 40).

[8] According to Sozomenus, *Historia ecclesiastica*, 3.14: PG 67, 1077c, Eustathius of Sebaste initiated and promoted (ἄρξαι) the monastic life (μοναχικὴ πολιτεία) in Armenia, Paphlagonia and Pontus. As historians we should notice that Sozomenus draws his information from a secondhand source ("it is said"). Similarly a secondary source is quoted for the ascription of Basil's *Asceticon* to Eustathius, ibid.: 1080A. The major studies on Eustathius include the "rehabilitation" of F. Loofs, *Eustathius von Sebaste und die Chronologie des Basilius-Briefe* (Halle, 1898); E. Venables, "Eustathius of Sebaste," *DCB* (London, 1877), 2: 383-387; Clarke, *Monasticism*, pp. 46-47 and 159-162; Duchesne, *History*, 2: 304-307; E. Amand de Mendieta, *L'ascèse monastique de saint Basile* (Maredsous, 1949), pp. 52-61; J. Gribomont, "Eustathe de Sebaste," *DSp* (Paris, 1961), 4: 1709-1712; idem, "Eustathe le Philosophe et les voyages du jeune Basile de Césarée," *RHE* 54 (1959) 115-124; idem, "Eustathe de Sebaste," *DHGE* (Paris, 1967), 16: 26-33.

[9] On the synod of Gangra and its canons see C. J. Hefele - H. Leclercq, *Histoire des conciles* (Paris, 1907), 1: 1029-1245. An English translation of the twenty canons is available in F. Morison, *Saint Basil and His Rule* (Oxford, 1912), pp. 146-148.

Although Eustathius himself has left no writing from which we would be able to glean firsthand information on his views and the practices of his followers, several scholars, on the evidence of some of Basil's utterances, have tried to make of Basil a disciple of Eustathius.[10] First, in recalling his trip to Alexandria, the rest of Egypt, Palestine, Coelesyria and Mesopotamia in 356, Basil makes it quite clear that his visit to the south evoked only feelings of admiration for the monks he visited. In fact he expresses only sentiments like "I admired," "I was amazed," and "all this moved my admiration."[11] Perhaps for reasons of health, but maybe also of personal preference, Basil restrained himself from joining the Egyptian "athletes" in their extraordinary exploits.[12] In the same document addressed to Eustathius of Sebaste Basil explains:

> So when I beheld certain men in my own country striving to copy their ways, I felt that I had found a help to my own salvation. ... And though many were for withdrawing me from their society, I would not allow it, because I saw that they put a life of endurance before a life of pleasure; and, because of the extraordinary excellence of their lives, I became an eager supporter of them.[13]

Second, *Epistle 1* contains an array of complimentary epithets on behalf of Eustathius' philosophy, that is, his asceticism. Also, *Epistle 244*, written at a time when Basil had to explain to his friend the reasons for ending his long friendship and communion with Eustathius, reports that Basil "had served" Eustathius "from his boyhood" (δουλεύσας ἐκ παιδός).[14] If Basil's schools attached to his brotherhoods were indeed patterned, as seems to be

[10] See above, n. 8.

[11] *Ep.* 223.2: Courtonne, 3: 11.

[12] According to *Ep.* 1: Courtonne, 1: 3-4, Basil was kept in Alexandria because of poor health. J. Gribomont has proposed that this letter was written to Eustathius of Sebaste; see "Voyages" cited n. 8. Apart from preference and choice there are some more compelling reasons for excluding eremitism from the northern provinces of Asia Minor; see Maran, *Vita*, 6.2, the texts quoted from Sozomenus and Cassian. In addition see the text from Herodotus cited in the *Adversus Marcionem* of Tertullian in E. Ivanka, *Hellenisches und Christliches im frühbyzantinischen Geistesleben* (Vienna, 1948), pp. 32-33. Duchesne, after recognizing the suitability of the warm Egyptian climate for the desert-type asceticism, writes: "It was quite different north of the Taurus. In that cold climate, the desert meant the bare mountain-side, fatal to human life in winter. It was absolutely necessary that the ascetics should not go very far from inhabited places, and, as their wants were not so few as those of their brethren in the Thebaid, they were obliged to enter into closer communication with the rest of mankind" (*History*, 2: 410-411). Lietzmann mentions cultural differences; see his *History*, 4: 133. It should be noted that even during his initial "seclusion" Basil was not alone but in the company of his family, and later on of Gregory of Nazianzus.

[13] *Ep.* 223.3: Courtonne, 3: 11; Jackson, p. 263.

[14] *Ep.* 244.1: Courtonne, 3: 74.

the case, on the Eustathian model, an allusion could here be discerned to Basil's taking some of his early education in one of the Eustathian institutes flourishing in the area.[15] The primary aim of such convent schools "was so to train the children that at a later age they might choose the monastic life as their own career."[16]

Basil's early fascination with Eustathius' philosophy proved, however, to have lasting consequences. As Gregory of Nazianzus reports, both friends, while in Athens, often discussed their future and even promised to join one another later on in a life of "philosophy."[17] In his first letter to Eustathius written shortly after his return from Athens Basil expresses a "passionate longing" to put himself under the guidance of this admired master of asceticism.[18] Neither the brilliant teachers of Athens nor the extraordinary exploits of the monks of Egypt made Basil change his mind.

Whereas it is quite likely that Basil came under the influence of Eustathius, it is not so evident how much Basil owed to his master. In any event, this indebtedness could not have gone beyond an Eustathian influence on Basil's conceptions related to asceticism and organizational matters.[19] Basil's faith however, developed independently of Eustathius, along the lines set by the teaching of Gregory Thaumaturgus.[20] The breach of friendship and communion between the two most prominent exponents of Christian asceticism in Asia Minor was to be caused exclusively by irreconcilable differences regarding faith and not by ascetic practices.[21]

---

[15] Cf. *Reg. fus.* 15: 952-956D, and the brief but pertinent comment of Clarke, *Monasticism*, pp. 101-102. See also E. Amand de Mendieta, "Le système cénobitique basilien comparé au système cénobitique pachômien," *RHR* 152 (1957) 63-64. Basil moved to Caesarea for further education after the death of his father about 346. This was also the time of the Synod of Gangra in which the Eustathians were blamed, among other things, for admitting children to their brotherhoods without the consent of the parents; see canon 16. In Sebaste, where the Eustathians were known for running hospices and schools, Basil's family probably had an estate; see Clarke, *Monasticism*, pp. 24 and 61. Probably in reference to Basil's early training under the Eustathians, Gregory of Nazianzus observes: "He was trained in general education, and practised in the worship of God, and, to speak concisely, led on by elementary instruction to future perfection" (*Or.* 43.12 cited in Clarke, ibid., p. 20). See also *Reg. br.* 292: 1288A-B, and the interpretation of S. Giet, *Les idées et l'action sociales de saint Basile* (Paris, 1941), pp. 197-198.

[16] Clarke, *Monasticism*, p. 121.

[17] Cf. Gregory of Nazianzus, *Ep.* 1: Gallay, 3.

[18] Cf. *Ep.* 1: Courtonne, 1: 3.

[19] Among the possible imitations could be mentioned the *Ptochotrophium* (see *Ep.* 94: Courtonne, 1: 205-206) built on the pattern of a similar complex presided over by Eustathius' disciple Aerius in Sebaste (see Duchesne, *History*, 2: 315-316).

[20] See *Epp.* 204.6: Courtonne, 2: 178; 223.3: ibid., 3: 12.

[21] Cf. *Epp.* 223.1: Courtonne, 3: 8 ff. and 226.1: ibid., 23 f.

Appendix C

The Background of the Basilian Ascetics

In any analysis of Basil's ascetic writings it is important from the ecclesial viewpoint to answer the following question: Were all the ascetics to whom Basil addresses himself in his ascetic works members of organizations living a community life (ὁ χοινωνιχὸς βίος) distinct from ordinary Christian life (ὁ χοινὸς βίος), or were there also some living the ascetic life in the world? The distinction between cenobites and secular Christians is recognized in the *Great Asceticon* from which we borrowed the above terminology.[1] However, one may legitimately wonder whether things were always thus.[2] Since our concern here is primarily Basil's ecclesial awareness, it would be improper to base conclusions on statements in his works meant exclusively for people belonging to one segment of the Christian church. Therefore before making use of Basil's ascetic writings we need to be sure whether he had intended his teaching also for members of the church who lived the ascetic life in the world, that is, who after their "consecration" continued to stay with their families.

The question of the relationship between ecclesial and "ascetic" life in Basil is difficult to solve.[3] It could perhaps be of some help to compare the requirements of the ascetic life as described especially in the earlier edition of the *Asceticon* with the obligations which all Christians incur as a result of baptism.[4] J. Bernardi wonders whether the small number of the baptized

---

[1] For ὁ χοινὸς βίος see *Reg. fus.* 6.2: 928ᴀ; for ὁ χοινωνιχὸς βίος, *Reg. fus.* 7.2: 932ᴀ; see also ibid., for ἡ τῆς ζωῆς χοινωνία in the same sense.

[2] The *Great Asceticon* is certainly from the time of Basil's episcopate. The shorter interrogations were preserved in it from the first edition almost unaltered, with many more added. The longer interrogations underwent considerable revision and expansion. Besides, the *Interrogations 25-54*, which deal with organizational matters, were inserted for the first time.

[3] Cf. J. Gribomont, "S. Basile," *Théologie de la vie monastique* (Paris, 1961), p. 107.

[4] Although we generally concentrate on the *Small Asceticon*, for it is there where Basil for the most part presents the ascetic life as applicable to all Christians, we draw also from other later sources on matters that are not affected by chronological development and that are rather of general principle.

during Basil's time was not attributable to Basil's insistence on the acceptance of ascetic life as part of the baptismal renunciation and commitment.[5] This could well have been the case. Regarding the early ministry of Basil in Pontus, Rufinus reports that through his preaching Basil induced "almost the whole province to put away all unnecessary worldly cares, to come together into one, to build monasteries, to devote time to singing psalms and hymns and to prayers, to attend to the needs of the poor and to provide them with proper houses and the necessities of life, and finally, to hold in high esteem and to furnish recruits for the life of virginity."[6] Rufinus' testimony may not be totally accurate.[7] However, independently of it we find Basil saying in his *Epistle 199* that the number of professed virgins during his lifetime has increased considerably.[8] Also in *Epistle 207* Basil writes to the clergy of Neocaesarea:

> We are accused because we maintain men in the practice of true religion [τῆς εὐσεβείας ἀσκητάς] who have renounced the world and all those cares of this life, which the Lord likens to thorns that do not allow the word to bring forth fruit. Many of this kind carry about in the body the deadness of Jesus; they have taken up their own cross, and are followers of God.[9]

Women also are reported to have chosen

> to live the gospel life, preferring virginity to wedlock. ... I wish you to know that we rejoice to have assemblies of both men and women, whose conversation is in heaven and who have crucified the flesh with the affections and lusts thereof; they take no thought for food and raiment, but remain undisturbed beside their Lord, continuing night and day in prayer. Their lips speak not of the deeds of men: they sing hymns to God continually, working with their own hands that they may have to distribute to them that need.[10]

What is still more remarkable is that in Caesarea as well not only the ascetics-cenobites but

---

[5] *La prédication des Pères cappadociens. Le prédicateur et son auditoire* (Paris, 1968), p. 395.

[6] This free translation of Rufinus' account from *Historia ecclesiastica*, 2.9, is based on W. K. L. Clarke's paraphrase, *St. Basil the Great. A Study in Monasticism* (Cambridge, 1913), p. 56.

[7] For some of the inaccuracies found in his *History*, see Clarke, *Monasticism*, p. 51.

[8] Cf. *Ep.* 199, c. 18: Courtonne, 2: 155. It should be noted that neither here nor in *Ep.* 207, quoted below, does Basil claim any personal credit for the increasing number of virgins and ascetics. On the prehistory of asceticism in Pontus see Clarke, *Monasticism*, p. 46.

[9] *Ep.* 207.2: Courtonne, 2: 185; Jackson, p. 247.

[10] Ibid.

the people [ὁ λαός] go at night to the house of prayer, and in distress, affliction, and continual tears, making confession to God, at last rise from their prayers and begin to sing psalms. ... And so after passing the night in various psalmody, praying at intervals as the day begins to dawn, all together, as with one voice and one heart, raise the psalm of confession to the Lord, each forming for himself his own expressions of penitence.[11]

The preface to the *Small Asceticon* seems to indicate that not only the elite of Basil's disciples but the people who attended the service of worship and the instruction in the local church were prepared to interrogate Basil "concerning that which belongs to sound faith and the true method of right conduct according to the gospel of our Lord Jesus Christ."[12] If they were of the close circle of Basil's followers, they would appear, at any rate, to have regularly received instruction about their duties "in common with the whole church."[13]

In his works Gregory of Nazianzus speaks of two types of asceticism he and Basil found in Pontus early in their career.[14] One was the solitary, βίος ἐρημικός; the other Gregory designates as μιγάς, a term of obscure meaning.[15] Its most plausible translation seems to be "ascetic life lived in the world."[16] According to Gregory, Basil managed to merge both types nicely into a third one, the cenobitic.[17] Since traces of a more advanced cenobitic life can be found mainly in the *Great Asceticon*, with only a very few traces in the *Small Asceticon*, we may conclude that, at least at the beginning of his career, Basil did not contemplate the practice of ascetic life as being necessarily confined to Christians living communally. The contents of his sermons and of the first eleven interrogations of his *Small Asceticon* show that in principle Basil considered the ascetic ideal to be applicable to all Christians.[18] Thus, throughout his works, all Christians are urged to consecrate their possessions in the churches presided over by the local bishops in order that what is above necessity (χρεία) might be shared with

---

[11] Ibid. See the penetrating analysis of this passage in J. Mateos, "L'office monastique à la fin du IVe siècle: Antioche, Palestine, Cappadoce," *OCh* 47 (1963) 81 ff.

[12] *Proem. in reg. br.*: 1080A.

[13] Ibid. Also *Ep.* 207.3: Courtonne, 2: 186 and *In ps.* 114.1: 484A speak of the vigils. Cf. the appropriate comments of Mateos, "L'office," p. 86, n. 84.

[14] Cf. *Carm.* 11.300 ff. quoted by Clarke, *Monasticism*, p. 46.

[15] See the texts and a discussion in Clarke, ibid., pp. 111-113; also Maran, *Vita*, 4.4-5.

[16] I follow Clarke's opinion, *Monasticism*, p. 112, against others quoted there. See also *PGL*, s.v.

[17] See for the evidences Maran, *Vita*, 4.4-5 and Clarke, *Monasticism*, pp. 109-113.

[18] If, as Bernardi suggests, Basil's homilies were re-worked and made public *ca.* 376, his views expressed in the *Small Asceticon* remained basically the same.

the poor and needy.[19] All Christians are to show unconditional obedience to God and his commandments in imitation of Christ and the Holy Spirit, seeking always what is of benefit for the others.[20] Although acknowledging the existence and excellence of virginity, Basil hardly ever advises it directly. He urges, however, the freeing of the soul from all passions, the constant memory of God and of his benefits, and the continuous offering of prayers of thanksgiving.[21]

This sampling of some of the most characteristic virtues proposed by Basil for people living in community and in the world provides, I believe, sufficient evidence for the fact that his ideal of ascetic perfection was intended for all Christians.[22] Only at the time of the *Great Asceticon* does there seem to be emerging a difference in the status of Christians living in the world and cenobites.[23] But even then, the so-called ascetic profession

[19] Cf. *Hom.* 11.5: 381D-384A; *Interrog.* 29 (*Reg. br.* 85: 1144A); *Ep.* 236.7: Courtonne, 3: 54; *Hom.* 6.7: 276B-C. Cf. also *Reg. mor.* 48.6: 772B-D; *Interrog.* 5: 497B; *Reg. br.* 92: 1145C-D. For Basil, possession and production are for use ($\chi\rho\varepsilon\acute{\iota}\alpha$) only, not profit. Thus, what is above necessity ($\chi\rho\varepsilon\acute{\iota}\alpha$) is not only "superfluous" (S. Giet, *Les idées et l'action sociales de s. Basile* [Paris, 1941], pp. 138-140) but "scandalous" and "sinful" if used for personal purposes (see J. Gribomont, "Un aristocrate révolutionnaire, évêque et moine: s. Basile," *Aug.* 17 [1977] 185-186). The Christian has no option but to share his possessions and profits with others. (Giet, *Idées,* pp. 127-131, incorrectly suggests that for Basil the sharing of properties is an [evangelical] "counsel." That the distinction between counsels and precepts was unknown to Basil, see Gribomont, "Un aristocrate," pp. 186-187.)

[20] Among other texts see the genesis of the act of obedience in *Reg. br.* 1: 1080C ff. (= *Interrog.* 12); *Reg. mor.* 37: 757A; *De jud.,* 4-8: 660B ff. See also J. Gribomont, "Obéissance et évangile selon saint Basile le Grand," *VSSt* 21 (1952) 192-215, esp. pp. 200-212; M. M. van Molle, "Vie commune et obéissance d'après les institutions premières de Pachôme et Basile," *VSSt* 23 (1970) 196-225; see also *In ps.* 14, 2.5: 277C ff., and I. Hausherr, "Vocation chrétienne et vocation monastique selon les Pères," in *Etudes de spiritualité orientale* (Rome, 1969), p. 475.

[21] See *Hom.* 4 ($\pi\varepsilon\rho\grave{\iota}$ $\varepsilon\mathring{\upsilon}\chi\alpha\rho\iota\sigma\tau\acute{\iota}\alpha\varsigma$) and 5, esp.: 220C-237A; 244A-261A; *In ps.* 33.1: 352B-C; *Reg. mor.* 56.1-4: 784C-785C; 55.2: 784A.

[22] Besides Basil's homilies and ascetic collections, *Epistles 18, 116, 117* and *299* apply to people living the ascetic life in the world the same categories as to cenobites; see Gribomont, "S. Basile," p. 107. See also Hausherr, "Vocation chrétienne," p. 443: "Telle se présente la spiritualité de saint Basile: comme une spiritualité de réponse d'amour aux bienfaits dont l'amour de Dieu nous a comblés. Ici encore il n'est fait mention de rien de particulier à telle ou telle catégorie de chrétiens; c'est la foi et l'espérance communes qui fondent l'obligation commune d'aimer Dieu." Cf. R. A. Norris in J. Macquarrie, ed., *A Dictionary of Christian Ethics* (London, 1967), p. 28.

[23] See J. Gribomont, "Le renoncement au monde dans l'idéal ascétique de saint Basile," *Irénikon* 31 (1958) 300-305. See also *Reg. fus.* 25-54, the only ones to bear traces of some codification. However, rather than being intentional, this transition to a more institutionalized form of asceticism in Basil seems to be an improvisation to meet the new circumstances. "A vrai dire, plus on va vers le *Grand Asceticon,* plus on voit s'organiser une société particulière; *mais c'est le fait, non le droit*" (Gribomont, "S. Basile," p. 106; italics mine).

(ὁμολογία) was to be nothing other than "a reconfirmation of the baptismal promises."[24]

According to Rufinus, it would seem that the method Basil used to recruit his cenobites was preaching. *Interrogation 4* of the *Small Asceticon*, repeated in the *Great Asceticon* as *Longer Rule 8*, makes it clear that ascetics are won to their communities in the same fashion as all Christians are said to become members of the local churches; namely, through the preaching of the gospel, the renunciation of Satan and his works, and the reception of the same spirit of adoption.[25] They are asked to consecrate their private possessions to the Lord and his church, a commitment that is demanded of every Christian.[26] The local church leaders seem to be at the time the only ones entrusted with the instruction of the ascetics and the distribution of the consecrated goods to the poor.[27] In the light of these facts, it should come as no surprise that Basil refers to all his followers, living either the cenobitic life or the ordinary life, with one and the same name, Christians.[28]

---

[24] U. Neri, "Studio sulla teologia del *De baptismo*" (Rome, 1965; diss. dactylogr.). This work was made available to me by J. Gribomont, Pontifical University Anselmiana, Rome. I am in full agreement with the conclusions of this author: "Per Basilio, nessuna delle categorie essenziali che caratterizzano tradizionalmente la vita monastica è esclusivamente propria a tale stato. Già il battesimo, infatti, significa: rinuncia definitiva al mondo; vita angelicale; intimità di discepolo col Cristo; mistico sposalizio col Signore; impegno solenne di fedeltà; totale consacrazione a Dio; promessa di perfetto adeguamento al Vangelo" (ibid., pp. 85 ff.). On ὁμολογία as "monastic" profession see *Reg. fus.* 15.4: 956B; *Reg. br.* 2: 1081c; *Epp.* 46.2: Courtonne, 1: 117; 199, c. 18: ibid., 2: 156; as baptismal promise of loyalty see *De sp. s.* 26: Pruche, 336; 27: ibid., 340 f.; *Hom.* 13.5: 436c.

[25] Cf. *Interrog.* 4: 496c with *In ps.* 33.8: 369B.

[26] See *Interrog.* 4: 496c and n. 19, above.

[27] See above, n. 19.

[28] In his works, Basil never refers to his followers or disciples by the name of "monks," but either "brethren" or "complete Christians" or simply "Christians." See *Reg. fus.* 3.1: 917A; *Hom.* 6.1: 216c and *Reg. fus.* 7.3: 932c for a statement that man is not a solitary (μοναστικόν) but a sociable (κοινωνικόν) being.

Appendix D

Conditions for a Profitable and Enduring Success of the Proclamation

Proclamation (κήρυγμα) of the gospel, whatever form it may assume—that of prophetic utterances about God or of testimony (μαρτυρία) exemplified in virtuous life—is the moment of grace and salvation for many. According to Basil, the preacher, through his work of preparing souls to surrender to the will of Christ, heals the wounds occasioned by sin and restores to them the life of divine grace.

Preaching originates with the Holy Spirit through whose intervention alone the church of Christ is built in the world. Apostolic succession (διαδοχή) for Basil is an uninterrupted continuity in the handing down of the same message initially delivered by the Spirit of God to the prophets and apostles. Although the responsibility for ensuring the identity of contents tends in Basil to become more and more an office of the bishop and clergy, in principle this need not always be so, as the Spirit is free and sovereign (ἐλευθερός; κύριος) to speak through the agency of any spiritual and charismatic man. The main condition is to speak with authority, that is, to have one's own charisma of the word and teaching recognized (ἐγκρι-θέντα) by someone who in his turn is acknowledged as possessing them.

As the main objective of preaching is not so much to persuade as to prepare souls to fall under the rule of Christ—faith being a free decision of every individual[1]—by way of conclusion I propose to summarize in this appendix Basil's ideas on the conditions for a profitable and enduring success in this proclamation. Unless such requirements are met, proclamation is doomed to remain an unfulfilled human commitment to collaborate with the Holy Spirit in the edification of the church of Christ.

---

[1] One of the cornerstones of Basilian theology which cannot be discussed here in more detail is that human freedom (προαίρεσις) should play in the restoration of the divine life the same role it played in its destruction (see *Hom.* 9.3: 332D ff.; ibid., 5: 337D ff.; and 6: 344A-345C).

First Condition: Internal Quiet (ἡσυχία). The *Homily on the Words, "Take Heed to Thyself"* begins by exhorting the hearers to create in the interior of their hearts an atmosphere of absolute calm in order to ensure to the words of the preacher an enduring success,

> When our thought seizes upon a meaningful word, carried by that word as by a ferry, it crosses the air and passes from the one who utters it to the one who listens to it. If it finds concentrated calm and quiet [ἡσυχία], the word lands upon the ears of the hearers as in a calm and stormless harbour. But if it is hit as by some rough storm by the confusion raging in the hearers, it dissolves in the air, capsizes and drowns. Create then for the word a stillness, with silence. Perhaps you will be able to find in it something profitable and worthy of being taken along. The word of truth is hard to catch, and can easily escape those who are inattentive.[2]

Mere physical presence during sermons is of no avail, if not accompanied by the laying aside of all unnecessary worries and cares of life.[3]

Second Condition: Purity of Heart. Only a heart emptied and free from sin and unnecessary cares (μέριμναι) is adequate to receive the words of God. "Just as he who intends to write on the wax, first smooths it down and thus puts on whatever forms he wishes, so also the heart which is to admit clearly the divine words must be made clean of the opposite thoughts."[4] Κάθαρσις as a necessary means for the acquisition of γνῶσις, true knowledge, was already recommended by Greek philosophers.[5] For Basil purity of heart is the only possible means for the reception of the evangelical message. It produces in the mind that stillness of which we spoke earlier.

> 'Be still and see that I am God.' So long as we are engaged in affairs outside God, we are not able to make progress in the knowledge of God. Who, anxious about the things of the world and sunk deep in the distractions of the flesh, can be intent on the words of God and be sufficiently accurate in such mighty objects of contemplation? Do you not see that the word which fell among the thorns is choked by the thorns? The thorns are the pleasures of the flesh and wealth and glory and the cares of life. He who desires the knowledge of God will have to be outside of all these things, and being freed from his

---

[2] *Hom.* 3.1: Rudberg, 23. See *Ep.* 2.2: Rudberg, 157 for the notion of ἡσυχία.
[3] See *Hex.* 3.1: Giet, 190.
[4] *In ps.* 32.7: 341A-B; Way, p. 240.
[5] T. Špidlik, *La sophiologie de saint Basile* (Rome, 1961), p. 137, and R. R. Ruether, *Gregory of Nazianzus, Rhetor and Philosopher* (Oxford, 1969), pp. 2 and 136-149.

passions, thus to receive the knowledge of God. For, how could the thought of God enter into a soul choked by considerations which preoccupied it?[6]

Third Condition: Personal Meditation. To heal and vivify the soul the words of God must not only be listened to with attention but they also must be assimilated by each hearer. They should be recorded on the mind as on a column, that is, the hearing of them should not be casual nor should one allow them to become confused and obliterated through disregard and oblivion.[7] Basil interrupted his homily on the second day of creation to allow his listeners "to examine what they have just heard. May their memory retain it for the profit of their soul; may they by careful meditation inwardly digest and benefit by what I say."[8] The last words indicate that not only during but also after the sermon hearers should dwell upon a careful consideration of the message. They should try to experience the goodness of the Lord˙ through their internal senses.

> Since our Lord is true bread and His flesh is true meat, it is necessary that the pleasure of the enjoyment of the bread be in us through a spiritual taste. As the nature of honey can be described to the inexperienced not so˙much by speech as by the perception of it through taste, so the goodness of the heavenly Logos cannot be clearly taught by doctrines, unless, examining to a greater extent the dogmas of truth, we are able to comprehend by our own experience the goodness of the Lord.[9]

---

[6] *In ps.* 45.8: 428c-429a; Way, p. 307. See *Ep.* 210.6: Courtonne, 2: 196; *Hex.* 1.1: Giet, 86.

[7] See *In ps.* 59.2: 464c.

[8] *Hex.* 3.10: Giet, 240-242; Jackson, p. 71.

[9] *In ps.* 33.6: 364c-365a; Way, p. 258.

Appendix E

Preaching and Letter-Writing

In antiquity the art of government was closely associated not only with the oratory, but also with written composition. Both rhetorical forms were diligently used by clear-sighted rulers. This tradition of Hellenistic extraction was soon adopted by Christian missionaries and preachers. Through their letters intended for the communities they founded or which they never visited in person, the first apostles have left the most convincing proofs of the validity, usefulness and relevance of the written word as a means of leadership, instruction and propaganda among Christian believers. Clement of Rome, Ignatius of Antioch, Polycarp of Smyrna, to name only a few, followed undeviatingly in the footsteps of their predecessors by having recourse in the government of their churches not only to preaching but also to letter-writing. Many other bishops banished from their sees did the same in the subsequent centuries. The most celebrated case in the fourth century was Athanasius of Alexandria, who for about sixteen of his forty-five years as bishop of that city communicated with his people by means of the written word only.

As a disciple of the best rhetoricians of Athens, Basil also excels in the use of this alternate method of exercising leadership. For him the written word occupies the same place of honour as the spoken. Gregory of Nazianzus informs us that his friend employed a double method of defending the Christian truth.

> Those who engaged in hand-to-hand conflicts he overthrew at close range by word of mouth. Those who engaged at a distance he struck with arrows of ink, no less significant than the characters in the tables of the law, legislating not for one small Jewish nation, concerning meat and drink, temporal sacrifices, and purifications of the flesh, but for every nation and every portion of the earth, concerning the true doctrine from which comes our salvation.[1]

---

[1] *Or.* 43.43: PG 36, 553A; McCauley, p. 64.

Gregory is far from overemphasizing the importance of the written word if we consider that a great part of what he knew about his friend came to him from the reading of Basil's writings. Also, had it not been for Basil the author, future generations would have had no means of knowing Basil the preacher. Thanks to the pen, Basil himself came to know many people with whom he would never have become acquainted otherwise. I propose to investigate here the value ascribed by Basil to the written word in general as well as its role in the defense and propagation of Christian faith and ideals, concluding with some remarks concerning the style and material execution of the manuscripts.

The Written Word. Its Value and Characteristics

The written word, compared with the spoken, seems to possess less persuasive power. Writing lacks the warmth and immediacy which characterize so well live human relations. In a personal encounter it is always much easier to add words of clarification in case they are needed to make our statements better understood.[2] Precisely because of such a contingency, Basil on one occasion refused to delineate further some dogmatic propositions, inviting the recipient of his letter instead to pay him a personal visit "that we may talk of these high topics face-to-face, instead of committing them to lifeless letters."[3]

Basil appreciates, however, the power of written communication to overcome the isolation of space and time. He shares memorable thoughts with two of his ex-pupils:

> Bodily separation is no hindrance to instruction. The Creator, in the fulness of His love and wisdom, did not confine our minds within our bodies, nor the power of speaking to our tongues. Ability to profit derives some advantages even from lapse of time; thus we are able to transmit instruction, not only to those who are dwelling far away, but even to those who are hereafter to be born. And experience proves my words: those who lived many years before teach posterity by instruction preserved in their writings; and we, though so far separated in the body, are always near in thought, and converse together with ease. Instruction is bounded neither by sea nor land, if only we have care for our souls' profit.[4]

As a Christian, Basil considers the art of writing as a providential device, a divine gift which allows man, limited by space and time, to overcome his

---

[2] See *Epp.* 156.2: Courtonne, 2: 83; 112.1: ibid., 13.
[3] *Ep.* 9.3: Courtonne, 1: 39; Jackson, p. 123; see also *Ep.* 138.2: Courtonne, 2: 55.
[4] *Ep.* 294: Courtonne, 3: 169; Jackson, p. 317; see *De leg.* 2: 565A.

individual insufficiency and contingency. Often impeded by the over-whelming demands of his work and frequent illness, and a victim of time, Basil was constrained to resort to the διαχονία τῶν γραμμάτων.[5] He con-verted letters into apostolic means. Reviewing their contents we find that Basil used them to bring comfort to the persecuted, to those who suffered losses or injustices; to explain in more detail some articles of the symbol of faith, e.g., the consubstantiality of Christ, his divinity and humanity, the non-creaturehood of the Spirit; to establish the validity of some ecclesia-stical ordinances; to clarify the principles of evangelical life, and also to defend the rights of the oppressed. It seems as though almost every class of person was a recipient of his letters: bishops, magistrates, officers, generals, soldiers, presbyters, ascetics, laymen, youngsters, pagans and heretics. Although in Basil's time letters had to be delivered by couriers or trust-worthy friends who could often describe the situation better by word of mouth, the written signs had the advantage of preserving for a longer time the words or the memory of certain events.[6]

Although the art of writing can be an instrument of wide and varied ap-plication, Basil considers that among Christians it should be used only for the purpose of "the edification of the church."[7] On this score it is worth-while to take a closer look at his criticisms of the books that Diodorus of Tarsus sent him for review. Of the two writings, Basil decided to keep the shorter one.[8] With that liberty of a mature personality that he demanded, Basil explains to his friend the motives for his preference.

The first of the two books of Diodorus is better "because it is at once full of thought, and so arranged that the objections of opponents, and the an-swers to them, stand out distinctly. Its simple and natural style seems to me to befit the profession of a Christian who writes less for self-advertisement than for the general good."[9] The second book ideologically possesses the same force as the first, but the unnecessary artifices of style require more time and sometimes more mental labour for the reader both to gather its meaning and retain it in memory. "The abuse of our opponents and the support of our own side, which are thrown in, although they may seem to add some charms of dialectic to the treatise, do yet break the continuity of thought and weaken the strength of the argument, by causing interruption

---

[5] See *Epp.* 297: Courtonne, 3: 172; 219.1: ibid., 2; 206: ibid., 2: 182.
[6] See *Ep.* 205: Courtonne, 2: 181.
[7] *Ep.* 135.2: Courtonne, 2: 50.
[8] Ibid., 51.
[9] Ibid., 1: 49, 200.

and delay."[10] There are two ways of writing dialogues. If someone like Theophrastus and Aristotle is aware "of not being gifted with the graces of Plato," he should use dialogues only for exposition of his thought.

> Plato, on the other hand, with his great power of writing, at the same time attacks opinions and incidentally makes fun of his characters, assailing now the rashness and recklessness of a Thrasymachus, the levity and frivolity of a Hippias, and the arrogance and pomposity of a Protagoras. When, however, he introduces unmarked characters into his dialogues, he uses the interlocutors for making the point clear, but does not admit anything more belonging to the characters into his arguments. An instance of this is in the *Laws*.[11]

Christians may in their apologetic works use the form of dialogues, but only under two conditions: that no offence result for the persons whose faults we blame; and that the only purpose for using such literary device be not vain glory but the good of others.[12]

Basil not only was dedicated to the critical review of the contents of works sent to him, but he also made observations regarding the material preparation and technical execution of the manuscripts. To a copyist he wrote, "Words are of a swift-flying nature. In order to catch them in their speedy flight the writer needs signs. Therefore you, my child, write with accuracy and use the correct punctuation. Because an insignificant error can seriously alter a discourse, but the care of the copyist conveys with accuracy the spoken words."[13] Another letter gives practical advice on how to prepare a manuscript. Basil complains of having difficulty in deciphering the handwriting of one of his copyists; to another he indicates on what syllables some words should be accentuated.[14]

Such meticulous care of detail and such a thorough knowledge of the Greek language clearly indicate Basil's concern that Christian writers should not be accused of carelessness and impropriety in writing. Although Basil deliberately tried to use plain vocabulary in his homilies and other works, the style of his writings is nonetheless elegant and impeccable. Gregory of Nazianzus, an accomplished stylist and rhetorician himself, rightly praises Basil's propriety of expression, the logical construction of sentences and the perfect balance of style.[15] To a disciple, Nicobulus, who

---

[10] Ibid.
[11] Ibid.
[12] Ibid., 2: 50.
[13] *Ep.* 333: Courtonne, 3: 201.
[14] *Epp.* 334: Courtonne, 3: 201; 236.3: ibid., 51.
[15] *Or.* 43.65: PG 36, 581D ff.

requested from him advice in how to write letters, Gregory thought it most convenient to send him a collection of Basil's letters.[16] According to the same Gregory, people of all social standings, magistrates, teachers and students sought in Basil's works the rules of accurate thinking and elegant speech, whereas the candidates for the ministry looked for spiritual food in them to nourish their vocation.[17] Five centuries later, the noted Hellenist Photius acknowledged in Basil's writings the same virtues: purity of style, order and lucidity of thought, fluency of diction and persuasive force. According to Photius, in the study of rhetoric the works of Basil can well replace those of Plato and Demosthenes. In reviewing Basil's letters, the Byzantine librarian discovered not only the most outstanding testimony to Basil's piety and religious spirit but also the most perfect model of letter-writing.[18]

[16] *Ep.* 53: Gallay, 49.
[17] *Or.* 43.66: PG 36, 584D-585A.
[18] *Bibliotheca* 141, 143, 191: Henry, 2: 109-110; 3: 73.

A Select Bibliography

A. Editions and English Translations of Basil's Works

For an alphabetical listing with short references, see the List of Abbreviations, pp. ix-xii.

Boulenger, Fernand, ed. & trans. *Saint Basile, Aux jeunes gens sur la manière de tirer profit des lettres helléniques.* Paris: Les Belles Lettres, 1935.

Boyd, Hugh Stuart, trans. *Select Passages of the Writings of St. Chrysostom, St. Gregory Nazianzen, and St. Basil.* 3rd ed. London: Hatchard, 1813.

——. *The Catholic Faith; a Sermon by St. Basil.* London: Rivingston, 1825.

Carr, John, trans. *The Forty-Sixth Psalm with the Commentary of St. Basil.* Lincoln: Brumby, 1847.

Clarke, William Kemp Lowther, trans. *The Ascetic Works of St. Basil.* London: SPCK, 1925.

Courtonne, Yves, ed. & trans. *Saint Basile, Homélies sur la richesse.* Paris: Firmin-Didot, 1935.

——. *Saint Basile, Lettres.* 3 vols. Paris: Les Belles Lettres, 1957, 1961, 1966.

Deferrari, Roy Joseph, ed. & trans. *St. Basil, The Letters.* 4 vols. London: Loeb, 1926, 1928, 1930, 1934 (with *Address to Young Men on Reading Greek Literature,* 4: 363-435).

Garnier, Julien, and Prudentius Maran, edd. & trans. *Sancti Basilii Magni Opera omnia.* 3 vols. Paris: Coignard, 1721, 1722, 1730; rpt. in Migne, *Patrologiae graecae cursus completus* 29-32, Paris, 1857, 1886, and now also Turnhout: Brepols, 1959-1961, with Introductions by J. Gribomont, and (to volume 30) by the Monks of Chevetogne.

Giet, Stanislas, ed. & trans. *Basile de Césarée, Homélies sur l'Hexaéméron.* 2nd ed. SCh 26bis. Paris: Editions du Cerf, 1968.

Hörner, Hadwiga, ed. *Auctorum incertorum, vulgo Basilii vel Gregorii Nysseni, sermones de creatione hominis, sermo de paradiso.* Leiden: Brill, 1972.

Jackson, Blomfield, trans. *The Treatise De Spiritu Sancto, The Nine Homilies of the Hexaemeron and the Letters of Saint Basil the Great.* SLNPF, series 2, volume 8. New York, 1895; rpt. Grand Rapids: Wm. B. Eerdmans, 1968.

Johnston, Charles Francis Harding, ed. *The Book of St. Basil the Great on the Holy Spirit.* Oxford: Clarendon, 1892.

Junod, Eric, ed. & trans. *Origène, Philocalie 21-27: Sur le libre arbitre.* SCh 226. Paris: Editions du Cerf, 1976.

Kenrick, Francis Patrick, trans. *A Treatise on Baptism; with an Exhortation to Receive it, Translated from the Works of St. Basil the Great.* Philadelphia: Fithian, 1843.

Lewis, George, trans. *St. Basil the Great, On the Holy Spirit.* London: Religious Tract Society, 1888.

———. trans. *The Philocalia of Origen: A Compilation of Selected Passages from Origen's Works, Made by St. Gregory of Nazianzus and St. Basil of Caesarea.* Edinburgh: Clark, 1911.

Maguire, John M., trans. *Scripture Ethics, by St. Basil the Great.* London: Bagster, 1871.

Maloney, Edward Raymond, ed. *St. Basil the Great, To Students on Greek Literature.* New York: American Book Company, 1901.

Neri, Umberto, ed. & trans. *Basilio di Cesarea, Il battesimo.* Brescia: Paideia, 1976.

Padelford, Frederick Morgan, ed. & trans. *Essays on the Study and Use of Poetry by Plutarch and Basil the Great.* New York: Holt, 1902.

Pruche, Benoît, ed. & trans. *Basile de Césarée, Traité du Saint-Esprit.* 2nd ed. SCh 17bis. Paris: Editions du Cerf, 1968.

Robinson, Joseph Armitage, ed. *The Philocalia of Origen.* Cambridge: University Press, 1893.

Rufinus Tyrannius, trans. *[Asceticum parvum].* PL 103: 483-554.

Rudberg, Stig Y., ed. "Lettres 2, 150, 173." In *Etudes sur la tradition manuscrite de s. Basile,* pp. 151-211. Lund: Lundequitska, 1953.

———. *L'homélie de Basile de Césarée sur le mot: "Observe-toi toi même."* Stockholm: Almquist, 1962.

Smets, Alexis, and Michel van Esbroeck, edd. & trans. *Basile de Césarée, Sur l'origine de l'homme (Homélies x et xi de l'Hexaéméron).* SCh 160. Paris: Editions du Cerf, 1970.

St. Charles' House, trans. *Excerpts from the Works of St. Basil the Great, Archbishop of Caesarea, Confessor, Bishop, Doctor of the Church.* St. Charles, Ill.: St. Charles' House, 1971.

Trevisan, Piero, ed. & trans. *San Basilio, Commento al profeta Isaia.* 2 vols. Turin: Società editrice internazionale, 1939.

Wagner, Monica, trans. *St. Basil, Ascetical Works.* New York: Fathers of the Church, 1950.

Way, Agnes Clare, trans. *St. Basil, Letters.* 2 vols. New York: Fathers of the Church, 1951, 1955.

———. *St. Basil, Exegetic Homilies.* Washington, D.C.: Catholic University Press, 1963.

Wilson, Nigel Guy, ed. & trans. *St. Basil on the Value of Greek Literature.* London: Duckworth, 1975.

B. Other Texts

Aubineau, Michel, ed. & trans. *Grégoire de Nysse, Traité de la virginité.* SCh 119. Paris: Editions du Cerf, 1966.

Boulenger, Fernard, ed. & trans. *Grégoire de Nazianze, Discours funèbres en l'honneur de son frère Césaire et de Basile de Césarée.* Paris: Picard, 1908.

Clémencet, Charles and Armand Benjamin Caillau, edd. & trans. *Sancti Gregorii Nazianzeni Opera omnia.* PG 35-38.

Gallay, Paul, ed. & trans. *Saint Grégoire de Nazianze, Lettres* 1. Paris: Les Belles Lettres, 1964.

——. ed. *Gregor von Nazianz, Briefe.* GCS. Berlin: Akademie Verlag, 1969.

——. ed. & trans. *Grégoire de Nazianze, Lettres théologiques.* SCh 208. Paris: Editions du Cerf, 1974.

Henry, René, ed. & trans. *Photius, Bibliothèque.* Paris: Les Belles Lettres, 1959—.

Jaeger, Werner, et al., edd. *Gregorii Nysseni Opera.* Leiden: Brill, 1960—. (For works not comprised by any of the modern editions see PG 44-46).

Maraval, Pierre, ed. & trans. *Grégoire de Nysse, Vie de sainte Macrine.* SCh 178. Paris: Editions du Cerf, 1971.

Martin, Joseph, ed. *Sancti Aurelii Augustini De doctrina christiana.* CCSL 32. Turnhout: Brepols, 1962.

McCauley, Leop., et al., trans. *Funeral Orations by St. Gregory Nazianzen and St. Ambrose.* New York: Fathers of the Church, 1953.

Miller, Walter, ed. & trans. *Cicero, De officiis.* London: Heinemann, 1928.

Petschenig, Michael, ed. *Johannis Cassiani De institutis coenobiorum.* CSEL 17. Vienna: Tempsky, 1888.

Stein, James Aloysius, ed. & trans. *Gregory of Nyssa, Encomium on His Brother St. Basil.* Washington, D.C.: Catholic University Press, 1928.

Valesius, Henricus, ed. & trans. *Hermiae Sozomeni Historia ecclesiastica.* PG 67, 844-1629.

C. Studies and General Works

Abramowski, Luise. "Das Bekenntnis des Gregor Thaumaturgus bei Gregor von Nyssa und das Problem seiner Echtheit." *ZKG* 87 (1976) 145-166.

Adams, Jeremy Duquessay. *The "Populus Dei" of Augustine and Jerome. A Study in the Patristic Sense of Community.* New Haven: Yale University Press, 1971.

Aghiorgoussis, Maximos. "Applications of the Theme 'Eikon Theou' (Image of God) according to St. Basil the Great." *GOTR* 21 (1976) 265-288.

Agresta, Apollinare. *Vita del protopatriarca san Basilio Magno.* Rome, 1658.

Aland, Kurt. "The Relation between Church and State in Early Times: A Reinterpretation." *JThS* 19 (1968) 115-127.

Alevisopoulos, A. *Das Gute und das Böse in der Sicht Basileios des Grossen im Zusammenhang mit seiner Welterklärung.* Diss. Mainz, 1963.

Alexa, G. "Sf. Vasile cel Mare în colindele religioase romîneste." *Studii Teologice* 11 (1959) 73-84.

Allard, Paul. *Saint Basile.* Paris: Lecoffre, 1903.

Altaner, Berthold. "Augustinus und Basilius der Grosse. Eine quellenkritische Untersuchung." *RB* (1950) 17-24.

——. *Patrologie. Leben, Schriften und Lehre der Kirchenväter.* 6th ed. rev. by A. Stuiber. Freiburg-im-Breisgau: Herder, 1966; pp. 290-298: "Basil of Caesarea."

Amand de Mendieta, Emmanuel. "Essai d'une histoire critique des éditions générales grecques et gréco-latines de s. Basile de Césarée." *RB* 52 (1940) 141-161; 53 (1941) 119-151; 54 (1942) 124-144; 56 (1945/46) 126-173.

——. *L'ascèse monastique de saint Basile. Essai historique.* Maredsous: Editions de Maredsous, 1949.

—— & M. Ch. Moons. "Une curieuse homélie grecque inédite sur la virginité, adressée aux pères de famille." *RB* 63 (1953) 18-69; 211-238.

——. "Damase, Athanase, Pierre, Mélèce et Basile. Les rapports de communion ecclésiastique entre les Eglises de Rome, d'Alexandrie, d'Antioche et de Césarée de Cappadoce." *L'Eglise et les Eglises (1054-1954).* Chevetogne, 1954, 1: 261-277.

——. "La virginité chez Eusèbe d'Emèse et l'ascétisme familial dans la première moitié du ive siècle." *RHE* 50 (1955) 777-820.

——. "Le système cénobitique basilien comparé au système cénobitique pachômien." *RHR* 152 (1957) 31-80.

—— & S. Y. Rudberg. *Eustathius. Ancienne version latine des neuf homélies sur l'Hexaéméron de Basile de Césarée.* Berlin: Akademie Verlag, 1958.

——. "Basile de Césarée et Damase de Rome. Les causes de l'échec de leurs négociations." In *Biblical and Patristic Studies in Memory of R. P. Casey*, pp. 122-166. Freiburg-im-Breisgau: Herder, 1963.

——. *The "Unwritten" and "Secret" Apostolic Traditions in the Theological Thought of Saint Basil of Caesarea.* (Scottish Journal of Theology Occasional Papers, 13.) Edinburgh: Oliver & Boyd, 1965.

——. "The Pair 'Kerygma' and 'Dogma' in the Theological Thought of Saint Basil of Caesarea." *JThS* 16 (1965) 129-142.

——. "L'authenticité des lettres ascétiques 42 à 45 de la correspondance de s. Basile de Césarée." *RSR* 56 (1968) 241-264.

——. "L'authenticité de la lettre 45 de la correspondance de Basile de Césarée." *SP* 10 (Berlin, 1970) 44-53.

——. "Les deux homélies sur la création de l'homme que les manuscrits attribuent à Basile de Césarée ou à Grégoire de Nysse. Le problème de leur rédaction." In *Zetesis. Album amicorum aangeboden aan E. de Strycker*, pp. 695-716. Antwerp: De Nederl. Boekhandel, 1974.

——. "La plus ancienne tradition manuscrite (ixe et xe siècles) des homélies de Basile de Césarée sur l'*Hexaéméron*." *SP* 16 (Berlin, 1976) 253-274.

——. "The Official Attitude of Basil of Caesarea as a Christian Bishop towards Greek Philosophy and Science." In Derek Baker, ed., *The Orthodox Churches and the West*, pp. 25-49. Oxford: Blackwell, 1976.

Angeli, Antonio. *Basilio di Cesarea.* Milan: Ancora, 1968.

Antoniades, Sophie. *Place de la liturgie dans la tradition des lettres grecques.* Leiden: Sijthoff, 1939.

Armstrong, Arthur Hilary. "The Theory of the Non-existence of Matter in Plotinus and the Cappadocians." *SP* 5 (Berlin, 1962) 427-429.

Aubineau, Michel. "Le thème du 'Bourbier' dans la littérature grecque profane et chrétienne." *RSR* 47 (1959) 185-214.

Baert, Fr. "S. Basilius Magnus." In *Acta Sanctorum Bollandiana*, 2: 807-938. Antwerp, 1698.

Balás, David L. Μετουσία Θεοῦ. *Man's Participation in God's Perfection according to St. Gregory of Nyssa.* Rome: Anselmianum, 1966.

——. "The Unity of Human Nature in Basil's and Gregory of Nyssa's *Against Eunomius.*" *SP* 16 (Berlin, 1976) 275-281.

Balthasar, Hans Urs von. *Présence et pensée. Essai sur la philosophie religieuse de Grégoire de Nysse.* Paris: Beauchesne, 1942.

Bamberger, John Eudes. "Μνήμη-Διάθεσις. The Psychic Dynamisms in the Ascetical Theology of Saint Basil." *OCP* 34 (1968) 233-251.

Bardenhewer, Otto. "Basilius der Grosse." In *Geschichte der Altkirchlichen Literatur*, 2nd ed., 3: 130-162. Freiburg-im-Breisgau: Herder, 1923.

Bardy, Gustave. "Saint Basile, évêque de Césarée de Cappadoce: Vie et œuvres." *DSp* (Paris, 1937), 1: 1276-1283.

——. *La théologie de l'Eglise de s. Irénée au concile de Nicée.* Paris: Editions du Cerf, 1947.

——. "Arianism," etc. In J. R. Palanque, et al., edd. *The Church in the Christian Roman Empire.* 2 vols. New York: Macmillan, 1953.

Bartelink, Gerard J. M. "Observations de saint Basile sur la langue biblique et théologique." *VCh* 17 (1963) 85-104.

Batiffol, Pierre. "L'ecclésiologie de saint Basile." *EO* 21 (1922) 9-30.

——. "*Cathedra Petri.*" *Etudes d'histoire ancienne de l'Eglise.* Paris: Editions du Cerf, 1938.

Bauer, Walter. *Orthodoxy and Heresy in Earliest Christianity.* Philadelphia: Fortress, 1971.

Bayle, Antoine. *Saint Basile, archevêque de Césarée (329-379), cours d'éloquence sacrée, 1869-1870.* Avignon: Seguin, 1878.

Baynes, Norman & Henry Moss, edd. *Byzantium: Introduction to Eastern Roman Civilization.* Oxford: University Press, 1948.

Belazzi, P. *Il fine ultimo dell'uomo in san Basilio Magno.* Alba, 1954.

Bellini, Enzo. *La chiesa nel mistero della salvezza in san Gregorio Nazianzeno.* Venegono Inferiore: La Scuola Cattolica, 1970.

——. "La posizione dei monaci e dei vergini nella chiesa secondo Gregorio Nazianzeno." *SC* 99 (1971) 452-466.

Benito y Durán, Angel. "El nominalismo arriano y la filosofía cristiana: Eunomio y san Basilio." *Augustinus* 5 (1960) 207-226.

——. "San Basilio Magno, punto de partida para el estudio de la autognoseología cristiana." *Augustinus* 6 (1961) 315-338.

——. "Filosofia de san Basilio en sus homilías sobre los Salmos." *SP* 3 (Berlin, 1962) 446-472.

——. "Huellas autognoseológicas basilianas en san Ambrosio y san Agustín." *Augustinus* 10 (1965) 199-225.

——. "El trabajo manual en la Regla de san Basilio." *TE* 15 (1971) 317-338.

——. "Los monacatos de san Basilio y san Agustín y su coincidencia en el pensamiento del trabajo corporal." *Augustinus* 17 (1972) 357-395.

Berger, Max. *Die Schöpfungslehre des hl. Basilius des Grossen.* Progr. Rosenheim: Niedermayer, 1897.

Berlocco, Francesco. *La creazione in Basilio Magno.* Palermo, 1956.

Bernardakis, G. "Notes sur la topographie de Césarée de Cappadoce." *EO* 11 (1908) 22-27.

Bernardi, Jean. "La date de l'*Hexaéméron* de saint Basile." *SP* 3 (Berlin, 1962) 165-169.

——. *La prédication des Pères cappadociens. Le prédicateur et son auditoire.* Paris: Presses universitaires de France, 1968.

Berry, Christopher J. "On the Meaning of Progress and Providence in the Fourth Century." *The Heythrop Journal* 18 (1977) 257-270.

Bessières, Mario. *La tradition manuscrite de la correspondance de saint Basile.* Oxford: Clarendon Press, 1923.

Bethune-Baker, James Franklin. *The Meaning of Homoousios in the Constantinopolitan Creed.* Cambridge: University Press, 1901.

Betz, Johannes. *Die Eucharistie in der Zeit der griechischen Väter.* Freiburg: Herder, 1955.

Beyer, Hermann W. Ἐπίσκοπος. *TDNT* (Grand Rapids, 1964), 2: 608-622.

Blomenkamp, P. *Klemens von Alexandrien und Basilius der Grosse. Ein ideengeschichtlichen Versuch.* Diss. Cologne, 1958.

Blond, Georges. "L''hérésie' encratite vers la fin du IVe siècle." *RSR* 32 (1944) 157-210.

Bobrinskoy, Boris. "Liturgie et ecclésiologie trinitaire de s. Basile." *VC* 89 (1969) 1-32.

Boer, S. de. "Basilius de Grote en de 'homoousie' van de Hl. Geest." *NTT* 18 (1964) 362-380.

——. *De anthropologie van Gregorius van Nyssa.* Assen: van Gorcum, 1968.

——. "Paradosis, dogma en kerygma naar de opvatting van Basilius de Grote." *NTT* 24 (1970) 333-372.

Bombay, L. "La portée de l'argumentation scripturaire dans les écrits d'Eunome et l'*Adversus Eunomium*." Diss. Rome: Gregorian, 1959.

Bonis, Constantine G. "The Problem concerning Faith and Knowledge as Expressed in the Letters of Saint Basil the Great to Amphilochius of Iconium." *GOTR* 5 (1959) 27-44.

——. Βασίλειος Καισαρείας ὁ μέγας ... Βίος καὶ ἔργα. Συγγράμματα καὶ διδασκαλία. Athens, 1975.

Bonnet, M. "Basile de Césarée et l'administration impériale." Diss. Grenoble, 1962.

Bori, Piere Cesare. *Koinōnia. L'idea della communione nell'ecclesiologia recente e nel Nuovo Testamento.* Brescia: Paideia, 1972.

———. *Chiesa primitiva. L'immagine della communità delle origini—Atti 2.42-47; 4.32-37—nella storia della chiesa antica.* Brescia: Paideia, 1974.

———. "La référence à la communauté de Jérusalem dans les sources chrétiennes de l'Orient et de l'Occident jusqu'au vᵉ siècle." *Istina* 19 (1974) 31-48.

Botte, Bernard, ed. *Etudes sur le sacrement de l'ordre.* Paris: Editions du Cerf, 1957.

Brightman, Frank Edward. "The Liturgy of Saint Basil." In *Liturgies Eastern and Western,* 1: 309-344; 400-411. Oxford: Clarendon, 1896.

Britz, Andrew. "The Renunciation of the World: Saint Basil's Call to Restoration." Diss. Collegeville, Minn.: Saint John's University, 1965.

Brown, Peter. *The World of Late Antiquity.* London: Thames & Hudson, 1971.

———. *Religion and Society in the Age of Saint Augustine.* London: Faber, 1971.

———. "Eastern and Western Christendom in Late Antiquity: A Parting of the Ways." In Derek Baker, ed., *The Orthodox Churches and the West,* pp. 1-24. Oxford: Blackwell, 1976.

Buonaiuti, Ernesto. "Attraverso l'epistolario di san Basilio." *RSCST* 4 (1908) 122-132.

Busch, L. "Basilius und die Medizin." *TB* 29 (1957) 111-121.

Busquets, A. M. "San Basilio, predicador de la limosna." *Paraula cristiana* 19 (1934) 16-31.

Büttner, Georg. *Beitrage zur Ethik Basileios' des Grossen.* Progr. Landshut, 1913.

Cadiou, René. "Basile dans sa correspondance." *REG* 70 (1957) 500-505.

———. "Le problème des relations scolaires entre saint Basile et Libanius." *REG* 79 (1966) 89-98.

Calasanctius, Pater (= Jos Joosen). *De beeldspraak bij den hl. Basilius den Groote.* Nijmegen: Dekker, 1941.

Callahan, John F. "Basil of Caesarea. A New Source for Saint Augustine's Theory of Time." *HSCP* 63 (1958) 437-454.

———. "Greek Philosophy and the Cappadocian Cosmology." *DOP* 12 (1958) 29-58.

Campbell, James Marshall. *The Influence of the Second Sophistic on the Style of the Sermons of Saint Basil the Great.* Diss. Washington, D.C.: Catholic University of America, 1922.

Campenhausen, Hans von. "Saint Basil." In *The Fathers of the Greek Church,* pp. 84-100. New York: Pantheon, 1959.

———. *Ecclesiastical Authority and Spiritual Power in the Church of the First Three Centuries.* London: Black, 1969.

Capelle, Bernard. "La procession du Saint-Esprit d'après la liturgie grecque de saint Basile." *OS* 7 (1962) 69-76.

Cavalcanti, Elena. "Il problema del linguaggio teologico nell'*Adversus Eunomium* di Basilio Magno." *Aug* 14 (1974) 527-539.

———. *Studi eunomiani.* Rome: Pontificio Istituto orientale, 1975.

———. "'Excerpta' e temi sullo Spirito Santo in Ps. Basilio, *Adv. Eunomium, IV-V.*"
In *Forma futuri. Studi in onore di Michele Pellegrino*, pp. 1003-1021. Turin:
Bottega d'Erasmo, 1975.

Cavallera, Ferdinand. *Le schisme d'Antioche.* Paris: Picard, 1905.

Cavallin, Anders. *Studien zu den Briefen des hl. Basilius.* Diss. Lund: Gleerupska
universitetsbokhandeln, 1944.

Cayré, Fulbert. "Le divorce au IVᵉ siècle dans la loi civile et les canons de saint
Basile." *EO* 19 (1920) 295-321.

Cesaro, Maria. "Natura e cristianesimo negli *Exaemeron* di san Basilio e di
sant'Ambrogio." *Didaskaleion* 7 (1929) 53-123.

Chadwick, Henry. *The Early Church.* London: Penguin Books, 1967.

Chadwick, Owen. *John Cassian.* 2nd ed. Cambridge: University Press, 1968.

Chitty, Derwas James. *The Desert a City. An Introduction to the Study of Egyptian
and Palestinian Monasticism.* Oxford: Blackwell, 1966.

Chreptak, V. I. *Otnošenie sv. Vasilija Velikogo k Cerkvi.* Diss. Leningrad: Spiritual
Academy, 1967.

Christophe, Paul. *L'usage chrétien du droit de propriété dans l'écriture et la
tradition patristique.* Paris: Lethielleux, 1964.

Christou, Panayotis C. "L'enseignement de saint Basile sur le Saint-Esprit." *VC* 89
(1969) 86-99.

Clarke, William Kemp Lowther. *Saint Basil the Great. A Study in Monasticism.*
Cambridge: University Press, 1913.

———. *Saint Basil.* London: SPCK, 1921.

Cochrane, Charles Norris. *Christianity and Classical Culture. A Study of Thought
and Action from Augustus to Augustine.* Oxford: Clarendon Press, 1940.

Colibă, M. "Regulile monahale ale sf. Vasile cel Mare în istoria vietii religioase
monahale şi a cultului creştin." *Studii teologice* 17 (1965) 241-253.

Collégialité épiscopale, La. Histoire et théologie. Paris: Editions du Cerf, 1965.

Colombás, García M. *El monacato primitivo. 1: Hombres. Hechos. Costumbres. In-
stituciones.* BAC 351. Madrid: Editorial Católica, 1974.

Colson, Jean. *L'épiscopat catholique. Collégialité et primauté dans les trois premiers
siècles de l'Eglise.* Paris: Editions du Cerf, 1963.

Coman, J. "La démonstration dans le *Traité sur le Saint-Esprit* de s. Basile le
Grand." *MEPREO* 44 (1963) 218-221.

Conevski, I. K. "Vuzgledut na sv. Vasily Veliki za Čurkvata." *Godišnik na duchov-
nata Akademija Sofia* 36 (1961) 247-304.

Congar, Yves Marie Joseph. *After Nine Hundred Years; the Background of the
Schism between the Eastern and Western Churches.* New York: Fordham University, 1959.

——— et al., edd. *L'épiscopat et l'Eglise universelle.* Paris: Editions du Cerf, 1964.

Constantelos, Demetrios J. *Byzantine Philanthropy and Social Welfare.* New Bruns-
wick/N. J.: Rutgers University Press, 1968.

Conzelmann, Hans. Χάρισμα. *TDNT* (Grand Rapids, 1974), 9: 402-406.

Corneanu, N. "Les efforts de saint Basile pour l'unité de l'Eglise." *VC* 90 (1969) 43-67.

Cossu, Giovanni M. "Il motivo formale della carità in san Basilio Magno." *BBGG* 14 (1960) 3-30.

———. "L'amore naturale verso Dio e verso il prossimo nell'insegnamento di san Basilio Magno." *BBGG* 14 (1960) 87-107.

Courtonne, Yves. *Saint Basile et l'hellénisme. Etude sur la rencontre de la pensée chrétienne avec la sagesse antique dans l'Hexaéméron de Basile le Grand.* Paris: Firmin-Didot, 1934.

———. *Un témoin du IVᵉ siècle oriental. Saint Basile et son temps d'après sa correspondance.* Paris: Les Belles Lettres, 1973.

Crovini, Mario. "I malintesi di un famoso episodio storico del secolo quarto: Basilio e papa Damaso." *SC* 56 (1928) 321-344.

Dagron, Gilbert. "L'Empire romain d'Orient au IVᵉ siècle et les traditions politiques de l'hellénisme: Le témoignage de Thémistios." In *Travaux et mémoires*, 3: 1-242. Paris: de Boccard, 1968.

———. *Naissance d'une capitale. Constantinople et ses institutions de 330 à 451.* Paris: Presses universitaires de France, 1974.

D'Alès, Adhémar. "Le prince du siècle scrutateur des âmes selon s. Basile." *RSR* 23 (1933) 325-328.

Daniélou, Jean. "'Conspiratio' chez Grégoire de Nysse." In *L'homme devant Dieu. Mélanges H. de Lubac*, 1: 295-308. Paris: Aubier, 1963.

———. "L'évêque d'après une lettre de Grégoire de Nysse." *ED* 20 (1967) 85-98.

Davids, A. J. M. "On Ps.-Basil, *De baptismo*." *SP* 16 (Berlin, 1976) 302-306.

Décarreaux, Jean. *Monks and Civilization. From the Barbarian Invasions to the Reign of Charlemagne.* London: Allen & Unwin, 1964.

Dehnhard, Hans. *Das Problem der Abhängigkeit des Basilius von Plotin.* Diss. Berlin: de Gruyter, 1964.

Delhougne, Henri. "Autorité et participation chez les Pères du cénobitisme. Le cénobitisme basilien." *RAM* 46 (1970) 3-32.

Demopulos, H. Ὁ φωστὴρ τῆς Καισαρείας (ὁ μέγας Βασίλειος). Athens, 1964.

Denomy, Alexander Joseph. "An Old French Version of the Julian Episode in the Life of Saint Basil." *MS* 18 (1956) 105-124.

D'Ercole, Giuseppe. *Communio-Collegialità-Primato e Sollicitudo Omnium Ecclesiarum dai Vangeli a Costantino.* Rome: Herder, 1964.

———. "Il fondamento dei poteri episcopali nelle fonti del sec. II al sec. IV." *ED* 20 (1968) 335-368.

Deseille, Placide. "Les origines de la vie religieuse dans le christianisme." *Lumière et vie* 19 (1970) 25-53.

———. "Eastern Christian Sources of the Rule of St. Benedict." *Monastic Studies* 11 (1975) 73-122.

Diekamp, Franz. "Ein angeblicher Brief des heiligen Basilius gegen Eunomius." *ThQ* 77 (1895) 277-285.

——. "Literargeschichtliches zur Eunomianischen Kontroverse." *BZ* 18 (1909) 1-13; 190-194.

Dirking, Augustin. *Sancti Basilii Magni de divitia et paupertate sententiae quam habeant rationem cum veterum philosophorum doctrina. Commentatio philologica.* Münster, 1911.

——. "Tertullian und Basilius." *ThG* 4 (1912) 189-201.

——. "Die Bedeutung des Wortes Apathie bei Basilius dem Grossen." *ThQ* 134 (1954) 202-212.

Dix, Gregory. *Le ministère dans l'Eglise ancienne.* Neuchâtel: Delachaux, 1955.

Dodds, Eric Robertson. *Pagan and Christian in an Age of Anxiety. Some Aspects of Religious Experience from Marcus Aurelius to Constantine.* New York: Norton, 1970.

Dörries, Hermann. "Das Asketikon des Basilius." In *Symeon von Mesopotamien. Die Ueberlieferung der messalianischen "Makarios" Schriften,* pp. 451-465. Leipzig: Hinrichs, 1941.

——. *De Spiritu Sancto. Der Beitrag des Basilius zum Abschluss des Trinitarischen Dogmas.* Göttingen: Ruprecht, 1956.

——. "Basilius und das Dogma vom hl. Geist." *LR* 6 (1956) 247-262.

——. "Die Beichte im alten Mönchtum." In *Judentum, Urchristentum, Kirche. Festschrift Joachim Jeremias,* pp. 235-259. Berlin, 1960.

Doresse, Jean & Emmanuel Lanne. *Un témoin archaïque de la liturgie de s. Basile.* En annexe: Bernard Capelle, *Les liturgies "basiliennes" et s. Basile.* Louvain: Publ. Univers., 1960.

Downey, Glanville. "Philanthropia in Religion and Statecraft in the Fourth Century after Christ." *Historia* 5 (1955) 199-208.

Drack, Basil. "Beschauliches und tätiges Leben bei Mönchtum nach der Lehre Basilius des Grossen." *FZPhTh* 7 (1960) 297-309; 8 (1961) 92-108.

Duchatelez, K. "La 'koinonia' chez s. Basile le Grand." *Communio* 6 (1973) 163-180.

Duchesne, Louis. *The Early History of the Christian Church.* 3 vols. London: Murray, 1909, 1912, 1924.

Dunn, James D. G. *Jesus and the Spirit. A Study of the Religious and Charismatic Experience of Jesus and the First Christians as Reflected in the New Testament.* London: SCM, 1975.

Eickhoff, H. *Zwei Schriften des Basilius und Augustinus als geschichtliche Dokumente der Vereinigung von klassischen Bildung und Christentum.* Schlesswig, 1897.

Eirenides, D. Βίος τοῦ ἐν ἁγίοις πατρὸς ἡμῶν Βασιλείου τοῦ μεγάλου. Athens, 1881.

Engberding, Hieronymus. *Das Eucharistische Hochgebet der Basileiosliturgie.* Münster, 1931.

——. "Die Verehrung des hl. Basilius des Grossen in der byzantinischen Liturgie." *COVG* 2 (1937) 16-22.

——. "Das anaphorische Fürbittgebet der Basiliusliturgie." *OCh* 49 (1965) 18-37.

Ernst, V. "Basilius des Grossen Verkehr mit den Occidentalen." *ZKT* 16 (1896) 626-664.

Evdokimov, Paul. *L'Orthodoxie*. Neuchâtel: Delachaux, 1959.

Ewell, John Louis. *Basil and Jerome Compared*. New York, 1913.

Fedwick, Paul Jonathan. "The Function of the προεστώς in the Earliest Christian κοινωνία." *Recherches de théologie ancienne et médiévale* 48 (1977) forthcoming.

———. *Svijatyj Vasylyj Velykyj i chrystijanske askytychne zyttija*. (Analecta OSBM, Opera historica, 39.) Toronto: Basilian Press, 1978.

———. "A Commentary of Gregory of Nyssa or the 38th Letter of Basil of Caesarea." *OCP* 44 (1978) 31-51.

———. "The Quotations of Basil of Caesarea in the Florilegium of the Pseudo-Antony Melissa." *OCP*, forthcoming.

Fedyniak, Sergius. *Mariologia apud Patres Orientales (Basilium Magnum, Gregorium Nazianzenum, Gregorium Nyssenum)*. 2nd ed. Rome: Apud Curiam generalem Ordinis Basiliani, 1958.

Felci, C. *L'ideale della povertà nell'ascetismo e nel monachesimo primitivo*. Rome, 1956.

Festugière, André Marie Jean. "Basile et Chrysostome ont-ils été élèves de Libanius?" In *Antioche païenne et chrétienne*, pp. 409-410. Paris: de Boccard, 1959.

Fialon, Eugène. *Etude historique et littéraire sur saint Basile*. 2nd ed. Paris: Ernest Thorin, 1869.

Florovsky, Georges. "The Function of Tradition in the Ancient Church." *GOTR* 9 (1963) 181-200.

Forlin Patrucco, Marcella. "Povertà e ricchezza nell'avanzato IV secolo: la condanna dei mutui in Basilio di Cesarea." *Aevum* 47 (1973) 225-234.

———. "Aspetti del fiscalismo tardo-imperiale in Cappadocia. La testimonianza di Basilio di Cesarea." *Athenaeum* 51 (1973) 294-303.

———. "Aspetti di vita familiare nel IV secolo negli scritti dei Padri Cappadoci." In *Etica sessuale e matrimonio nel cristianesimo delle origini*, pp. 158-179. Milan, 1976.

Fossa, V. "Evangelium Sancti Matthaei in operibus S. Basilii Magni." Diss. Rome: Pontificium Athenaeum Anselmianum, 1964.

Fox, Margaret Mary. *The Life and Times of Saint Basil the Great as Revealed in His Works*. Diss. Washington, D.C.: Catholic University of America, 1939.

Fragonard, Marie Madeleine. "Patristique et pensée protestante: De l'*Hexaéméron* de s. Basile à *La création* d'Agrippe d'Aubigné." *Revue d'histoire littéraire de la France* 77 (1977) 3-23.

Franck, Lisbeth. "Sources classiques concernant la Cappadoce." *Revue hittite et asianique* 24 (1966) 5-122.

Frank, S. "Gehorsam und Freiheit im frühen Mönchtum." *Römische Quartalschrift* 64 (1969) 234-245.

Fremantle, Anne. "Saint Basil." *Month* 19 (1958) 154-163.

Frings, H. J. *Medizin und Arzt bei den griechischen Kirchenvätern.* Diss. Bonn, 1959; pp. 2-23: "St. Basil."

Gagé, Jean. *Les classes sociales dans l'Empire romain.* Paris: Payot, 1964.

Gallay, Paul. *La vie de s. Grégoire de Nazianze.* Lyon: Vitte, 1943.

Gallicet, E. "Intorno all'attribuzione a Basilio delle due omelie *De creatione hominis.*" *Atti della Accademia delle Scienze di Torino* 109 (1975) 319-342.

Galtier, Paul. "Le Tome de Damase." *RSR* 26 (1936) 404-410.

Ganshof, François Louis. "Note sur l'élection des évêques dans l'Empire romain au IVᵉ siècle et pendant la première moitié du Vᵉ." *Revue internationale des droits de l'Antiquité* 4 (1950) 367-498.

Gaudemet, Jean. *La formation du droit séculier et du droit de l'Eglise aux IVᵉ et Vᵉ siècles.* Paris: Sirey, 1957.

——. *L'Eglise dans l'Empire romain (IVᵉ-Vᵉ siècles).* Paris: Sirey, 1958.

Gaume, Fratres. "The Letters and Times of Basil of Caesarea." *NAR* 90 (1860) 356-395.

Geerard, Mauritius. "Basilius Caesariensis." In *Clavis Patrum Graecorum*, 2: 140-178 (nos. 2835-3005). Turnhout: Brepols, 1974.

Gelsinger, Michael S. H. "The Epiclesis in the Liturgy of Saint Basil." *EChQ* 10 (1954) 243-248.

Geoghegan, Arthur Turbitt. *The Attitude towards Labor in Early Christianity and Ancient Culture.* Diss. Washington, D.C.: Catholic University of America, 1945; pp. 175-181: Basil of Caesarea.

Georgescu, M. "Idei morale şi sociale în *Commentarul la Psalmi* al sf. Vasile cel Mare." *Studia Bucureşti* 10 (1958) 463-474.

Ghellinck, Joseph de. "Un cas de conscience dans les conflits trinitaires sur le Saint-Esprit." In *Patristique et Moyen Age*, pp. 313-338. Paris-Gembloux, 1948.

Giacchero, Marta. "L'influsso di Plutarco sulla condanna basiliana del prestito ad interesse." In *Tetraonyma, Miscellanea graeco-romana L. de Regibus, et al.*, pp. 157-174. Genova: Pubblicazioni dell'Istituto di filologia classica, 1966.

Gibson, Arthur. "Saint Basil's Liturgical Authorship." Diss. Washington, D.C.: Catholic University of America, 1965.

Giet, Stanislas. *Les idées et l'action sociales de s. Basile.* Paris: Gabalda, 1941.

——. *Sasime. Une méprise de s. Basile.* Paris: Gabalda, 1941.

——. "S. Basile et les pouvoirs publics." *VS* 69 (1943) 349-360.

——. "De s. Basile à s. Ambroise. La condamnation du prêt à intérêt au IVᵉ siècle." *RSR* 32 (1944) 95-128.

——. "La doctrine de l'approbation des biens chez quelques-uns des Pères." *RSR* 35 (1948) 55-91.

——. "S. Basile et le concile de Constantinople de 360." *JThS* 6 (1955) 94-99.

——. "Basile, était-il sénateur?" *RHE* 60 (1965) 429-444.

Girardi, Mario. "Le 'nozioni comuni sullo Spirito Santo' in Basilio Magno." *VChr* 13 (1976) 269-288.

Gnesko, Modestus. "De monastica professione paupertatis apud sanctum Basilium M." Diss. Rome, 1951.

Goemans, Monald. *De hl. Basilius de Grote en de geneeskunde.* Nijmegen, 1951.

Goppelt, Leonhardt. *Apostolic and Post-Apostolic Times.* London: Black, 1970.

Gorce, Denys. *Les voyages, l'hospitalité et le port des lettres dans le monde chrétien des IVe et Ve siècles.* Paris: Picard, 1925.

Grandsire, A. "Nature et hypostases divines dans s. Basile." *RSR* 13 (1923) 130-152.

Grasso, Domenico. *Proclaiming God's Message.* Notre Dame: University Press, 1965.

Greenslade, Stanley Lawrence. *Schism in the Early Church.* London: SCM, 1953.

Gregg, Robert Clark. *Consolation Philosophy: Greek and Christian Paideia in Basil and the Two Gregories.* Diss. Cambridge, Mass.: Philadelphia Patristic Foundation, 1975.

Greer, Rowan A. "Hospitality in the First Five Centuries of the Church." *Monastic Studies* 10 (1974) 29-48.

Gribomont, Jean. "Obéissance et évangile selon s. Basile le Grand." *VSSt* 21 (1952) 191-215.

———. *Histoire du texte des Ascétiques de s. Basile.* Diss. Louvain: Publications universitaires, 1953.

———. "L'exhortation au renoncement attribué à s. Basile." *OCP* 21 (1955) 375-398.

———. "Le monachisme au IVe siècle en Asie Mineure: de Gangres au Messalianisme." *SP* 2 (Berlin, 1957) 400-416.

———. "Les *Règles morales* de s. Basile et le Nouveau Testament." *SP* 2 (Berlin, 1957) 416-426.

———. "Le renoncement au monde dans l'idéal ascétique de s. Basile." *Irénikon* 31 (1958) 282-307; 460-475.

———. "Eustathe le Philosophe et les voyages du jeune Basile de Césarée." *RHE* 54 (1959) 115-124.

———. "In tomos 29, 30, 31, 32 PG ad editionem operum s. Basilii Magni introductio." Photost. rpt. PG 29-32, Turnhout: Brepols, 1959.

———. "In tomum 29, 31, 32 PG adnotationes." Photost. rpt. PG 29-32, Turnhout: Brepols, 1959, 1961.

———. "Eustathe." *DSp* (Paris, 1961), 4: 1708-1712.

———. "Saint Basile." In *Théologie de la vie monastique,* pp. 99-113. Paris: Aubier, 1961.

———. "L'origénisme de s. Basile." In *L'homme devant Dieu. Mélanges H. de Lubac,* 1: 281-294. Paris: Aubier, 1963.

———. "Le paulinisme de s. Basile." In *Studiorum Paulinorum congressus internationalis catholicus 1961,* 2: 481-490. Rome: Pontificium Institutum Biblicum, 1963.

———. "Le monachisme au sein de l'Eglise en Syrie et en Cappadoce." *SM* 7 (1965) 7-24.

——. Review of H. Dehnhard, *Das Problem...* (see above) in *RHE* 60 (1965) 487-492.

——. "Basil, St." *NCE* (New York, 1966), 2: 143-146.

——. "Eustathe de Sebaste." *DHGE* (Paris, 1967), 16: 26-33.

——. "Esotérisme et tradition dans le *Traité du Saint-Esprit* de s. Basile." *Oecumenica* 2 (1967) 22-56.

——. "Le *Panégyrique de la virginité*, œuvre de jeunesse de s. Grégoire de Nysse." *RAM* 43 (1967) 249-266.

——. "Le dossier des origines du Messalianisme." In *Epektasis. Mélanges J. Daniélou*, pp. 611-625. Paris: Beauchesne, 1972.

——. "Les lemmes de citation de s. Basile, indice de niveau littéraire." *Aug* 14 (1974) 513-526.

——. "Antonio l'eremita, San." *DIP* (Rome, 1974), 1: 700-703.

——. "Asceta"; "Ascetismo ecclesiale premonastico." *DIP* (Rome, 1974), 1: 915-917; 924-926.

——. "Basilio, San." *DIP* (Rome, 1974), 1: 1101-1109.

——. "Les succès littéraires des Pères grecs et les problèmes d'histoire des textes." *SE* 22 (1974/1975) 23-49.

——. "Intransigencia e irenismo en san Basilio. Introducción al *De Spiritu Sancto.*" *Estudios trinitarios* 9 (1975) 227-243.

——. "Rome et l'Orient. Invitations et reproches de saint Basile." *Seminarium* 27 (1975) 336-354.

——. "Un aristocrate révolutionnaire, évêque et moine: saint Basile." *Aug* 17 (1977) 179-191.

Grillmeier, Aloys. *Christ in Christian Tradition. 1: From the Apostolic Age to Chalcedon (451).* 2nd ed. Atlanta: Knox Press, 1975.

Gronau, Karl. *Poseidonius, eine Quelle für Basilius' Hexaemeron.* Braunschweig, 1912.

Grumel, Venance. "Saint Basile et le siège apostolique." *EO* 21 (1922) 280-292.

Guillén-Preckler, Fernando. "Basilio di Cappadocia e l'occidente. Ricerca storico-teologica." *Communio* 6 (1973) 5-32.

Hall, Stuart G. "Le fonctionnaire impérial excommunié par Athanase d'Alexandrie vers 371. Essai d'identification." In Charles Kannengiesser, ed., *Politique et théologie chez Athanase d'Alexandrie*, pp. 157-159. Paris: Beauchesne, 1974.

Hands, Arthur Robinson. *Charities and Social Aid in Greece and Rome.* London: Thames & Hudson, 1968.

Hanson, Richard Patrick Crosland. *Tradition in the Early Church.* London: SCM, 1962.

——. "Basil's Doctrine of Tradition in Relation to the Holy Spirit." *VCh* 22 (1968) 241-255.

Hanssens, Jean Michel. *La liturgie d'Hippolyte. Ses documents, son titulaire, ses origines et son caractère.* Rome: Pontificium Institutum Orientalium Studiorum, 1959.

Hardy, Edward R. "Basil the Great, Saint." *The New Encyclopedia Britannica. Macropaedia* 2: 747-748. Chicago: Benton, 1974.

Harl, Margaret. "Les trois quarantaines de la vie de Moïse, schéma idéal de la vie du moine-évêque chez les Pères Cappadociens." *REG* 80 (1967) 407-412.

Harnack, Adolf von. *History of Dogma.* 7 vols. New York: Dover, 1961.

———. *The Mission and Expansion of Christianity in the First Three Centuries.* 2 vols. London: Williams, 1904/1905.

Hatch, Edwin. *The Influence of Greek Ideas on Christianity.* New York: Torch-books, 1957.

———. *The Organization of the Early Christian Churches.* New York: Franklin, 1972.

Hauschild, Wolf Dieter. *Die Pneumatomachen. Eine Untersuchung zur Dogmengeschichte des vierten Jahrhunderts.* Diss. Hamburg, 1967.

———. *Basilius von Caesarea, Briefe,* 2. Stuttgart: Hiersemann, 1973.

Hauser-Meury, Marie Madeleine. *Prosopographie zu den Schriften Gregors von Nazianz.* Bonn: Hanstein, 1960.

Hausherr, Irénée. "Les grands courants de la spiritualité orientale." *OCP* 1 (1935) 114-138.

———. "L'erreur fondamentale et la logique du Messalianisme." *OCP* 1 (1935) 328-360.

———. *Etudes de spiritualité orientale.* Rome: Pontificium Institutum Orientalium Studiorum, 1969.

Hayes, Walter Martin. *The Greek Manuscript Tradition of (Ps.) Basil's Adversus Eunomium IV-V.* Leiden: Brill, 1972.

Hawkaluk, Alexander. "De nominibus Dei apud sanctum Basilium Magnum." Diss. Rome: Anselmianum, 1965.

Hefele, Karl Josef & Henri Leclercq. *Histoire des conciles d'après les documents originaux.* 10 vols. Paris: Letouzey, 1907-1938.

Heising, Alkuin. "Der Hl. Geist und die Heiligung der Engel in der Pneumatologie des Basilius von Caesarea." *ZKTh* 87 (1965) 257-308.

Hengsberg, W. *De ornatu rhetorico, quem Basilius Magnus in diversis homiliarum generibus adhibuit.* Diss. Bonn, 1957.

Henry, Paul. *Les états du texte de Plotin.* Paris: Desclée, 1938.

Hermant, Godefroy. *La vie de s. Basile le Grand, archevêque de Césarée en Cappadoce, et celle de s. Grégoire de Nazianze, divisées en douze livres.* 2 vols. Paris: Dezallier, 1679.

Herter, H. "Basileios der Grosse und das Problem der profanen Bildung." In *Proceedings of the First International Humanistic Symposium at Delphi 1969,* 1: 252-260. Athens, 1970-1971.

Hertling, Ludwig. *Communio, Church and Papacy in the Early Christianity.* Chicago: Loyola University Press, 1972.

Holl, Karl. ["Basil's Ascetic Ideal"]. In *Enthusiasmus und Bussgewalt beim griechischen Mönchtum. Eine Studie zu Symeon den Neuen Theologen,* pp. 138-170; 258-273. Leipzig: Hinrichs, 1898; rpt. 1968.

——. ["Basil's Trinitarian Teaching"]. In *Amphilochius von Ikonium in seinem Verhältnis zu den grossen Kappadoziern*, pp. 116-158. Tübingen: Mohr, 1904; rpt. 1969.

Hornus, Jean Michel. "La divinité du Saint-Esprit comme condition du salut personnel selon Basile." *VC* 89 (1968) 33-62.

Houdret, Jean Philippe. "Palamas et les Cappadociens." *Istina* 19 (1974) 260-271.

Hübner, Reinhard. "Gregor von Nyssa als Verfasser der sog. *Ep.* 38 des Basilius. Zum unterschiedlichen Verständnis der ousia bei den Kappadozischen Brüdern." *Epektasis. Mélanges Jean Daniélou*, pp. 463-490. Paris: Beauchesne, 1972.

Humbertclaude, Pierre. *La doctrine ascétique de s. Basile*. Paris: Beauchesne, 1932.

Ibañez, Javier. "Aspecto eclesiológico en la teología de Basilio de Cesarea." *STh* 2 (1970) 7-38.

Ivanka, Endre von. *Hellenisches und Christliches im frühbyzantinischen Geistesleben*. Vienna: Herder, 1948.

Ivanov, N. "Velikij stolp pravoslavija svatitel Vasilij, archiepiskop Kesarij Kappadokijskoj." *Žurnal moskovskoj patrijarchij* 1 (1959) 40-50.

Jacks, Leo Vincent. *St. Basil and Greek Literature*. Diss. Washington, D.C.: Catholic University of America, 1922.

Jackson, Blomfield. "Sketch of the Life and Works of Saint Basil," in *SLPNF* 8: xiii-lxxvii.

Jäger, Werner. "Basilius und der Abschluss des trinitarischen Dogmas." *ThL* 83 (1958) 255-258.

——. *Early Christianity and Greek Paideia*. Oxford: University Press, 1961.

Jahn, Albert. *Basilius Magnus plotinizans*. Bern: Jennium, 1838.

Janin, Raymond. *Saint Basile, archevêque de Césarée et docteur de l'Eglise*. Paris, 1929.

Janini Cuesta, José. "La penitencia medicinal desde la *Didascalia Apostolorum* a san Gregorio de Nisa." *Revista Española de Teología* 7 (1947) 337-362.

Jerphanion, Guillaume de. "Ibora-Gazioura? Etude de géographie pontique." In *Mélanges de la Faculté Orientale* (Beirut, 1911), 5: 333-354.

——. "Histoires de saint Basile dans les peintures cappadociens et dans les peintures romaines du Moyen Age." *Byzantion* 6 (1931) 535-558.

Jones, Arnold Hugh Martin. *The Later Roman Empire 284-602: A Social, Economic, and Administrative Survey*. 3 vols. Oxford: Blackwell, 1964.

——. *Were Ancient Heresies Disguised Social Movements?* Philadelphia: Fortress, 1966.

——. *The Decline of the Ancient World*. London: Longmans, 1966.

——. *The Cities of the Eastern Roman Provinces*. 2nd. ed. Oxford: Clarendon, 1971.

——, et al., edd. *Prosopography of the Later Roman Empire*. 1: *A.D. 260-395*. Cambridge: University Press, 1971.

Jounel, Pierre. "Les ordinations." In A. G. Martimort, ed., *L'Eglise en prière. Introduction à la liturgie*, pp. 477-513. Paris: Desclée, 1961.

Jülicher, Adolf. "Basileios." A. Pauly & G. Wissowa, edd. *Real-Encyclopädie der classischen Altertumswissenschaft* (Stuttgart, 1897), 3: 52-54.

Junod, Eric. "Remarques sur la composition de la *Philocalie* d'Origène par Basile de Césarée et Grégoire de Nazianze." *RHPR* 52 (1973) 149-156.

Jursuk, M. "Sv. Vasilij Velikij i ego borba z arianstvom v dijatelnosti pasteria i v bogoslovskich trudach." Diss. Moscow, 1958.

Käsemann, Ernst. *Essays on New Testament Themes*. London: SCM, 1964.

——. *New Testament Questions of Today*. London: SCM, 1969.

Karayannopulos, John. Review of B. Treucker, *Politische* ... (see below) in *BZ* 65 (1963) 356-359.

Karmiris, John. Ἡ ἐκκλησιολογία τοῦ μεγάλου Βασιλείου. Athens, 1958.

Kelly, John Norman Davidson. *Early Christian Doctrines*. 4th ed. London: Black, 1968.

——. *Early Christian Creeds*. 3rd ed. London: Longmans, 1972.

Kittel, Gerhart, et al., edd. *Theological Dictionary of the New Testament*. 10 vols. Eng. trans. & ed. by Geoffrey W. Bromiley. Grand Rapids: Eerdmans, 1964-1976.

Klose, C. R. W. *Ein Beitrag zur Kirchengeschichte: Basilius der Grosse nach seinem Leben und seiner Lehre*. Stralsund, 1835.

Knorr, Uwe Walter. "Basilius der Grosse. Sein Beitrag zur christlichen Durchdringung Kleinasiens." Diss. Tübingen, 1968.

——. "Einige Bemerkungen zu vier unechten Basilius-Briefen." *ZKG* 80 (1969) 375-381.

Kötting, Bernhard. *Peregrinatio religiosa. Wahlfahrten in der Antike und das Pilgerwesen in der alten Kirche*. Regensburg-Münster, 1950.

Konidaris, G. "Ὁ μέγας Βασίλειος πρότυπον οἰκουμενικοῦ ἐκκλησιαστηκοῦ ἡγέτου." *Parnassos* 8 (1966) 31-46.

Kopecek, Thomas A. "Social Class of the Cappadocian Fathers." *CH* 42 (1973) 453-466.

——. "Cappadocian Fathers and Civic Patriotism." *CH* 43 (1974) 293-303.

——. "Curial Displacements and Flight in Later Fourth-Century Cappadocia." *Historia* 23 (1974) 319-342.

Kourkoula, K. Αἱ περὶ θείου κηρύγματος ἰδέαι τοῦ μεγάλου Βασιλείου. Salonika, 1964.

Kovalyk, Volodimir. *Obnova ljubove na osnovi navchania sv. Vasilija Velikoho*. Buenos Aires: Padres Basilianos, 1959.

Kranich, Anton. *Der hl. Basilius in seiner Stellung zum "Filioque."* Braunsburger, 1882.

——. *Die Ascetik in ihrer dogmatischen Grundlage bei Basilius den Grossen*. Paderborn: Schöningh, 1896.

Kretschmar, Georg. "Ein Beitrag zur Frage nach dem Ursprung frühchristlicher Askese." *ZTK* 61 (1964) 27-67.

Krivocheine, Basile. "L'ecclésiologie de s. Basile le Grand." *MEPREO* 17 (1969) 75-102.

Küng, Hans. *The Church.* New York: Image Books, 1976.

Kuljov, Vasilij Nikiforovich. "Uchenie sv. Vasilija Velikogo o cheloveke." Diss. Leningrad, 1966.

Ladner, Gerhart Burian. *The Idea of Reform: Its Impact on Christian Thought and Action in the Age of the Fathers.* Cambridge, Mass.: Harvard University Press, 1959.

Lafontaine, Jacques. "Nouvelles notes cappadociennes." *Byzantion* 33 (1963) 121-183.

Lagarde, André (=Joseph Turmel). "La confession dans s. Basile." *RHLR* 8 (1922) 534-548.

Lampe, Geoffrey William Hugo, ed. *A Patristic Greek Lexicon.* Oxford: University Press, 1961-1965.

Laube, Adolfus. *De litterarum Libanii et Basilii commercio.* Vratislava: Nischkowski, 1913.

Laun, Ferdinand. "Die beiden Regeln des Basilius, ihre Echtheit und ihre Entstehung." *ZK* 44 (1925) 1-61.

Lavros, Jean. "Les idées anthropologiques et l'activité morale de s. Basile." Dipl. Lille, 1958.

Lazzati, Giuseppe. *L'Aristotele perduto e gli scrittori cristiani.* Milan: Vita e pensiero, 1933.

——. "Basilio di Cesarea insegnò retorica?" *SMSR* 38 (1973) 284-292.

Lèbe, Léon. "S. Basile et ses *Règles morales.*" *RB* 75 (1965) 193-200.

——. "S. Basile. Note à propos des *Règles monastiques.*" *RB* 76 (1966) 116-119.

Lebon, Joseph. "Le Pseudo-Basile (*Adv. Eunomius, IV-V*) est bien Didyme d'Alexandrie." *Le Muséon* 50 (1938) 61-83.

——. "Le sort du consubstantiel nicéen." *RHE* 47 (1952) 485-529; 48 (1953) 632-682.

Leclercq, Henri. "Cénobitisme." *DACL* (Paris, 1910), 2: 3047-3248.

——. "Monachisme." *DACL* (Paris, 1934), 11: 1774-1947.

Lecuyer, Joseph. *Etudes sur la collégialité épiscopale.* Le Puy: Mappus, 1964.

Leggio, Efremo. *L'ascetica di s. Basilio.* Turin, 1934.

Legrand, Hervé Marie. "The Revaluation of Local Churches: Some Theological Implications." *Concilium* 71 (1972) 53-64.

Lemerle, Paul. *Le premier humanisme byzantin. Notes et remarques sur enseignement et culture à Byzance des origines au xe siècle.* Paris: Presses universitaires de France, 1971.

Leroy, Julien. "Experience of God and Primitive Cenobitism." *Monastic Studies* 9 (1972) 59-81.

L'Huillier, P. "Les sources canoniques de s. Basile." *MEPREO* 44 (1963) 210-217.

Lialine, Clément. "Eastern and Western Monasticism." *Monastic Studies* 1 (1963) 59-83.

Liddell, Henry George & Robert Scott. *A Greek-English Lexicon.* Oxford: University Press, 1940; rpt. 1968 with Supplement.

Lietzmann, Hans. *History of the Early Church.* 4 vols. Cleveland: World, 1961.

——. *Apollinaris von Laodicea und seine Schule.* Tübingen, 1904; rpt. Hildesheim-New York: Olms, 1970.

Lilienfeld, Fairy von. "Basilius der Grosse und die Mönchsväter der Wüste." *Zeitschrift der deutschen morgenländischen Gesellschaft* 17 (1969) 418-435.

Lohn, Ladislaus, "Doctrina s. Basilii de processionibus divinarum personarum." *Gregorianum* 10 (1929) 329-364; 461-500.

——. "Nauka sw. Bazylego o pochodzeniu Sw. Ducha również i od Syna na podstawie iii. ks. przeciw Eunomjuszowi." *Przenglad teologiczny* 10 (1929) 407-427.

Lohse, Bernhard. *Askese und Mönchtum in der Antike und der alten Kirche.* München: Oldenbourg, 1969.

Loofs, Friedrich. *Eustathius von Sebaste und die Chronologie der Basiliusbriefe.* Halle: Niemeyer, 1898.

Lossky, Vladimir. *Essai sur la théologie mystique de l'Eglise d'Orient.* Paris: Aubier, 1944.

Lot-Borodine, Myrrha. *La déification de l'homme selon la doctrine des Pères grecs.* Paris: Editions du Cerf, 1970.

Lubatschiwskyj, M. J. "Des hl. Basilius liturgischer Kampf gegen den Arianismus. Ein Beitrag zur Textgeschichte der Basiliusliturgie." *ZKTh* 66 (1942) 20-38.

Luneau, Auguste. *L'histoire du salut chez les Pères de l'Eglise. La doctrine des âges du monde.* Paris: Beauchesne, 1964.

Maier, Johannes. *Die Eucharistielehre der drei grossen Kappadozier.* Freiburg-im-Breisgau: Herder, 1915.

Malingrey, Anne Marie. *"Philosophia." Etude d'un groupe de mots dans la littérature grecque, des Présocratiques au ive siècle après J.C.* Paris: Klincksieck, 1961.

Malunowiczowna, L. "Le problème de l'amitié chez Basile, Grégoire le Théologien et Jean Chrysostome." *Rocznik humanisteczny* 16 (1968) 107-132.

Maran, Prudentius. *Vita s. Basilii Magni.* PG 29, v-clxxvii. See Julien Garnier and Prudentius Maran, edd. & trans. *Sancti Basilii Magni Opera omnia.*

Marrou, Henri Irénée. *History of Education in Antiquity.* New York: Sheed & Ward, 1956.

Martimort, Aimé Georges, ed. *L'Eglise en prière. Introduction à la liturgie.* Paris: Desclée, 1961.

Martin, Victor. *Essai sur les lettres de s. Basile le Grand.* Nantes, 1865.

Martland, T. R. "A Study of Cappadocian and Augustinian Trinitarian Methodology." *Anglican Theological Review* 47 (1965) 252-263.

Mateos, Juan. "L'office monastique à la fin du ive siècle: Antioche, Palestine, Cappadoce." *OCh* 47 (1963) 53-88.

May, Gerhard. "Einige Bemerkungen über das Verhältnis Gregors von Nyssa zu Basilius dem Grossen." In *Epektasis. Mélanges Jean Daniélou*, pp. 509-515. Paris: Beauchesne, 1972.

——. "Basilius der Grosse und der römische Staat." In *Bleibendes im Wandel. Studien Hans von Campenhausen*, ed. B. von Möller & G. Ruhbach, pp. 47-70. Tübingen: Mohr, 1973.

Mazzarino, Santo. *Aspetti sociali del quarto secolo; ricerche di storia tardo-romana.* Rome: Bretschneider, 1951.

Meer, Frederik van der & Christine Mohrmann. *Atlas of the Early Christian World.* London: Nelson, 1958.

Meester, Placidus de. "Authenticité des liturgies de s. Basile et de s. Jean Chrysostome." *DACL* (Paris, 1925), 6: 1596-1604.

Melcher, Robert. *Der 8. Brief des hl. Basilius ein Werk des Evagrius Pontikus.* Diss. Münster: Aschendorff, 1923.

Mellis, L. *Die ekklesiologischen Vorstellungen des hl. Basilius des Grossen.* Oberhausen, 1973.

Meredith, Antony. "Orthodoxy, Heresy and Philosophy in the Latter Half of the Fourth Century." *The Heythrop Journal* 16 (1975) 5-21.

———. "Asceticism—Christian and Greek." *JThS* 27 (1976) 313-332.

Merki, Hubert. Ὁμοίωσις Θεῷ. *Von der platonischen Angleichung an Gott zur Gottähnlichkeit bei Gregor von Nyssa.* Freiburg in der Schweiz: Paulusverlag, 1952.

Metz, René. *La consécration des vierges dans l'Eglise romaine.* Paris: Presses universitaires de France, 1957.

Michaud, E. "S. Basile de Césarée et s. Cyrille d'Alexandrie sur la question trinitaire." *Revue internationale de théologie* 16 (1898) 354-371.

Mitchell, J. F. "Consolatory Letters in Basil and Gregory Nazianzen." *Hermes* 96 (1968) 299-318.

Mitchell, Leonel L. "Alexandrian Anaphora of St. Basil of Caesarea: Ancient Source of 'A Common Eucharistic Prayer'." *Anglican Theological Review* 58 (1976) 194-206.

Moffatt, Ann. "The Occasion of St. Basil's *Address to Young Men.*" *Antichton* 4 (1972) 74-86.

Molle, M. M. van. "Essai de classement chronologique des premières règles de vie commune connue en chrétienté." *VSSt* 21 (1968) 108-127.

———. "Confrontation entre les règles et la littérature pachômienne postérieure." *VSSt* 21 (1968) 394-424.

———. "Aux origines de la vie communautaire chrétienne, quelques équivoques déterminantes pour l'avenir." *VSSt* 22 (1969) 101-121.

———. "Vie commune et obéissance d'après les institutions premières de Pachôme et Basile." *VSSt* 23 (1970) 196-225.

Momigliano, Arnaldo, ed. *The Conflict between Paganism and Christianity in the Fourth Century.* Oxford: University Press, 1963.

Monaci Cavetonienses (Chevetogne). "In tomum 30 Patrologiae graecae ad editionem operum s. Basilii Magni adnotationes." Photost. rpt. PG 29-32, Turnhout: Brepols, 1960.

Mongelli, S. "Eustazio di Sebaste, Basilio e lo scisma macedoniano." *Nicolaus* 3 (1975) 455-469.

Monticelli, P. F. "Collegialità episcopale ed occidente nella visione di s. Basilio Magno. Le nozioni di πλῆθος e ἀξιόπιστον." *Annali della Facoltà di Magistero di Bari,* 6 (1967) 1-38.

Morison, Ernest Frederick. *Saint Basil and His Rule. A Study in Early Monasticism.* Oxford: University Press, 1912.

Moser, Karl. *Die Lehre des hl. Basilius über den Glauben.* Diss. Rome: Pontificia Università Gregoriana, 1940.

Mossay, Justin. *Les fêtes de Noël et d'Epiphanie d'après les sources littéraires cappadociennes du ɪᵛᵉ siècle.* Louvain: Abbaye du Mont-César, 1965.

Mouratidos, Constantine. "Χριστοκεντρικὴ ποιμαντικὴ ἐν τοῖς ἀσκητικοῖς τοῦ μεγάλου Βασιλείου." *Theologia* 33 (1962) 54-82.

——. "Ποιμαντικαὶ ἀρχαὶ καὶ μέθοδοι ἐν τῇ ἀσκητικῇ διδασκαλίᾳ τοῦ μεγάλου Βασιλείου." *Ephemerios* 15 (1965) 967-1022.

Muraille, Philippe. "L'Eglise, peuple de l'oikouménè d'après s. Grégoire de Nazianze. Notes sur l'unité et l'universalité." *EThL* 44 (1968) 154-178.

Murphy, Francis Xavier. "Moral and Ascetical Doctrine in Saint Basil." *SP* 16 (Berlin, 1976) 320-326.

Murphy, Margaret Gertrude. *Saint Basil and Monasticism.* Diss. 2nd ed. New York: A.M.S. Press, 1971.

Musurillo, Herbert. "The Problem of Ascetical Fasting in the Greek Patristic Writers." *Traditio* 12 (1956) 1-64.

Nagel, Peter. *Die Motivierung der Askese in der alten Kirche und der Ursprung der Mönchtum.* Berlin, 1966.

Nager, Franz. *Die Trinitätslehre des hl. Basilius des Grossen.* Paderborn, 1912.

Naldini, Mario. "Paideia origeniana nella '*Oratio ad adolescentes*' di Basilio Magno." *VChr* 13 (1976) 297-318.

Neuhäusler, Engelbert. *Der Bischof als geistlicher Vater nach den frühchristlichen Schriften.* Münster: Kösel, 1964.

Newman, John Henry. "Trials of Basil"; "Labours of Basil"; "Basil and Gregory." In *Essays and Sketches,* 3: 5-28; 29-50; 51-73. New York: Longmans, 1948.

Nock, Arthur Darby. *Conversion. The Old and the New in Religion from Alexander the Great to Augustine of Hippo.* Oxford: University Press, 1961.

Noethlichs, Karl Leo. "Materialen zum Bischofsbild aus den spätantiken Rechtsquellen." *Jahrbuch für Antike und Christentum* 16 (1973) 28-59.

Nothomb, D. M. "Charité et unité. Doctrine de saint Basile le Grand sur la charité envers le prochain." *POCh* 4 (1954) 309-321; 5 (1955) 3-13.

O'Connor, Terence. *The Communio as Revealed in the Writings of Saint Basil the Great.* Diss. Rome, 1952.

Oliver, H. H. "The Text of the Four Gospels as Quoted in the *Moralia* of Basil the Great." Diss. Atlanta, Ga.: Emory University, 1961.

Onory, Sergio Machi. *Vescovi e città (sec. ɪᵛ-ᵛɪ).* Bologna: Zanichelli, 1933.

Orphanos, Marcos A. *Creation and Salvation according to Saint Basil of Caesarea.* Athens: Gregorios Parisianos, 1975.

Osborn, Eric Francis. "Basil the Great" (Ethics). In *Ethical Patterns in Early Christian Thought,* pp. 84-113. Cambridge: University Press, 1976.

Otis, Brooks. "Cappadocian Thought as a Coherent System." *DOP* 12 (1958) 95-124.

——. "Gregory of Nyssa and the Cappadocian Conception of Time." *SP* 16 (Berlin, 1976) 325-357.

Papadopolou-Tsanana, Olympia. Ἡ ἀνθρωπολογία τοῦ μεγάλου Βασιλείου. Diss. Salonika, 1970.

Papakonstantinos, Th. Ὁ μέγας Βασίλειος, ἡ δογματική αὐτοῦ διδασκαλία. 3rd ed. Athens, 1931.

Pargoire, Jules. "Basile de Césarée." *DACL* (Paris, 1910), 2: 501-510.

Parsons, Wilfrid. "The Influence of Romans 13 on Pre-Augustinian Christian Political Thought." *Theological Studies* 1 (1940) 337-364.

Parys, Michel van. "Quelques remarques à propos d'un texte controversé de s. Basile au concile de Florence." *Irénikon* 40 (1967) 6-14.

——. "Exégèse et théologie trinitaire: Prov. 8.22 chez les Pères cappadociens." *Irénikon* 43 (1971) 493-514.

Paverd, Frans van de. "Die Quellen der kanonischen Briefe Basileios des Grossen." *OCP* 38 (1972) 5-63.

Pekar, Athanasius Basil. *St. Basil the Great. His Life and His Work.* New York: Good Shepherd Publications, 1963.

——. *Doskonalyj chrystijanyn. Chernechyj ideal sv. Vasilija.* New York: Basilian Fathers Press, 1968.

Pelikan, Jaroslav. *Historical Theology. Continuity and Change in Christian Doctrine.* New York: Corpus, 1971.

——. *The Christian Tradition. A History of the Development of Doctrine.* 1: *The Emergence of the Catholic Tradition (100-600).* 2: *The Spirit of Eastern Christendom (600-1700).* Chicago: University Press, 1971, 1974.

Pellegrino, Michele. "Basilio, san." *EC* (Vatican, 1949), 2: 971-978.

Pépin, Jean. *Théologie cosmique et théologie chrétienne.* Paris: Presses universitaires de France, 1964.

Petit, Pierre. "Emerveillement, prière et Esprit chez s. Basile le Grand." *CC* 35 (1973) 81-108; 218-238.

Pfister, J. Emile. "A Biographical Note: The Brothers and Sisters of St. Gregory of Nyssa." *VCh* 18 (1964) 108-113.

Pichler, Theodore. *Das Fasten bei Basileios dem Grossen und die antiken Heidentum.* Innsbruck: Wagner, 1955.

Piganiol, André. *L'empire chrétien (325-395).* 2nd ed. Paris: Presses universitaires de France, 1972.

Pitt, W. E. "The Origin of the Anaphora of the Liturgy of St. Basil." *JEH* 12 (1961) 1-13.

Pluta, A. "Ist die syrische Mönchskonzeption der 'īhīdājūtā' im Sinne von 'Christförmigkeit' Leitbild des Basilius?" In *Festschrift F. Loidl,* E. Kovács, ed., 3: 204-220. Wiesbaden: Hollinek, 1971.

Polman, Andries Derk Rietema. *The Word of God according to St. Augustine.* Grand Rapids: Eerdmans, 1961.

Popescu, Ioan C. *Activitatca oratorica a sf. Vasile cel Mare.* Bucharest, 1908.

Pozzo, Giuseppe del. *Dilucidazioni critico-storiche sulle relazioni degli antichi e moderni scrittori della vita de s. Basilio Magno.* Rome, 1747.

Prestige, George Leonard. *St. Basil the Great and Apollinaris of Laodicea.* London: SPCK, 1956.

Probst, Ferdinand. *Liturgie des 4. Jahrhunderts und deren Reform.* Münster, 1893.

Pruche, Benoît. "L'originalité du traité de s. Basile sur le Saint-Esprit." *RSPT* 32 (1948) 207-221.

———. "Autour du *Traité du Saint-Esprit* de s. Basile de Césarée." *RSR* 52 (1964) 204-232.

———. "*Dogma* et *kerygma* dans le *Traité sur le Saint-Esprit* de s. Basile de Césarée en Cappadoce." *SP* 9 (Berlin, 1966) 257-262.

———. "Didyme l'Aveugle est-il bien l'auteur des livres *Contre Eunome* IV et V attribués à s. Basile de Césarée?" *SP* 10 (Berlin, 1970) 151-155.

Puech, Aimé. "S. Basile." In *Histoire de la littérature grecque chrétienne,* 3: 235-317. Paris: Les Belles Lettres, 1930.

Quasten, Johannes. *Patrology.* 3 vols. Westminster, Md.: Newman Press, 1950, 1953, 1960. For a more up-dated bibliography see the Spanish ed. BAC 206, 217, Madrid: Editorial Católica, 1962.

Rahner, Karl, et al., edd. *Sacramentum Mundi. An Encyclopedia of Theology.* 6 vols. New York: Herder, 1968.

Ramsay, William Mitchell. *The Historical Geography of Asia Minor.* London, 1890; rpt. New York: Cooper Square, 1972.

———. "Glycerius the Deacon." In *The Church in the Roman Empire before A.D. 170,* pp. 443-464. New York: Putnam, 1893.

———. "Basil of Caesarea." *The Expositor* 5 (1896) 49-61.

———. "Life in the Days of St. Basil the Great." In *Pauline and Other Studies,* pp. 369-406. London: Hodder & Stoughton, 1906.

Régamey, Pie Raymond. "Carismi." *DIP* (Rome, 1975), 2: 299-315.

Reicke, Bo. Προΐστημι. *TDNT* (Grand Rapids, 1963), 6: 700-703.

Reilly, Gerald F. *Imperium and Sacerdotium according to St. Basil the Great.* Diss. Washington, D.C.: Catholic University of America, 1945.

Rendina, Sergio. *La contemplazione negli scritti di s. Basilio.* Diss. Rome: Gregorian, 1959.

Richard, Marcel. "S. Basile et la mission du diacre Sabinus." *AB* 67 (1949) 170-202.

———. "La lettre 'Confidimus quidem' du Pape Damase." *Annuaire de l'Institut de philologie et d'histoire orientales* 11 (1951) 323-340.

Riedmatten, Henri. "La correspondance entre Basile de Césarée et Apollinaire de Laodicée." *JThS* 7 (1956) 199-210; 8 (1957) 53-70.

Ring, Oskar. *Drei Homilien aus der Frühzeit Basilius' des Grossen. Grundlegendes zur Basiliusfrage.* Paderborn: Schöningh, 1930.

Ritter, Adolf Martin. *Das Konzil von Konstantinopel und sein Symbol. Studien zur Geschichte und Theologie des Zweiten ökumenischen Konzils von Konstantinopel 381.* Göttingen: Ruprecht, 1965.

------. *Charisma im Verständnis des Joannes Chrysostomos und seiner Zeit. Ein Bei-trag zur Erforschung der griechisch-orientalischen Ekklesiologie in der Früh-zeit der Reichskirche.* Göttingen: Ruprecht, 1972.

Rivas, H. L. "El conocimiento analógico de Dios en los Santos Padres de Capado-cia." *RT* 6 (1959) 68-74.

Rivière, Jean. *S. Basile, évêque de Césarée.* 2nd ed. Paris: Gabalda, 1925.

Roggisch, W. M. *Platons Spuren bei Basilius dem Grossen.* Diss. Bonn, 1949.

Roman, Jerome. *The Flaming Pillar of Cappadocian Caesarea.* Rome: Sorelle An-cille della Beata Maria Vergine, 1963.

Ronnat, Jean Marie (= Jean Marie Leroux). *Basile le Grand.* Paris: Editions ouvrières, 1955.

Rostovtzeff, Michael. *The Social and Economic History of the Roman Empire.* 2nd ed. Oxford: Clarendon, 1957.

Rothenhäusler, M. "Der hl. Basilius und die klösterliche Profession." *Benedik-tinische Monatschrift* 4 (1922) 280-290.

Rouillard, Edouard. "La tradition manuscrite des *Homélies diverses* de s. Basile." *SP* 3 (Berlin, 1961) 116-123.

------. "Peut-on retrouver le texte authentique de la prédication de s. Basile?" *SP* 7 (Berlin, 1966) 90-101.

------. "Recherches sur la tradition manuscrite des *Homélies diverses* de s. Basile." *Revue Mabillon* 57 (1967) 1-16; 45-55.

Rousseau, Olivier. "La rencontre de s. Ephrem et s. Basile." *OS* 2 (1957) 261-284; 3 (1958) 73-90.

Roux, Léon. *Etude sur la prédication de Basile le Grand, archevêque de Césarée.* Strasbourg, 1867.

Rudberg, Stig Y. *Etudes sur la tradition manuscrite de s. Basile.* Diss. Lund: Lun-dequitska, 1953.

------. "Welche Vorlage benutzte Erasmus für seine editio princeps der Basilius-Homilien?" *Eranos* 58 (1960) 20-28.

------. "The Manuscript Tradition of the *Moral Homilies* of St. Basil." *SP* 3 (Berlin, 1961) 124-128.

------. "'Morceaux choisis' de Basile sélectionnés par Syméon Métaphraste." *Eranos* 62 (1964) 100-119.

------. Review of Y. Courtonne, *S. Basile, Lettres...* (see above). *Gnomon* 40 (1968) 776-778.

------. "'Du är luften som jag andas.' Om relationerna mellan tvà 300-talsfäder, Basilius och Gregorius." *Religion och Bibel. Nathan Söderblom-sällskapets ärsbok 1974*, pp. 43-50. Stockholm, 1975.

Ruether, Rosemary Radford. *Gregory of Nazianzus. Rhetor and Philosopher.* Ox-ford: Clarendon, 1969.

Rutka, Theophil. *Sw. Bazyliusz Wielki zycia zakonneto w Cerkwie swietej wschodniej Patriarcha i Fundator.* Calissii, 1686.

Saddington, D. B. "The Function of Education according to Christian Writers of the Latter Part of the Fourth Century." *Acta classica* 8 (1965) 86-101.

Salmona, Bruno. *Il filosofare nei luminari di Cappadocia.* Milan: Marzorati, 1974.

Samaritani, A. "I sacramenti in s. Basilio di Cesarea." *PC* 36 (1957) 1123-1132.

Sammartano, Nino. "Basilio: Pedagogia." *EC* (Vatican, 1949), 2: 978-979.

Savramis, Demosthenes. ʽΗ ἀρχὴ 'ora et labora' κατὰ τὸν μέγαν Βασίλειον." *Theologia* 38 (1967) 42-51.

———. "Basilius der Grosse als Vermittler zwischen Himmel und Erde." *Kyrios* 10 (1970) 65-75.

Scazzoso, Piero. *Reminiscenze della Polis platonica nel cenobio di s. Basilio.* Milan: Istituto Italiano, 1970.

———. "L'umanesimo di s. Basilio." *Aug* 12 (1972) 391-405.

———. "La componente ecclesiologica del linguaggio trinitario di s. Basilio." *Aug* 13 (1973) 507-514.

———. "S. Basilio e la Sacra Scrittura." *Aevum* 47 (1973) 210-224.

———. "Rifflessioni sull'ecclesiologia orientale." *VM* 27 (1973) 38-117.

———. *Introduzione alla ecclesiologia di s. Basilio.* Milan: Studia patristica mediolanensia, 1975.

Schäffer, J. *Basilius des Grossen Beziehungen zum Abendlande.* Münster, 1907.

Schillebeeckx, Edouard, ed. *The Unifying Role of the Bishop.* New York: Herder, 1972.

Schmidt, Karl Ludwig. Ἐκκλησία. *TDNT* (Grand Rapids, 1965), 3: 501-536.

Schönborn, Christoph von. "La 'Lettre 38 de s. Basile' et le problème christologique de l'iconoclasme." *RSPT* 60 (1976) 446-450.

Scholl, Eugen. *Die Lehre des hl. Basilius von der Gnade.* Freiburg-im-Breisgau: Herder, 1881.

Schucan, Luzi. *Das Nachleben von Basilius Magnus "Ad adolescentes." Ein Beitrag zur Geschichte des christlichen Humanismus.* Diss. Geneva: Droz, 1973.

Schwartz, Eduard. "Zur Kirchengeschichte des vierten Jahrhunderts." *ZNW* 34 (1935) 129-213.

———. "Ueber die Sammlung des cod. Veronensis 60." *ZNW* 35 (1936) 1-23.

Schweizer, Eduard. *Church Order in the New Testament.* London: SCM, 1961.

———. Πνεῦμα; πνευματικός. *TDNT* (Grand Rapids, 1965), 6: 389-455.

———. *Jesus.* Richmond, Va.: Knox, 1971.

Scrima, André. "Ascesi monastica orientale." *DIP* (Rome, 1974), 1: 906-913.

Shear, Theodore Leslie. *The Influence of Plato on St. Basil.* Baltimore: Furst, 1906.

Simonetti, Manlio. "La tradizione nella controversia ariana." *Aug* 12 (1972) 37-50.

———. *La crisi ariana nel IV secolo.* Rome: Augustinianum, 1975.

Smith, John Holland. *The Death of Classical Paganism.* New York: Scribner's, 1976.

Smith, Richard Travers. *St. Basil the Great.* London: SPCK, 1879.

Soell, Georg. "Die Mariologie der Kappadozier im Lichte der Dogmengeschichte." *ThQ* 131 (1951) 163-188; 288-319; 426-457.

Solovij, Meletyj. "Duch Vasylijanskoho monashestva v mynulomu i suchasnomu." In *Propamijatna knyha Otciv Vasylijan u Kanadi,* pp. 37-66. Toronto: Basilian Press, 1953.

Sorsoli, Cirillo. "Dottrina trinitaria in s. Basilio Magno." In Ermanno Ancilli, ed., *Il mistero del Dio vivente*, pp. 144-162. Rome: Teresianum, 1968.

Spanneut, Michel. "Eunome." *DHGE* (Paris, 1963), 15: 1399-1405.

Špidlik, Thomas. *La sophiologie de saint Basile*. Rome: Pontificium Institutum Orientalium Studiorum, 1961.

———. "L'eternità e il tempo, la *zoé* e il *bíos*, problema dei Padri Cappadoci." *Aug* 16 (1976) 107-116.

Staats, Reinhart. "Die Asketen aus Mesopotamien in der Rede des Gregor von Nyssa, 'In suam ordinationem'." *VCh* 21 (1967) 165-179.

Stam, John Edward. *Episcopacy in the Apostolic Tradition of Hippolytus*. Diss. Basel: Rheinhardt, 1969.

Ste. Croix, Geoffrey de. "Early Christianity Attitudes to Property and Slavery." In *Church, Society and Politics*, ed. Derek Baker, pp. 1-38. Oxford: Blackwell, 1975.

Stevenson, James, ed. *A New Eusebius. Documents Illustrative of the History of the Church to A.D. 337*. London: SPCK, 1968.

———. *Creeds, Councils, and Controversies. Documents Illustrative of the History of the Church A.D. 337-461*. London: SPCK, 1973.

Stiernon, Daniel. "Basilio il Grande. Vita, opere, culto, reliquie, iconografia." In *Bibliotheca Sanctorum*, 2: 910-944. Rome: Istituto Giovanni XXIII, 1962.

Strachey, Marjorie. *Saints and Sinners of the Fourth Century*. London: Kimber, 1958.

Suárez, G. C. "La vida religiosa en s. Basilio Magno." *Confer* 11 (1972) 149-161.

Szymusiak, Jan Marie, ed. & trans. *Athanase d'Alexandrie, Apologie à l'empereur Constance, Apologie pour sa fuite*. SCh 56. Paris: Editions du Cerf, 1958.

Tadin, Marin. "La *Lettre 91* de s. Basile a-t-elle été adressée à l'évêque d'Aquilée Valérien?" *RSR* 37 (1950) 457-468.

Tamburrino, Pio. "Osservazione sulla sezione cristologica dell'*Hom. in ps.* 44 di s. Basilio." *RCCM* 11 (1966) 229-239.

———. "Die Beziehung 'Monasterium'-'Kirche' im frühen pachomianischen Mönchtum." *Erbe und Auftrage* 43 (1967) 5-21.

———. "L'opera dei sei giorni, visione patristica del cosmo." In *Simposio cristiano*, pp. 86-103. Milan, 1971.

Taylor, Justin. "St. Basil the Great and Pope St. Damasus." *DR* 91 (1973) 186-203; 262-274.

Teja, Ramón. "La Iglesia y la Economía en el siglo IV. El pensamiento económico de los Padres Capadocios." *Revista de la Universidad de Madrid* 20, 79 (1971) 113-127.

———. "Invasiones de godos en Asia Menor antes y después de Adrianópolis." *Hispania antiqua* 1 (1971) 169-177.

———. "Las villas de Hispania y Capadocia en el siglo IV y su entorno económico-social." In *12 Congreso nacional de arqueología, Jaén 1971*, pp. 611-624. Zaragoza: Seminario de arqueología, 1973.

——. *Organización económica y social de Capadocia en el siglo* IV, *según los Padres Capadocios.* Salamanca: Universidad de Salamanca, 1974.

——. "El deporte en la Capadocia romana." *Zephyrus* 25 (1974) 479-496.

Telfer, William. *The Office of a Bishop.* London: Darton, 1962.

Thornton, Lionel Spencer. *The Common Life in the Body of Christ.* 4th ed. London: Dacre, 1963.

Tieck, William Arthur. "Basil of Caesarea and the Bible." Diss. New York: Columbia University, 1953.

Tillemont, Louis Sébastien Le Nain de. "S. Basile." In *Mémoires pour servir à l'histoire ecclésiastique des six premiers siècles.* Paris: Robustel, 1703, 9: 1-304; 628-691.

Torrance, Thomas. "Spiritus creator." *VC* 89 (1969) 33-62.

Treu, Kurt. "Φιλία und ἀγάτη. Zur Terminologie der Freundschaft bei Basilius und Gregor von Nazianzus." *Studii classice* 3 (1961) 421-427.

Treucker, Barnim. *Politische und sozialgeschichtliche Studien zu den Basilius-Briefen.* Diss. Bonn: Habelt, 1961.

Troeltsch, Ernst. *The Social Teachings of the Christian Churches.* 2 vols. New York: Macmillan, 1931.

Trunk, J. *De Basilio Magno sermonis attici imitatore.* Progr. Ehingen, 1911.

Tsamis, Demetrios. Ἡ πρωτολογία τοῦ μεγάλου Βασιλείου. Salonika: Centre for Byzantine Studies, 1970.

Tsanana, H. A. Τὰ ἐν τῇ Ἐκκλησίᾳ χαρίσματα τοῦ Ἁγίου Πνεύματος κατὰ τὸν μεγάλον Βασίλειον. In *Theological Symposium. P. K. Christou Festschrift,* pp. 121-141. Salonika, 1967.

Unterstein, K. *Die natürliche Gotteserkenntnis nach der Lehre der kappadozischen Kirchenväter Basilius, Gregor von Nazianzus und Gregor von Nyssa.* Progr. Straubing, 1902-1903.

Uspenskij, M. "Molitvy Eucharistii Vasilija Velikogo i Joanna Zlatousta v chine pravoslavnoj Liturgii." *SP* 5 (Berlin, 1962) 152-171.

Vallée, L. *Dissertatio qua expenditur celebris locus s. Basilii Magni de processione Spiritus Sancti a Patre Filioque.* Paris, 1721.

Vandenbroucke, François. "Jalons pour une théologie du monachisme." *Studia monastica* 11 (1960) 159-192.

Vandenbusche, E. "La part de la dialectique dans la théologie d'Eunomius, le technologue." *RHE* 40 (1944-1945) 47-72.

Veilleux, Armand. "The Abbatial Office in Cenobitic Life." *Monastic Studies* 6 (1968) 3-45.

Veloso, Gerardo. "Some Monastic Legislation of St. Basil: A Textual Study of the *Small Asceticon*, the *Big Asceticon* and the *Three Canonical Letters*." *PhS* 7 (1972) 244-269.

Venables, Edmund. "Basil of Caesarea." *DCB* (London, 1877), 1: 282-297.

——. "Eustathius of Sebaste." Ibid., 2: 383-387.

Verhees, Jacques. "Pneuma, Erfahrung und Erleuchtung in der Theologie des Basilius des Grossen." *Ostkirchliche Studien* 25 (1976) 43-59.

——. "Die Bedeutung der Tranzendenz des Pneuma bei Basilius." Ibid., 285-302.

Viller, Marcel & Karl Rahner. *Aszese und Mystik in der Väterzeit.* Freiburg-im-Breisgau: Herder, 1939.

Vischer, Lukas. *Basilius der Grosse. Untersuchungen zu einem Kirchenvater des vierten Jahrhunderts.* Diss. Basel: Rheinhardt, 1953.

——. "Das Problem der Freundschaft bei den Kirchenvätern." *Theologische Zeitschrift* 9 (1953) 173-200.

Völker, Walther. *Gregor von Nyssa als Mystiker.* Wiesbaden: Steiner, 1955.

Vogel, Cyrille. "Chirotonie et chirothèsie. Importance et relativité du geste de l'imposition des mains dans la collation des ordres." *Irénikon* 45 (1972) 7-21; 207-238.

Vogt, Hermann Josef. *Das Kirchenverständnis des Origenes.* Diss. Cologne-Vienna: Böhlau Verlag, 1974.

Vööbus, Arthur. *History of Asceticism in the Syrian Orient. A Contribution to the History of Culture in the Near East.* 1: *The Origin of Asceticism. Early Monasticism in Persia.* (CSCO 184). 2: *Early Monasticism in Mesopotamia and Syria.* (CSCO 197). Louvain: Secrétariat du Corpus SCO, 1958, 1960.

Vorgrimler, Herbert, ed. *Commentary on the Documents of Vatican 2.* 4 vols. New York: Herder, 1967-1969.

Vries, Wilhelm de. "Die Ostkirche und die Cathedra Petri im IV. Jahrhundert." *OCP* 40 (1974) 114-144.

Wawryk, Basilius Boris. *Doctrina Sancti Basilii Magni de inspiratione Sacrae Scripturae.* Diss. Rome: Gregorian University, 1943.

Way, Agnes Clare. *The Language and Style of the Letters of Saint Basil.* Diss. Washington, D.C.: Catholic University of America, 1927.

Weijenborg, Reimond. *De authenticitate et sensu quarumdam epistolarum Sancto Basilio Magno et Apollinario adscriptarum.* Rome: Antonianum, 1958/1959.

——. "Autour de quelques textes de saint Basile. Observations critiques sur certaines positions mariologiques faussement attribuées à saint Basile de Césarée." *Ephemerides Mariologicae* 25 (1975) 381-395.

Weiss, Hugo. *Die grossen Kappadozier als Exegeten.* Braunsberg: Martens, 1872.

Wickham, L. R. "The Date of Eunomius' *Apology*: A Reconsideration." *JThS* 20 (1969) 231-240.

Wilken, Robert L. "The Spirit of Holiness: Basil of Caesarea and Early Christian Spirituality." *Worship* 42 (1968) 77-87.

Winslow, Donald F. "Christology and Exegesis in the Cappadocians." *CH* 40 (1971) 389-396.

Wittig, Josef. *Des hl. Basilius d. Gr. geistliche Uebungen auf der Bischofskonferenz von Dazimon 374/375, im Anschluss an Isaias 1-16.* Breslau, 1922.

——. *Die Friedenspolitik des Papstes Damasus I. und der Ausgang der arianischen Streitigkeiten.* Breslau, 1912.

Yakymyshyn, Severian Steven. "The Virtue of Charity as Revealed in the Writings of St. Basil the Great." Diss. Rome: Gregorian, 1958.

Yamamura, Kei. "Development of the Doctrine of the Holy Spirit in Patristic Philosophy: St. Basil and Gregory of Nyssa." *SVThQ* 1 (1974) 3-21. Originally published in *Shisaku* (*Meditation*), Annual of the Assocation of Philosophical Studies, Tohuku University, 5: 71-100. Tokyo, 1972.

Zaccherini, Gian Battista. "Il problema economico e i problemi sociali nel pensiero e nell'azione di un Padre della Chiesa del IV secolo: San Basilio di Cesarea." Diss. Bologna: Istituto per le scienze religiose, 1959.

Zucchetti, Fausta. "Eustazio di Sebaste e Basilio di Cesarea." *RR* 2 (1926) 17-22.

General Index

Abramius, bishop of Batnae, 148.

Abramowski, Luise, 3n.

Aburgius, lay compatriot, 142, 143, 147, 148.

accountant, letter to, 146.

Aegea, city (now Ayas), 149.

Aerius, ascetic, 160n.

Aetius (d. *ca.* 370), Christian sophist, 138.

Alexander, Egyptian bishop, 128.

Alexandria, 108, 109n., 128, 136, 146, 157, 159; synod of, 139.

altar, as sign of ecclesiastical communion, 121n.

Amand de Mendieta, Emmanuel (David; 1907-1976), xiii-xiv, 4n., 11n., 18n., 21n., 22n., 28n., 31n., 32n., 63n., 73, 83n., 108n., 109n., 111n., 114n., 153, 154, 156n., 158n., 160n.

Ambrose (*ca.* 339-397), bishop of Milan, 147, 148.

Amphilochius (*ca.* 340-395), bishop of Iconium, 47n., 57, 64, 145, 147, 148, 149.

Amun, eremite, 157.

Ancyra (now Ankara), 143; synod of, 137.

Andronicus, general, 145.

Annesi (now Sounisa? Turkey), village, 134, 136, 137, 138, 139.

Anomoeans, 3, 58, 103, 105, 126, 137, 138, 151, 153.

Anthimus, bishop of Tyana, 115n., 144.

Antioch (Antakya), 53, 54, 65, 110, 139, 146; church divided, 47n., 108; presbyters of, 44n.

Antiochus, nephew of Eusebius of Samosata, 147.

Antipater, governor of Cappadocia, 146, 147.

Antony (251?-356), hermit of Egypt, 135, 156 and n., 157.

apatheia, 23.

Apollinarians, 153; *see also* Apollinaris of Laodicea.

Apollinaris of Laodicea (*ca.* 310-*ca.* 390), 70n., 96, 110, 111, 112, 121, 126, 134, 135, 138, 139.

Apophthegmata patrum (4th-5th cent.), 157.

Apostolic Constitutions (4th cent. Syria), 79n.

Arada, island, 128.

Arcadius, bishop, 143.

Arcadius, *comes rei privatae,* 141.

Arians, 3, 5-6, 58, 75n., 95, 103, 105, 106, 113, 121, 126, 143, 149, 153, 154; *see also* Arius.

Arinthaeus, general, 147, 152.

Aristotle (384-322 BC), Greek philosopher, 5, 16n., 172.

Arius, (*ca.* 250-*ca.* 336), heresiarch, 68; his work *Thalia,* 3n.; *see also* Arians.

Armenia, kingdom of, 104, 123, 146, 158n.

ascetism and Arianism, 37; and baptism, 15n., 18n.; and Bible, 157; and Christian life, 4; and children, 15n.; and church, 6-7, 12-23; Egyptian, 23, 30-31, 135, 156-158; Eustathian, 4, 44, 66, 150, 158-160; family type, 4 and n.; and married people, 15 and n.; Pachomian, 30-31, 156-158; as "philosophy," 19, 138; secular and monastic, 163-165; and slaves, 15n.; universal calling to, 15, 20; urban, 4, 23; *see also* Basil: life; charisma; church.

ascetics, as in body of Christ, 23-32; as brotherhood, 23-24; called "Christians," 165 and n.; relations with pagans, 71n.; Basil's letters to, 141, 148, 149.

Hübner, Reinhard, 155.
Humbertclaude, Pierre, xv n., 24n.
hypostasis, 69n.; and ousia, 94, 108n., 139.

Iconium (now Konya), 147, 148; Synod of (376), 149.
Ignatius (ca. 35-ca. 107), bishop of Antioch, 69, 169.
Illyria, Synod of (375), 148.
Imperium et sacerdotium, 38-39.
Innocent, monk, 152.
Irenaeus (ca. 130-ca. 200), bishop of Lyons, 93.
Italy, 109n.
Ivanka, Endre von (1902-1974), 38n., 159n.
Izois, bishop, 71.

Jackson, Blomfield (1839-1906), ix, 53n., 61n.
Jerome (ca. 342-420), 23n., 113.
Jerusalem, apostolic community of, 14, 20, 22, 24 and n., 83.
John, unknown friend of Basil, 139.
Jones, Arnold Hugh Martin (1904-1970), 53n., 104n., 115n., 136, 144.
Jounel, Pierre, 79n.
Jovian (ca. 332-364), emperor, 14n., 140.
Jovinus, bishop of Perrha in Syria, 145.
Jovinus, count, 147.
Julian (332-363), emperor, xvi, 1n., 12-14, 37, 95n., 103, 135, 139, 140.
Julitta, martyr, 145.
Julitta, widow, 145.

Käsemann, Ernst, 24-28, 39n.
Karayannopulos, John, 104n.
Kelly, John Norman Davidson, 1n., 5n., 70n.
kerygma, 126; and dogma, 63, 72-75, 111n.
koinonia, 17, 20-22, 25.
Kopecek, Thomas Alan, 38n., 52n., 53n.

Lacizae, town in Armenia, 153.
Lampsacus (now Lapseki), city in Mysia, Synod of (ca. 364), 140.
Laodicea (now Latakia), city in Syria, 149.

Laun, Ferdinand, 12n.
Lazzati, Giuseppe Maria, 135.
leader (*proestos*), 9n., 41n.; of the word: 77 ff.; calling of, 79-82; function of, 89-90; instrument of the Holy Spirit, 77, 80; mission of, 82-84; teaching of, 83-84; tested, 87; see also *proestos*.
Leggio, Efremo, 71n.
Legrand, Hervé Marie, 1n.
Leontius, unknown friend of Basil, sophist, 141.
Letoius, bishop of Melitene, 154.
letter, of communion, 49, 122; of enthronement or enthronistic, 116, 122; means of communication, 169-173; synodal, 122.
Libanius (314-ca. 393), sophist of Antioch, 95n., 141.
Liberius, pope of Rome (352-366), 4n., 137, 141.
Licinius (d. ca. 324), Augustus, 103.
Lietzmann, Hans (1875-1942), 13n., 14n., 18n., 111n., 143, 144, 148, 149, 152, 157, 159n.
logos, 90; Christ as, 84, 168; of the church, 92, 95; as creator, 77; of love, 33, 119; scriptural, 152; *spermatikos*, 16, 118.
Loofs, Friedrich (1858-1928), 61n., 142, 143, 144, 146, 148, 152, 158n.
love (*agape*), 16-17, 74n., 118, 126-128; charismatic, 132; constitutive element of church unity, 64; distinguishing mark of Christians, 17, 115; for God and for neighbours, 119-120; "grown cold," 62 and n., 126; spiritual and material, 126-127; supremacy of, 118-119; various manifestations, 127-128.

Macarius, otherwise unknown, 139.
Pseudo-Macarius, 23n.
Macrina the Elder, grandmother of Basil, 3 and n., 68.
Macrina the Younger (ca. 327-379), sister of Basil, 133, 137.
Magnenianus, count, 147.
Malingrey, Anne Marie, 16n.
Mamant, martyr, 146.
man, his body a tomb, 28; image and

Index Graecitatis

Index of Biblical Passages

Index of the Works of Basil of Caesarea

INDEX TO DUBIOUS OR SPURIOUS WORKS OF BASIL

Index of Other Sources

Athanasius of Alexandria, *Epistola ad Palladium*: 63n., 75n.
Augustine of Hippo, *De doctrina christiana* **4. 59**: 88.
Cassian, John, *Institutiones* **11. 18**: 157n.
Cicero, *De officiis* **1. 17**: 23n.
Firmilian, *Epistula* **175. 25**: 23n.
Gregory of Nazianzus, *Carmen* **1. 1**: 88.
    11: 163.
    Epistulae **1**: 160n.
      2: 138.
      53: 173n.
      58: 63n.
      97: 123n.
    Invectivae contra Julianum: 14n., 95n.
    Orationes **20**: 14n.
      42: 14n., 129.
      43: 14n., 40, 52 and n., 53n., 55n., 129, 153.
      43. 5-6: 3n.
      43. 12: 134, 160n.
      43. 23: 59.
      43. 27: 81n., 136.
      43. 29: 14n.
      43. 31: 56, 57.
      43. 33: 55n.
      43. 35: 38.

      43. 40: 101n.
      43. 41: 55n., 62-63, 101-102.
      43. 43: 57, 169.
      43. 46: 37n.
      43. 47: 55n.
      43. 65: 172.
      43. 66: 173n.
      43. 67: 92.
      43. 68: 104n.
      43. 68-69: 63n.
    Oratio apologetica: 79n.
    Oratio contra arianos **3**: 37n.
Gregory of Nyssa, *Epistula* **13. 4**: 135.
    De virginitate: 28n., 44n.
    Vita Gregorii Thaumaturgi: 3n.
    Vita Macrinae: 3n., 5-8, 23n.
Hilary of Poitiers, *Ad Constantinum Augustum* **1. 6**: 37n.
    Fragmenta historica **2. 3**: 37n.
Hippolytus of Rome, *Traditio apostolica*: 79n.
Julian the Apostate, *Epistula* **84**: 13n.
    89: 13 and n.
Photius, *Bibliotheca* **141. 143. 191**: 173.
Rufinus, *Historia ecclesiastica* **2. 9**: 162.
Sozomenus, *Historia ecclesiastica* **3. 14**: 158n., 159n.

Made in the USA
Monee, IL
05 April 2021